BEST *of* ELVIS

BY SUSAN DOLL

PUBLICATIONS INTERNATIONAL, LTD.

Louis Weber, C.E.O.
Publications International, Ltd.
7373 North Cicero Avenue
Lincolnwood, Illinois 60646

Permission is never granted for commercial purposes. Manufactured in U.S.A.

8 7 6 5 4 3 2 1

ISBN 0-7853-1982-4

Library of Congress Catalog Card Number: 96-69042

Susan Doll holds a Ph.D. in Radio, Television, Film Studies from
Northwestern University. In addition to teaching film courses at several
Chicago-area colleges, she is the author of *Elvis: A Tribute to His Life, The
Films of Elvis Presley, Elvis: Rock 'n' Roll Legend,* and *Marilyn: Her Life and
Legend.*

Jerry Osborne was contributing consultant for the collectibles and music
sections of the publication. He has been an avid collector of Elvis Presley
records and memorabilia for over 30 years and has produced Elvis record
price guides and reference books since 1977. Osborne has been a regular
contributor of Presley-related features to countless music publications, and
he writes the weekly music newspaper column *Mr. Music,* which is nationally syndicated by World Features Syndicate.

Special thanks to Bill Burk, Sharon Fox, and Robin Rosaaen for their
expertise on Elvis lore.

CONTENTS

BEST OF ELVIS ♦ 6

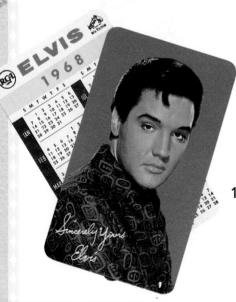

BEST OF ELVIS

EGEND. Icon of American Pop Culture. Larger-than-Life Superstar. Folk Hero. Myth. In writing about Elvis Presley two decades after his death, authors struggle to find words that adequately convey his influence and impact on our culture. Yet, no system of measurement seems sufficient to appraise that impact; no perspective seems broad enough to account for his durability. To best comprehend the potency of Elvis Presley, simply look at the facts and figures of his amazing career and the highlights of the phenomenon that surround him in death. The impact of Elvis Presley is best realized by sifting through the record-setting statistics, the astounding sales figures, and the fan following that he attracts 20 years after his death.

Best of Elvis consists entirely of lists—lists that detail the career highlights of the most recognizable performer of the 20th century, that offer insight into Elvis Presley the man, and that specify the most remarkable aspects of the post-death Elvis phenomenon. The lists vary in length and scope. Some are simple itemized lists; others are annotated lists in which each item is discussed at length. Divided into six chapters, *Best of Elvis* offers just that—the *best* of Elvis' life and career.

The main purpose of the book is to explore Elvis' remarkable career, his powerful image, and his controversial life to determine what could be considered the best. However, breaking down Elvis' life and career in this way serves other purposes. The format forces us to re-examine the most familiar aspects of Elvis' life and career. Why did a certain album, movie, song, or landmark make the list? What did that item mean to Elvis' life or career? Why is it important? Everyone knows that "Hound Dog" is Elvis' most recognizable song. Why? The music gates at Graceland are so familiar to fans, tourists, and passing visitors that many take them for granted. What makes them constitute one of the best sights to see at Graceland?

Determining the best of Elvis is admittedly a subjective undertaking. To minimize personal bias and subjectivity, criteria were developed to evaluate his recordings, movies, performances, and other creative efforts. In some of these lists, concrete data such as chart listings, sales statistics, box-office grosses, and awards were part of the criteria. The level of impact that a recording, movie, or performance had on Elvis'

career or on pop culture history also played a role in some of the decisions. To maintain greater objectivity, the opinions and contributions of Elvis biographers and music historians were researched, and the assistance of experts in certain fields, including music, collectibles, and Presleyana, were elicited. Even with these efforts, readers may not agree with all of the selections in *Best of Elvis*. And some of the lists are simply subjective by their very nature. Though certain selections on certain lists may be debatable, there is still plenty of information and analysis that makes for lively reading.

The first chapter involves Elvis' most significant contribution to popular culture—music. Some lists in "Music," such as Best Albums and Best Singles, seriously evaluate his most famous and popular recordings from the very beginning of his career to the mid-1990s. In doing so, these lists illustrate the diversity of his music and the expanse of his recording career—a career that is still thriving via repackaged and reissued material. Other lists in this chapter, including Best Elvis-Related Records and Best Elvis Tunes by Other Artists, attest to his influence on other artists and other genres of music. And, just for fun, Best Love Songs offers a little romance.

The selections for the music lists were based on a carefully assembled set of criteria. Part of that criteria involved a record's production values, which included sound quality, production personnel, the level of Elvis' participation, and the musicians who contributed to the recording. The criteria also included a record's significance to popular music, its significance to Elvis' career, and the statistics it generated (units sold, chart position, and gold or platinum status). For albums, the selection of songs was also taken into consideration. For example, did the record include any songs that were signature tunes for Elvis? Were any of the songs written by a significant songwriter? Did any of them capture Elvis' musical style from a given period?

Throughout the music chapter, industry terms are frequently used to indicate the importance of a recording. The RIAA, or the Recording Industry Association of America, is the organization that audits record companies and certifies record sales in order to issue gold and platinum records. Gold or platinum status is a gauge of a recording's popularity. Single records

and extended-play albums must sell one million units to qualify for gold status. Prior to 1975, long-playing albums had to reach $1 million in sales to qualify for gold status. After January 1, 1975, an LP compact disc was required to sell over 500,000 units to qualify for gold. An album or single achieves platinum status when it goes gold twice. The chart status in this book refers to the charts in *Billboard* magazine. Elvis' recordings have been on *Billboard*'s rhythm-and-blues, country, easy-listening, Top 100, and Hot 100 charts.

About half of Elvis' career was spent in Hollywood making musicals, and "Movies" acknowledges his big-screen career. Elvis' movies are often criticized because they tended to follow a set formula, but no Presley picture ever lost money, and video has opened a whole new market for them.

In his 31 Hollywood films, Elvis costarred with several notable actors and actresses. Some were Hollywood legends who had graced the silver screen in an earlier era, while others were just beginning promising careers that blossomed into stardom. Best Costars highlights those actors and actresses whose performances improved the film, those actresses who had a special chemistry with Elvis, and those character actors who turned their secondary roles into memorable screen performances. Elvis' movies may have a reputation for being lightweight, but they make amusing and colorful viewing for a variety of reasons. Perhaps a big-name star was featured in a bit role, or perhaps a film is special because of something that occurred behind the scenes. Some of the lists in "Movies," including Best Movie Trivia, Best Lines of Dialogue, and Best Movie Tunes, speak to the fun inherent in watching Elvis' movies.

Key movie lists include Best Movies, which consists of Elvis' best work on film, and Best Documentaries, which highlights the best films about him. Each item on these lists is discussed at length for a well-rounded view. The list of Best Movies not only examines Elvis' specific contributions to each film but also provides background information to better understand the Hollywood movie industry. Over the course of his acting career, Elvis' image changed, and the type of character he played changed with it. The evolution of his acting career and the changes that ensued are also examined for a complete picture of how Elvis fared in Hollywood. For a different approach to Elvis on film, Best Documentaries includes a selection of features that examine different aspects of Elvis' career in detail.

The criteria for selecting Best Movies and Best Documentaries included production values, which involves the caliber of acting, the contributions of behind-the-scenes personnel, and the quality of the script. For Best Movies, additional criteria involved the impact a film may have had on Elvis' entire Hollywood career. For Best Documentaries, the criteria included the level of accuracy and insight in the material, the amount of new information about Elvis, and how well the documentary explained his life and career.

A great deal of research was required to fill out the movie lists. Some of the research involved scrutinizing reviews, publicity articles, and promotional material of the era for accurate details and interesting trivia. Readers are sure to find a new approach to looking at his movies or a tidbit of information they didn't know before.

"Personal Elvis" contains familiar personal information about Elvis Presley, which provides insight into Elvis the man. Though much of the chapter focuses on Elvis' life at Graceland, some lists attempt to convey something about what Elvis thought and felt.

There are thousands of sights to see at Graceland, from the waterfall along the wall of the garish Jungle Room to the frayed handmade scrapbooks sent by fans in the Trophy Room. The items on the list titled Best Sights at Graceland were selected according to what they conveyed about Elvis' life. The many facets of his unique personality are suggested—though not entirely revealed—by the items discussed here. While some are fascinating and amusing, others are disturbing. Elvis' Proudest Achievements was a difficult list to compile because he left no autobiography or gave no definitive interview. The selections were culled from statements he made or from biographies of those who knew him. While all of his proudest achievements may never be known, those listed here offer some clue as to what Elvis thought of his life and career. Perhaps the most revealing list is Best Quotes About Elvis because the thoughts and ideas expressed here came straight from the man himself. Best Vehicles and Elvis' Favorites offer a more lighthearted look at Elvis' tastes and personality.

Once during a press conference, Elvis let his guard down to disclose how difficult it was to live up to his image. If "Personal Elvis" offers insight into Elvis the man, then "Public Elvis" addresses Elvis and his image. The lists in "Public Elvis" indicate how Elvis Presley the performer was presented to the public and how that public perceived him.

When Elvis became a household name in 1956, it was through a heated controversy over the effects of his image and music on the younger generation. Though the storm subsided after he went into the army, he continued to provoke controversy and inspire debate throughout his career. Best Controversies offers an in-depth examination of the major and minor conflicts that kept Elvis in the public eye. The medium of television had much to do with thrusting Elvis into that public eye. Though many fans and pop culture enthusiasts can recall with fondness Elvis' major television appearances, few realize the impact TV had on his career. Television was used to help launch his career back in 1956 and then later used to alter his image in order to attract a wider, more mainstream audience. Best TV Appearances highlights those small-screen performances that made an impact, whether by shaking up our culture, stimulating new audiences, or using new technology to span the continents.

Other media have also contributed to constructing and circulating Elvis' image. Best Headlines and Best Books offer a hint of how print material has contributed to the public perception of Presley. For sheer fun, Best Costumes shows how Elvis liked to present himself to the public in performance. Many familiar costumes are not included on the list, but those that are discussed are glorious examples of sartorial splendor. As a counterweight to Best Quotes by Elvis from the previous chapter, Best Quotes About Elvis offers divergent and conflicting viewpoints by those who knew him and those who knew of him.

The impact of the fans on Elvis' life and legend has rarely been discussed seriously. Often fans are misrepresented by the media and misunderstood by the general public. "Fans" attempts to present a more representative picture of Elvis' fans. The common threads that bond them together are that they are loyal and devoted and that they talk freely of the impact Elvis has had on their lives. Yet Elvis fans come from all walks of life and from all over the world. They represent diverse age groups, classes, and backgrounds. Best Fan Stories and Best Fan Clubs help dispel the negative stereotype of the fans. Though there are thousands of fascinating stories and hundreds of wonderful fan clubs, time and practical considerations prevented their inclusion here. Those few featured here are meant to stand in for the many.

The remaining lists in the chapter were compiled for the fans. Best Elvis Landmarks consists of a list of attractions that not only reveals something about Elvis' life but also offers interesting Presley places to visit. Best Fan Photos and Best Graffiti at Graceland depict fan forums that reveal the relationship between Elvis and his fans better than any writer or analyst ever could.

In 1957, Elvis proclaimed his goal during an interview: "Do something worth remembering." The final chapter, "Legend," addresses the many ways that Elvis is remembered. On a deeper level, it represents the impact he has had on American culture. From amusing Elvis collectibles to thought-provoking works of art, the life, career, and image of Elvis Presley have been endlessly interpreted in the public forum.

The Best Collectibles lists in this chapter have a different, broader function than they might in a book that showcases only Elvis collectibles. Here, the items on the lists have a historical perspective, with the individual lists representing specific periods of Elvis' career or aspects of the Elvis phenomenon. Dollar value and rarity were considered when compiling the lists, but they have less importance than they would have in a collectibles book. In some cases, items were selected because of the appeal they might have to the average fan or because they reflect the way Elvis' image was marketed during his career and after his death.

The Career Highlights list offers a quick glance at the cold, hard statistics and solid achievements that Elvis compiled during his lifetime, while Best Rumors and Myths offers just the opposite. Both lists are important in calculating Elvis' significance; the former speaks to his contributions to popular music, the latter hints at his impact on our culture.

The key list in "Legend" is Best Elvis Phenomena, which explores Elvis' role as an icon of popular culture. Fans pay tribute to him for personal reasons; impersonators exploit his image but fail to capture his essence; academics explore his significance to society; artists use his image to espouse sociopolitical points of view; while his image on a postage stamp signifies an identity as an important historical figure. No longer a mere performer, Elvis Presley has become ELVIS— an icon that conveys different meanings to different people.

From singer to legend, *Best of Elvis* addresses all phases of Elvis Presley's life and career. The statistics, facts, and key events that made up that career are astounding and thought-provoking. Pondering those facts and events will reveal the durability of his music, the intricacies of his image, and the complexity of the phenomena that surround him in death.

MUSIC

WHATEVER SOCIAL and cultural effect Elvis may have had, it was his music that made the most profound impact. A mixture of indigenous American styles and sounds, Elvis' innovative rockabilly remains as fresh now as it was in 1954. His later pop stylings may have become grandiose and exaggerated, but they still echo the sounds of the South . . . gospel, country, and rhythm and blues.

BEST ALBUMS
Elvis Presley

IN NOVEMBER 1955, Sam Phillips sold Elvis' contract to RCA Victor for $35,000, plus $5,000 in back royalties he owed Elvis. It was the largest amount paid for a single performer up to that time. Steve Sholes, RCA's premier A&R (artist and repertoire) man, had helped sign Elvis to the label. Sholes oversaw the company's specialty singles, which included country-western, gospel, and R&B, so he served as the producer of Elvis' first recordings for RCA. Moving to RCA was a major step in Elvis' career and a major investment for the company; at the very least, it meant going national and international in promotion and distribution. Sholes was aware that the execs at RCA were closely watching their unusual new artist, who didn't fit into any of the company's existing categories of music.

RCA rereleased Elvis' Sun singles in December 1955 and then arranged for Elvis to begin recording new material in Nashville the next month. Chet Atkins, RCA's head man in Nashville, organized the sessions, which started on January 10–11, 1956. Scotty Moore and Bill Black, who had worked with Elvis on the road and at Sun from the beginning, accompanied Elvis as usual. D.J. Fontana, who played with Elvis on tour, checked in as Elvis' drummer, though he had never recorded with the trio before. Atkins played rhythm guitar, Floyd Cramer was added at the piano, and gospel singers Ben and Brock Speer of the Speer Family and Gordon Stoker of the Jordanaires provided backing vocals.

A mix of rock 'n' roll and ballads, Elvis Presley *(RCA LPM-1254) reveals a talented young singer with a unique style exploring his musical tastes.*

The detached, professional air at the RCA sessions was intimidating to Moore and Black, who were used to the down-home atmosphere of Sun, while Sholes was unsure of how to duplicate Elvis' Sun sound. Stoker was unhappy because the rest of the Jordanaires had not been asked to join the session. In fact, everyone was nervous or unsettled except Elvis, who attacked his first number, Ray Charles' "I Got a Woman," with everything he had. In effect, Elvis *performed* the song while he recorded it, which so impressed the typically cool Atkins that he called his wife to come down to the studio because "it was just so damn exciting." Elvis went on to record "Heartbreak Hotel" and "Money Honey" that day. The RCA engineers approximated the Sun Studio's echo effect for "Heartbreak Hotel" by the creative placement of a speaker and a mike. The following day, Elvis recorded two ballads that Sholes had found for him, "I'm Counting on You" and "I Was the One."

Sholes was disconcerted by Elvis' off-handed, instinctual approach to recording, in which he sang a take, played it back, discarded it, and then sang another, repeating the process until he felt he had captured the tune. Elvis did not read music, nor did he have any professional experience at arranging it. He just instinctively knew what to do and when. RCA executives in New York were also troubled with the Nashville session. The recordings did not sound as much like Elvis' Sun records as they had wanted, and the two ballads were unlike anything Elvis had released before.

Elvis' informal approach to recording sessions sometimes flustered RCA execs. He often warmed up by playing the piano or singing gospel songs with friends or session musicians.

Elvis' deal with RCA made everyone smile. **From left:** *Elvis' former manager Bob Neal, the legendary Sam Phillips, RCA attorney Coleman Tilly, Elvis, and the Colonel.*

A second recording session was arranged in New York, in which Elvis covered Carl Perkins' "Blue Suede Shoes" and Little Richard's "Tutti Frutti." This time only piano player Shorty Long was used in addition to Scotty, Bill, and D.J., and the focus was on explosive rock 'n' roll numbers. Seven tracks from the Nashville and New York sessions were chosen for Elvis' first long-playing album, *Elvis Presley.* These were combined with five songs previously recorded at Sun but never released. Interestingly, "Heartbreak Hotel" was not included on the first album.

Sholes and RCA need not have worried about their new charge. Released on March 13, 1956, *Elvis Presley* sold over 360,000 copies by the end of April. At $3.98 per album, this made it RCA's first million-dollar album by a single artist. *Elvis Presley* also became the first album in music history to sell over a million copies. It reached number one on *Billboard*'s Top LPs chart, remaining there for ten weeks, and it launched a record five extended-play albums.

Critics have long struggled over whether Elvis' music began to go downhill after he left the innovative guidance of Sam Phillips for the mainstream glory of RCA. Detractors point to the ballads on his first album as evidence of his move toward pop music and away from the groundbreaking rockabilly of Sun. However, Elvis had just turned 21 when he began recording for RCA, and as a young artist, he was still developing his style. Elvis did not write music or compose lyrics. Rather, his talent was the uncanny ability to fuse diverse influences, ranging from the pop ballads of Dean Martin to the R&B of Arthur Crudup, into a unique sound that became polished rock 'n' roll at RCA. *Elvis Presley*, with its combination of ballads, rock 'n' roll covers, and unreleased Sun recordings, reveals a young singer developing his musical expression.

ELVIS PRESLEY

"Blue Suede Shoes"
"I'm Counting on You"
"I Got a Woman"
"One-Sided Love Affair"
"I Love You Because"
"Just Because"
"Tutti Frutti"
"Tryin' to Get to You"
"I'm Gonna Sit Right Down and Cry (Over You)"
"I'll Never Let You Go (Little Darlin')"
"Blue Moon"
"Money Honey"

BEST ALBUMS
Elvis

ELVIS' SECOND ALBUM, simply titled *Elvis*, was recorded on September 1–3, 1956, and released on October 19. It did not include "Hound Dog" and "Don't Be Cruel," his monumental single releases of that summer. Singles represented a large part of the record-buying scene during that period and were treated as releases unto themselves rather than as a means to promote albums. So, it was not unusual that these two major singles did not end up on Elvis' next album.

While Steve Sholes and Chet Atkins had guided Elvis' earlier sessions for RCA, Elvis was in the saddle this time around, and he thoughtfully mulled over each take of each song until he understood what he wanted. The result is an eclectic blend of songs that truly reflects the singer's personal taste in music as well the components of his style, and that is the album's strength and significance. The album included everything from rock 'n' roll tunes such as "Long Tall Sally" to old country weepies such as "Old Shep." The heart-stopping ballad "Love Me" proved a popular hit despite not being released as single. It was included on the extended-play record *Elvis, Volume 1*, which was a scaled-down version of *Elvis*. It became the first EP in history to sell a million copies.

Except for "So Glad You're Mine," all tracks were recorded at Radio Recorders in Los Angeles because Elvis was in Hollywood making his first film. For the rest of the 1950s and for much of the 1960s, Elvis recorded at this studio. Only Scotty Moore, Bill Black, and D.J. Fontana accompanied him on this album, while the Jordanaires provided background vocals. Elvis played piano on "Old Shep," marking the first time he played piano on a record. The LP entered *Billboard*'s chart at number seven. A month later, it reached the top of the chart, where it remained for five weeks.

David B. Hecht photographed the cover for Elvis *(RCA LPM-1382).*

ELVIS

"Rip It Up"
"Love Me"
"When My Blue Moon
   Turns to Gold Again"
"Long Tall Sally"
"First in Line"
"Paralyzed"
"So Glad You're Mine"
"Old Shep"
"Ready Teddy"
"Anyplace Is Paradise"
"How's the World
   Treating You"
"How Do You Think I Feel"

THE JORDANAIRES

Formed in 1948, the gospel quartet the Jordanaires have backed many diverse performers, including Kitty Wells, Hank Snow, and Ricky Nelson. The members have changed several times over the years. The four who backed Elvis Presley were Gordon Stoker (first tenor), Neal Matthews (second tenor), Hoyt Hawkins (baritone), and Hugh Jarrett (bass). In January 1956, Stoker was included as a backup singer on Elvis' first RCA recording session in a makeshift group with Ben and Brock Speer of the gospel-singing Speer Family. On another session later that year, Stoker was again hired to back Elvis without the rest of his quartet. When Elvis asked the tenor where the rest of the Jordanaires were, Stoker replied that he had been the only one asked. Elvis told him, "If anything comes of this, I want the Jordanaires to work all my sessions from now on, and my personal appearances, too." With that verbal agreement, the Jordanaires became "the Sound Behind the King" for over a decade.

BEST ALBUMS
Elvis' Christmas Album

"IT REALLY IS the best season of the year. The Christmas carols, trees and lights just grab you. There is something about Christmas and being home that I just can't explain. Maybe it's being with the family and with friends, time to read and to study. And, of course, there are the snowball fights and sleigh rides and, yes—just home." Elvis' heartfelt words about the holidays were revealed to his hometown newspaper, the *Memphis Press-Scimitar*, in 1966, though Christmas had been a special time for him since his childhood in Tupelo.

His love for the season prompted Elvis to put out several Christmas albums during his career, beginning with the November 19, 1957, release of *Elvis' Christmas Album*. In addition to such Christmas standards as "White Christmas," "Oh Little Town of Bethlehem, and "Silent Night," this album featured a couple of contemporary holiday tunes. During the recording sessions for the album, material ran short so Jerry Leiber and Mike Stoller retired to the mixing room for a while and came up with a clever piece called "Santa Claus Is Back in Town." Elvis' bluesy rendition of "Blue Christmas" made it a classic that would always be associated with him.

Elvis' Christmas Album hit the top of *Billboard*'s best-selling albums chart and eventually achieved sales of over $1 million. The next year, the album was released with a new cover and a new number, LPM-1951. This release made *Billboard*'s top-selling albums chart on three occasions—January 1961,

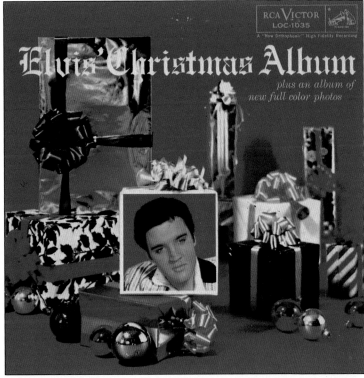

One deejay compared playing Elvis' Christmas Album *(RCA LOC-1035) to "having [stripper] Tempest Storm give Christmas presents to my kids."*

January 1962, and December 1967—which attests to its timeless popularity.

At the time of the album's initial release, Elvis was still generating controversy with his live performances, and many in the press and industry felt that it was in bad taste for a notorious rock 'n' roller to cut a Christmas album. Several disc jockeys refused to play any cuts from the album. At station KEX in Portland, Oregon, deejay Al Priddy was fired for playing Elvis' rendition of "White Christmas." Some radio stations banned the album outright, while WCFL of Chicago got carried away and banned all records by Elvis. Fortunately, the excitement over the Christmas album faded quickly, having been replaced by news that Elvis had received his draft notice.

ELVIS' CHRISTMAS ALBUM

"Santa Claus Is Back in Town"
"White Christmas"
"Here Comes Santa Claus"
"I'll Be Home for Christmas"
"Blue Christmas"
"Santa, Bring My Baby Back (to Me)"
"Oh Little Town of Bethlehem"
"Silent Night"
"Peace in the Valley"
"I Believe"
"Take My Hand, Precious Lord"
"It Is No Secret"

BEST ALBUMS
Elvis Is Back

SPECULATION RAN rampant about Elvis' future as the publicity surrounding his return from the army reached mammoth proportions. Among the many questions pondered by the press and public: What would Elvis' first recordings be like after two years away from the music scene? Would he still maintain his position as popular music's premier recording artist? Fans found the answer in his next album, *Elvis Is Back*, released in April 1960.

Elvis returned to a music scene very different than the one he had left. Smooth-sounding teen angels such as Bobby Vee, Bobby Rydell, Frankie Avalon, and Connie Francis caught the ears of young listeners, while a dance craze called the Twist propelled them across the dance floor. Elvis and his manager, Colonel Tom Parker, embarked on a campaign to mold his image around current trends and away from the controversy that had followed him before the army. The rebellious persona was cast aside for maturity; in his music, the innovation of his Sun Studio roots was replaced by the calculation of mainstream ambitions.

While many have criticized this change, it did not represent a decline in the quality of Elvis' music. On the contrary, *Elvis Is Back* represents a peak in the singer's career, when his maturity

The album Elvis Is Back *(RCA LPM-2231) opened up like a book. Bonus photos were included on the inside.*

and confidence led to a control and focus in his music. Like the pre-army *Elvis*, this album offered an eclectic collection of musical genres, from a sentimental duet with Charlie Hodge called "I Will Be Home Again" to the gritty "Reconsider Baby" with a bluesy sax solo by Boots Randolph. Once again, Elvis' talent of unifying disparate styles of music resulted in an innovative and successful album, and it reached number two on the charts.

Many of the songs chosen for this album had been provided through publishing companies owned by Elvis. In the future, this practice, combined with the Colonel's insistence that Elvis concentrate on soundtrack material, resulted in less-satisfying albums containing conventional songs with a homogenous sound.

ELVIS IS BACK

"Make Me Know It"	"Soldier Boy"
"Fever"	"Such a Night"
"The Girl of My Best Friend"	"It Feels So Right"
"I Will Be Home Again"	"The Girl Next Door"
"Dirty, Dirty Feeling"	"Like a Baby"
"Thrill of Your Love"	"Reconsider Baby"

BEST ALBUMS
Blue Hawaii

THE SOUNDTRACK to *Blue Hawaii* may have been miles away from rock 'n' roll or rhythm and blues, but it gave Elvis the song that he would close most of his 1970s concerts with— "Can't Help Falling in Love." Recorded at Radio Recorders in Hollywood in 1961, *Blue Hawaii* featured 14 songs, which was more than any other Elvis soundtrack. The material was not particularly creative, nor did it have the mix of sounds found on *Elvis Is Back*, but it is a solid example of that blend of pop and rock that defined Elvis' movie music. *Blue Hawaii*—the album and the movie— was aimed at a far wider audience than his studio recordings. Elvis' management was interested in appealing to the mainstream audience and generating spectacular sales. They were less concerned with the impact of his music or with his role as a musical innovator. This and other soundtrack albums were meant to serve a different purpose and appeal to different audiences. Unfortunately, as the decade wore on, the movie material declined in quality, reflecting poorly on all of the soundtracks.

Of the 14 songs on the album, most are pop-style tunes. Some of these were not written for the film but had been recorded and released previously, including "Moonlight Swim," "Blue Hawaii" and "Hawaiian Wedding Song." "Aloha Oe" was composed by Queen Liliuokalani of Hawaii in 1878. The title tune and "Aloha Oe" had been recorded in

Deejays picked Blue Hawaii *(RCA LPM-2426) as a favorite album of 1961.*

the 1930s by Bing Crosby during a craze for the allure of the tropical isles. The songs that were composed for the film were not rock 'n' roll, either, though "Rock-a-Hula Baby" is a playful pastiche of rock 'n' roll dance crazes. To capture a Hawaiian-style sound, special musicians were employed for the recording sessions. Percussionist Hal Blaine, whose expertise involved Hawaiian instruments, joined drummers D.J. Fontana and Bernie Mattinson. Steel guitar and ukelele players were also added.

Blue Hawaii became Elvis' biggest-selling movie soundtrack. It topped *Billboard*'s albums chart two months after its October 1961 release. It was the number-one album in the country for 20 weeks, which set a record for a rock performer or group that lasted until 1977 when Fleetwood Mac's *Rumors* broke it. *Blue Hawaii* remained on the albums chart for 79 weeks and was awarded double platinum status by the RIAA in March 1992.

BLUE HAWAII

"Blue Hawaii"	"Ku-u-i-po"
"Almost Always True"	"Ito Eats"
"Aloha Oe"	"Slicin' Sand"
"No More"	"Hawaiian Sunset"
"Can't Help Falling in Love"	"Beach Boy Blues"
"Rock-a-Hula Baby"	"Island of Love (Kauai)"
"Moonlight Swim"	"Hawaiian Wedding Song"

BEST ALBUMS
How Great Thou Art

FROM JANUARY 1964 to May 1966, Elvis recorded nothing but movie soundtracks, mostly in Hollywood. Unsatisfied with his life for complex professional and personal reasons, he did not venture into the Nashville studios to cut any album material. When he did finally decide to record new material, he returned to the studio with new musicians and a new producer, Felton Jarvis.

Elvis went to the RCA studios in Nashville in the spring of 1966 to make a gospel album, *How Great Thou Art*. As a child of the South, he was steeped in gospel music. Memphis was the center of white gospel music during the 1950s, and Elvis frequently attended all-night gospel sings at Ellis Auditorium as a teenager. Early in his recording career, he developed the lifelong habit of warming up before each session by singing gospel harmonies with the Jordanaires or with his companions.

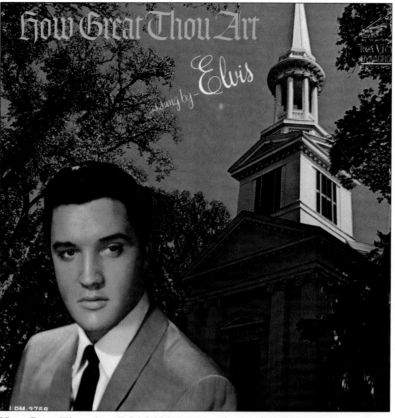

How Great Thou Art (RCA LPM-3758) used several studio musicians new to Elvis' recording sessions, including Charlie McCoy and Ray Stevens.

flamboyant dresser. Elvis was delighted when Hess and his latest quartet, the Imperials, joined him in the studio to record *How Great Thou Art*, along with a few secular songs that were released later. Also on board were the Jordanaires and a female backup group.

The arrangements for the gospel numbers consisted of Statesmen and Blackwood Brothers material. For most numbers, Elvis sang as the solo artist while one of the quartets backed him up. A high point of the sessions occurred when Elvis and Hess sang a duet on the Statesmen's famous "If the Lord Wasn't Walking by My Side."

Though Elvis loved all gospel, he particulary liked the four-part harmony style sung by male gospel quartets associated with the shapenote singing schools from the early part of the century. A quartet usually included first and second tenors, a baritone, and a bass. As a teenager, Elvis' favorite gospel quartets included the Blackwood Brothers, whom he knew personally, and the Statesmen, whose lead singer was the colorful Jake Hess. The Statesmen were known for their emotional, highly stylized delivery, and Hess had a reputation as a

How Great Thou Art proved to be a milestone in Elvis' career, winning him the first of his three Grammys, this one in the Best Sacred Performance category. He won Best Inspirational Performance for *He Touched Me* in 1972 and again in that category for the song "How Great Thou Art" from the album *Elvis Recorded Live on Stage in Memphis* in 1974.

Elvis created this album during a time of personal and professional struggle. He had been frustrated creatively by the formulaic movies and the conventional soundtrack music he recorded for them. It is altogether fitting that Elvis should record a gospel album at a time when he was at a creative and spiritual low. Gospel had inspired his interest in music, it had always calmed his nerves before a session or a performance, and now, as they say in the South, it called him back home.

A young Elvis performs at an all-night gospel sing with the Statesmen Quartet.

FELTON JARVIS

Chet Atkins served as Elvis' producer in a minimalist way until 1966 when he decided to get away from the night sessions that Elvis preferred when he recorded. Atkins introduced RCA staff producer Felton Jarvis to Elvis when the singer was scheduled to record *How Great Thou Art,* and Jarvis became Elvis' primary producer. Born in Atlanta, Charles Felton Jarvis had been something of an Elvis imitator in his youth, recording "Don't Knock Elvis" in 1959. Jarvis became a producer in 1963 with a Presley soundalike named Marvin Benefield, whom Jarvis renamed Vince Everett after Elvis' character in *Jailhouse Rock.*

Jarvis helped steer Elvis toward better material than the soundtrack albums he had been releasing for the last several years, though his hands were often tied by RCA's strict publishing policies. He left RCA in 1970 to devote his full attention to Elvis' recordings. After Elvis died, Jarvis produced sessions for Carl Perkins and coproduced the songs sung by Ronnie McDowell for the 1979 biopic *Elvis.* He died in 1981 at the age of 46.

BEST ALBUMS
From Elvis in Memphis

AFTER YEARS of starring in movie vehicles and recording mainly soundtrack material, Elvis fell into a rut, devoid of creativity and vitality. The decision to turn Elvis into a big-screen leading man via a series of musical comedies was arguably a good career move in the early 1960s, but by 1968, the movie formula was clearly a dead end. The television special *Elvis*, which aired in December 1968, turned his career around by introducing him to hipper recording material and new directions.

Inspired and invigorated by the success of his television special, Elvis walked through the door of tiny American Sound Studios in Memphis in January 1969 to make quality music that would garner him hit records. Elvis had not recorded in his hometown since he left Sun in 1955, but the musical atmosphere at RCA's Nashville studios had become stale. His friends and associates encouraged him to record at American Sound because Nashville would yield nothing for him at this time.

American Sound Studios, a small studio in a rundown neighborhood, was operated by Chips Moman. With Moman as producer, Elvis worked hard to record his first significant mainstream album in years. In retrospect, *From Elvis in Memphis* may be his most important album because it brought his recording career back from soundtrack purgatory and set a creative standard for the next few years.

The material that Moman brought to Elvis represented all styles of music. Some songs were from the pens of new coun-

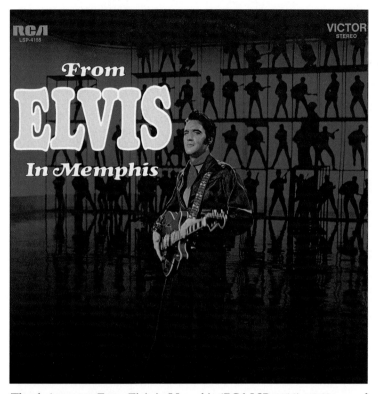

Thanks in part to From Elvis in Memphis *(RCA LSP-4155), 1969 proved to be the most successful year for Elvis' recording career since 1962.*

try songwriters who had been influenced by the innovative music scene of the 1960s. From Mac Davis came a song with socially conscious lyrics called "In the Ghetto," which was light-years away from the benign tunes Elvis had been recording. It became a top-ten hit for Elvis in the spring of 1969. Also recorded was Jerry Butler's rhythm-and-blues hit "Only the Strong Survive."

Though Elvis recorded 32 songs from a variety of genres, the 12 cuts on *From Elvis in Memphis* seem weighted toward modern country music. Elvis' intensely performed version of "Long Black Limousine," about a poor country girl who moves to the big city, turned a sentimental country song into a bitter social comment. Other passionately rendered country tunes on the album include Eddy Arnold's "I'll Hold You in My Heart (Till I Can Hold You in My Arms)" and "After Loving You." Also among the 32 tracks produced at American Sound Studios were the rock-flavored hits "Suspicious Minds" and "Kentucky Rain," which were not included on *From Elvis in Memphis*. "Suspicious Minds" was included on the follow-up release, *From Memphis to Vegas/From Vegas to Memphis*.

The house band at American Sound Studios included musicians who were steeped in all forms of Southern music. Both black and white artists recorded at American Sound, and the house band was generally the same no matter who recorded there. Many of these musicians, including guitarist Reggie

Young (who played Scotty Moore's old guitar on "Suspicious Minds"), bassist Tommy Cogbill, and pianist Bobby Wood, had grown up on Elvis' music. No more fitting group of musicians could have backed Elvis on his return to Memphis.

Released in May 1969, *From Elvis in Memphis* landed on *Billboard*'s Top LPs chart, where it peaked at number 13, and its Country LPs chart, where it reached the number-two position. A gold record was certified for the album in January 1970. Most importantly, *From Elvis in Memphis* helped alter Elvis' image. No longer the crooning movie star, he had returned to the music scene to reclaim his crown as the King of Rock 'n' Roll.

The interior of American Sound Studios.

The musicians at American Sound Studios. From left: *Bobby Wood, Mike Leech, Tommy Cogbill, Gene Chrisman, Elvis, Bobby Emmons, Reggie Young, Ed Kollis, and Dan Penn.*

FROM ELVIS IN MEMPHIS

"Wearin' That Loved on Look"
"Only the Strong Survive"
"I'll Hold You in My Heart (Till I Can Hold You in My Arms)"
"Long Black Limousine"
"It Keeps Right on a-Hurtin'"
"I'm Movin' On"
"Power of My Love"
"Gentle on My Mind"
"After Loving You"
"True Love Travels on a Gravel Road"
"Any Day Now"
"In the Ghetto"

CHIPS MOMAN

Born in 1936 in LaGrange, Georgia, Chips Moman made his name as one of the architects of the Memphis Sound, an edgier style of soul music descended from Memphis' blues and rhythm and blues. Settling in Memphis in the late 1950s, he helped establish soulful Stax Records in 1958. Six years later, Moman and fellow producer Bob Crewe founded American Sound Studios. Stax and American Sound became the premier champions of the Memphis Sound.

As a songwriter, Moman composed the gritty R&B tune "Dark End of the Street," which was recorded by Percy Sledge, Linda Ronstadt, and Roy Hamilton, as well as "Luckenback Texas," made famous by country outlaw Waylon Jennings. As a hands-on producer, Moman became an expert at finding the right material for the right performer. Moman produced a three-year string of hits for such diverse artists as Wilson Pickett, Dusty Springfield, B.J. Thomas, Neil Diamond, and the Box Tops. His work with Elvis in 1969 garnered the singer his first hit singles in years.

During the 1970s, Moman produced in Nashville but returned to Memphis in 1985 to open Three Alarm Studios. Partly because of his work with Elvis, Moman gained a reputation for reviving stagnating careers.

BEST ALBUMS
Reconsider Baby

THROUGHOUT HIS CAREER, Elvis recorded occasional blues songs or tunes that were at least reminiscent of the blues. Even during the 1960s when his music had the homogenous pop style typified by his soundtrack recordings, he managed to record "I Feel So Bad" and "Hi-Heel Sneakers." Released in 1985, *Reconsider Baby* offers a selection of the bluesier sounds Elvis recorded between 1955 and 1971, reminding us that the roots of his personal sound, even at its most mainstream, came from the indigenous musical styles of the South—in this case blues and rhythm and blues.

Some of the songs on this album are not the versions that were originally released, which adds a freshness to the collection. The version of "One Night" included here, for example, was an alternate take, and it features the original lyrics as sung by Smiley Lewis ("One night of sin..."). "Ain't That Loving You Baby" was also an alternate take, while "Merry Christmas Baby" was an alternate edit, and "Stranger in My Own Home Town" represented an alternate mix. The 1955 original Sun recording of "Tomorrow Night" is the version included here.

In 1960, Elvis recorded the insipid lullaby "Big Boots" for *G.I. Blues*, but he also recorded Lowell Fulson's nasty

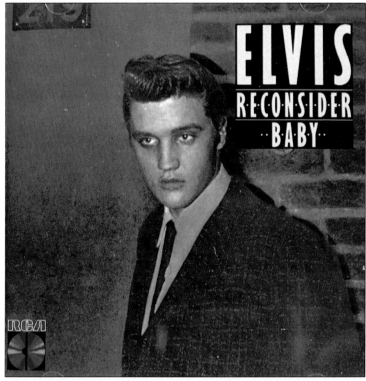

The songs featured on **Reconsider Baby** *(RCA AFL1-5418) reflect the bluesy, soulful edge of Elvis' eclectic music.*

"Reconsider Baby," accompanied by Boots Randolph's sexy-sounding sax. In 1966, he released "Yoga Is as Yoga Does," but he also cut a raw-sounding "Down in the Alley." Elvis' critics and detractors often quote John Lennon, who once quipped, "Elvis died when he went into the army." *Reconsider Baby* proves that there was a still an edge to Elvis' music long after he returned from the army.

Drummer Ronnie Tutt played on some of the cuts, most notably "Merry Christmas Baby." During a break in the vocals on that song, Elvis roars, "Wake up, Tutt."

RECONSIDER BABY

"Reconsider Baby"	"Ain't That Loving You Baby"
"Tomorrow Night"	"I Feel So Bad"
"So Glad You're Mine"	"Down in the Alley"
"One Night"	"Hi-Heel Sneakers"
"When It Rains, It Really Pours"	"Stranger in My Own Home Town"
"My Baby Left Me"	"Merry Christmas Baby"

BEST ALBUMS
The Top Ten Hits

IN THE YEARS after Elvis died, RCA continued to release Presley albums, but there was little attempt to treat the music as his legacy. Each executive who handled the Presley account treated it differently, but most viewed it as commercial output rather than as music history. Albums and songs were reissued, and original tapes were overdubbed. Sometimes

When Steve Sholes signed Elvis in 1955, little did he know that Elvis would remain a vital artist for RCA long after his death.

the instrumentation was overdubbed; sometimes a fake stereo effect was added; sometimes the background vocals were "enhanced." This changed in 1986, when the German publishing group Bertlesmann Music Group purchased RCA. The company now issues Elvis' music without vocal and instrumental enhancement, and it tends to package the material in contexts that acknowledge the significance of Elvis' music.

Presented as an "Elvis Presley Commemorative Issue," *The Top Ten Hits* is a two-record set originally released in June 1987. A poster was included in the packaging, and the set came with special commemorative innersleeves. In 1995, a compact-disc version of *The Top Ten Hits* was released (RCA 6383-2-R). Chart information, including the recording date, chart debut, and peak position, was included for the record set and the CD set.

Elvis' top-ten hits spanned the three decades of his career, and 38 of them are included here. The packaging of over three dozen top-ten singles into one set focuses on Elvis' career-long ability to chart hit records and indicates the diversity of his singles output. Organized chronologically by release date, *The Top Ten Hits* begins with Elvis' first number-one single, "Heartbreak Hotel," released in 1956, and ends with the platinum-selling hit "Burning Love," released in 1972. *The Top Ten Hits* was awarded gold status by the RIAA in 1992.

The Top Ten Hits (RCA 638-1-R) includes Elvis' biggest hit tunes.

THE TOP TEN HITS

"Heartbreak Hotel"
"I Want You, I Need You, I Love You"
"Hound Dog"
"Don't Be Cruel"
"Love Me Tender"
"Love Me"
"Too Much"
"All Shook Up"
"Teddy Bear"
"Jailhouse Rock"
"Don't"
"I Beg of You"
"Wear My Ring Around Your Neck"
"Hard Headed Woman"
"One Night"
"I Got Stung"
"A Fool Such As I"
"I Need Your Love Tonight"
"A Big Hunk o' Love"

"Stuck on You"
"It's Now or Never"
"Are You Lonesome Tonight?"
"Surrender"
"I Feel So Bad"
"Little Sister"
"His Latest Flame"
"Can't Help Falling in Love"
"Good Luck Charm"
"She's Not You"
"Return to Sender"
"Devil in Disguise"
"Bossa Nova Baby"
"Crying in the Chapel"
"In the Ghetto"
"Suspicious Minds"
"Don't Cry Daddy"
"The Wonder of You"
"Burning Love"

BEST ALBUMS
Elvis, the King of Rock 'n' Roll: The Complete 50s Masters

WHEN BMG PURCHASED RCA, they formed an international committee of record executives to clean up the Presley catalogue. Interested in presenting Elvis Presley's music as a chronicle of a culturally significant performer, the committee embarked on a multiproject goal that involved reissuing the music as close to its original form as possible.

Released in 1992, *Elvis, the King of Rock 'n' Roll: The Complete 50s Masters* represents BMG's first significant restoration effort. Producers Ernst Mikael Jorgensen and Roger Semon searched the RCA vaults from Nashville to Indianapolis to Hollywood to find what they needed for this retrospective of Elvis Presley's complete 1950s output. The pureness of the sound is a result of what the producers did not do to the master tapes as opposed to what they did do. The five-disc, 140-track compilation features all of Elvis' released recordings from that era as well as some alternate takes and rare live performances. A bound booklet by Presley biographer and music historian Peter Guralnik discusses the original recording sessions in depth.

The Complete 50s Masters went platinum in 1993, and it was given the Critics' 1993 Music Award for the Best Reissue

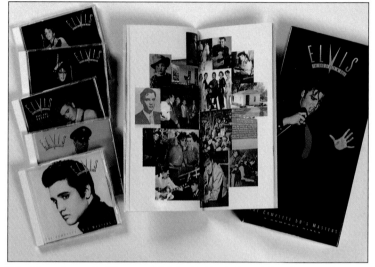

The Complete 50s Masters (RCA 66050-2) chronicles the most innovative phase of Elvis' career.

Album from *Rolling Stone* magazine. Most importantly, this boxed set affords the listener the opportunity to experience the development of Elvis' sound. It is as much music history as it is a retrospective of an artist's career.

THE 1950s: THE HILLBILLY CAT AND THE BLUE MOON BOYS

Essential to Elvis' sound in the 1950s was the trio of musicians who backed him up: Scotty Moore, Bill Black, and D.J. Fontana. Elvis, guitarist Moore, and bassist Black were dubbed the Hillbilly Cat and the Blue Moon Boys. Moore and Black had previously played with the country-western band the Starlight Wranglers, but they hitched their wagons to Elvis' star after recording "That's All Right" with the inexperienced young singer in July 1954. Moore's driving guitar sound helped create Elvis' style, while Black's antics on his stand-up bass added humor and excitement to their live act. After appearing with the group on the *Louisiana Hayride*, drummer D.J. Fontana joined them on the road, though he never played on any of Elvis' Sun recordings. After Elvis became a household name, Moore, Black, and Fontana were not given the respect and salary they were due. Moore and Black split with Elvis over this issue in September 1957. Though both were wooed back, things were never quite the same. Moore and Fontana recorded with Elvis after he returned from the army in 1960, but Black had already struck out on his own in 1958, enjoying moderate success with his own combo.

D.J. Fontana, Elvis, and Bill Black cut loose onstage, circa 1956.

BEST ALBUMS
Elvis Presley: From Nashville to Memphis: The Essential 60s Masters I

THIS COMPILATION of Elvis' 1960s work includes his recording sessions in Nashville and Memphis from that decade. It begins with Elvis' first sessions after his discharge from the army, which yielded the memorable album *Elvis Is Back*, and concludes with his historic sessions at American Sound Studios, which marked his successful comeback to the music scene after years of producing uninspired soundtrack albums. *The Essential 60s Masters I* leaves out the Hollywood movie soundtracks, which many consider the downfall of his music career.

The focus on Elvis' better material from that decade allows the listener to hear the maturing of a remarkable talent. Fans of Elvis will appreciate the approach to the packaging, which offers the tracks in sequence as they were recorded. The songs in this five-disc, 130-track set were digitally remastered and include 19 previously unreleased songs. Unfortunately, Elvis' work from this decade is oblivious to the innovative rock-music scene of the mid-1960s. However, when considering that his music and films were aimed at a broad audience during that decade, the homogenous pop stylings are accept-

The Essential 60s Masters I *(RCA 66160-2) showcases the mature sounds of a versatile singer.*

able. Peter Guralnik authored the extensive liner notes that accompany this compilation, and his straightforward discussions of the recording sessions are detailed and insightful.

THE 1960S: STALWARTS IN THE STUDIO

For most of the 1960s, Elvis did not perform live. The musicians who backed him did so in the studio, not on the stage. Despite a falling out with Elvis in 1957, guitarist Scotty Moore played with Elvis until 1968. Drummer D.J. Fontana stayed with Elvis till 1969. During the two years Elvis was in the army, Moore produced and played on some of Jerry Lee Lewis' records. Bassist Bill Black left Elvis' employ in February 1958 and formed the Bill Black Combo. Black's successful records included the instrumental "Smokie—Part 2" and "White Silver

Sands." Black died in 1965 of a brain tumor. In addition to Moore and Fontana, several Nashville session musicians contributed a consistent sound to Elvis' smooth, pop-styled music and soundtrack recordings. Nashville pianist Floyd Cramer, known for his slip-note style of playing, worked with Elvis from 1956 through 1968; Boots Randolph played saxophone and vibes on 21 recordings from 1960 through 1968; and, Charlie McCoy, a member of the Grand Ole Opry house band, played harmonica from 1965 to 1971.

During the 1960s, the Jordanaires provided background vocals on most of Elvis' recordings.

BEST ALBUMS
Elvis Presley: Walk a Mile in My Shoes: The Essential 70s Masters

THIS FIVE-DISK RETROSPECTIVE of Elvis' 1970s output features every single A- and B-side released between 1970 and August 1977. One disc features live recordings as a tribute to Elvis' concert performances. While continuing their goal of releasing the Elvis catalogue in its original form and context, the producers also hoped to counter the negative stereotype of a garish Elvis in his white jumpsuit belting out the same Vegas-style tunes over and over.

The Essential 70s Masters dispels that image by revealing how productive Elvis was during the 1970s, despite the drug abuse and health problems. Few artists recorded as much product as Elvis did during the last six years of his life. The 120 tracks included here also indicate that Elvis was a singer with eclectic tastes, just as he had been in the 1950s. He mastered all manner of songs and styles and made them his own, from the baroque "An American Trilogy" to the bluesy "Merry Christmas Baby" to the country confessional "You Gave Me a Mountain."

The Essential 70s Masters (RCA 66670-2) captures the Elvis of that decade—dramatic, flamboyant, larger-than-life.

A booklet by Elvis biographer Dave Marsh offers liner notes that are informative, though his prose is more embellished than that of Peter Guralnik, who wrote the booklets for *The Complete 50s Masters* and *The Essential 60s Masters I.*

THE 1970s: NEW FACES FOR A NEW SOUND

A consequence of Elvis' new direction in the 1970s was a change in the core group of musicians who recorded with him, many of whom accompanied him on the road. Chief among the musicians was lead guitarist James Burton, who had worked with Ricky Nelson. An accomplished and respected lead guitar player, Burton later worked with Gram Parsons and Emmylou Harris. Other band members included several Hollywood sessions musicians who had occasionally contributed to Elvis' movie soundtracks: There was bassist Jerry Scheff, who had worked with the Doors;

pianist Larry Muhoberac; and drummer Ronnie Tutt. Elvis' new sound was large-scale, almost operatic. In addition to musicians, he used a male gospel quartet and a female backup group in his recording sessions and on the road. At first the Imperials gospel quartet, with the legendary Jake Hess, backed Elvis vocally, but later J.D. Sumner and the Stamps Quartet took over that role. The Sweet Inspirations fulfilled the duties as female backup voices, and an additional soprano voice was offered by Kathy Westmoreland.

Soprano Kathy Westmoreland added a unique aural flair to Elvis' concerts.

BEST LOVE SONGS

Written by Maurice Mysels and Ira Kosloff, "I Want You, I Need You, I Love You" was recorded in Nashville on April 11, 1956. The song reached the top ten of the pop, country, and rhythm and blues charts. It was the first ballad recorded by Elvis for RCA that was released on a single as the A-side.

Jerry Leiber and Mike Stoller composed the torchy "Love Me" in 1954 as a spoof of country ballads. On September 1, 1956, Elvis recorded it straight and with feeling, turning it into a serious love song.

Elvis recorded "Love Me Tender" in Hollywood in the late summer of 1956 as the closing song for his first film, *Love Me Tender*.

George Weiss, Hugo Peretti, and Luigi Creatore wrote "Can't Help Falling in Love" for *Blue Hawaii*. Elvis recorded it in Hollywood on March 23, 1961.

Elvis recorded "It Hurts Me" in Nashville on January 12, 1964. The song was written by Joy Byers and Charlie Daniels, though Daniels is not always credited. Elvis recorded this song again for his 1968 TV special, *Elvis*, but it was not used.

"Until It's Time for You to Go" was written and originally recorded by Buffy Sainte-Marie in 1965 and was released by several artists before Elvis. Others who recorded it included Michael Nesmith (as Michael Blessing), the Four Pennies, and Neil Diamond. Elvis recorded this beautiful love song in Nashville in the early summer of 1971, and he sang it in the documentary *Elvis on Tour*.

Recorded on March 27, 1972, "Separate Ways" was biographical in that Elvis and Priscilla had just separated. Fans and biographers have often interpreted the song as a reflection of Elvis' feelings. It was composed for him by Richard Mainegra and Elvis' longtime friend and bodyguard Red West.

Mark James, Wayne Carson, and Johnny Christopher composed "Always on My Mind" especially for Elvis, though other singers have had success with it. Elvis was the first to record it, on March 29, 1972, but Brenda Lee's version was released first. In 1982, Willie Nelson scored a number-one country hit with it, while the Pet Shop Boys recorded a version in 1988.

Elvis recorded "It's Midnight" at legendary Stax Records in Memphis on December 10, 1973. It was written by Billy Edd Wheeler and Jerry Chestnut.

The most well-known version of "Unchained Melody" was released by the Righteous Brothers in 1965, though it was written in

1955 for the movie *Unchained*. Several performers recorded it in the 1950s, including Les Baxter, Roy Hamilton, Al Hibbler, and June Valli. Elvis sang this earnest love song in concert during the 1970s, and he was recorded performing it live in Ann Arbor, Michigan, on April 24, 1977. It was released posthumously.

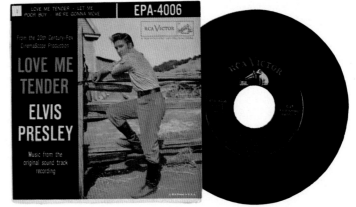

LOVE ME TENDER

Elvis was credited as coauthor of this love ballad, though it was actually composed by Ken Darby, who served as the vocal supervisor on the film. Darby's wife, Vera Matson, also received credit. The song was based on a ballad from the Civil War era called "Aura Lee" (sometimes spelled "Aura Lea"), which was written by W.W. Fosdick and George R. Poulton. "Aura Lee" became a favorite of the Union Army.

Almost 100 years later, the song became a favorite again with the public, this time reincarnated as Elvis' "Love Me Tender." Elvis' single release of the song achieved a first in music history when it received advance sales of over 1 million copies. The movie version of the song had slightly different lyrics and contained an additional verse. Elvis had always admired pop crooners such as Dean Martin, and "Love Me Tender" afforded him the opportunity to affect their gentle tones.

BEST SINGLES
"That's All Right"

ELVIS' FIRST RECORDING for Sun Records, "That's All Right," seemed to come about almost by accident. When Sun's owner and operator, Sam Phillips, needed a singer to record a ballad called "Without You," he remembered a young kid named Elvis Presley. Elvis had cut a couple of acetates at Phillips' Memphis Recording Service, and Phillips' assistant, Marion Keisker, had taped him for future reference. Phillips decided to let Elvis record "Without You," but the inexperienced singer wasn't able to master the new song. Elvis sang several other tunes for Phillips, who was sufficiently impressed to put him together with guitarist Scotty Moore for some seasoning. Moore, Elvis, and bass player Bill Black were working together at Sun on the evening of July 5, 1954, trying to find a sound that clicked. Nothing seemed to be working. During a break, Elvis began fooling around with Arthur "Big Boy" Crudup's country blues tune "That's All Right," singing it in a fast-paced, almost casual style. When Moore and Black jumped in, Phillips' voice boomed out from the control booth, "What are you doing?"

Phillips was excited by the trio's sound and recognized its potential. He recorded "That's All Right" that night and backed it a few days later with the bluegrass classic "Blue Moon of Kentucky." Elvis' approach to both songs differed from the originals. He used a more relaxed vocal style and higher key for "That's All Right" than Crudup had. He sped up the tempo for "Blue Moon of Kentucky" and omitted the high-pitched bluegrass singing style. Two elements were added to both songs that would make Elvis famous—syncopation and a "slapback" (electronically delayed) echo effect. Elvis' Sun style became the epitome of rockabilly.

"That's All Right" received extended airplay on Dewey Phillips' *Red Hot and Blue* radio program on WHBQ, and it was released as a single on July 19, 1954. The single did not chart nationally, but it launched the recording career of the most famous singer of the 20th century.

"That's All Right" (Sun 209) never reached the national charts, but it changed the course of popular music.

SAM PHILLIPS

Born and raised just outside Florence, Alabama, in 1923, Sam Cornelius Phillips was greatly influenced by his rural Southern roots. Working in the cotton fields with African-Americans, Phillips was exposed to gospel and blues music, and he experienced the poverty and hard life of many Depression-era Southern families. As a record producer, he would draw on those experiences to shape a new musical aesthetic—a purely Southern sound that combined black rhythm and blues and white country-western with a hardscrabble philosophy born of bad times. The new music that emerged—a Dixie-fried sound called rockabilly—would emanate from Phillips' Sun Records in the mid-1950s and influence all of rock 'n' roll.

Phillips' genius was recognizing talented singers and musicians—black and white—who could convey the aesthetic he envisioned. Of his desire to record Southern-based music, Phillips mused, "I just knew this was culture, and it was so embedded in these people because of hardship.... Generation after generation, these [Southern] people have been overlooked—black and white!" For his contributions in shaping modern music, Phillips was one of the first to be inducted into the Rock 'n' Roll Hall of Fame.

Elvis walked through the door of Sun Records a shy teenager, but under the guidance of Sam Phillips, he became Sun's premier recording artist. Top left: Bill Black, Elvis, and Scotty Moore were called the Hillbilly Cat and the Blue Moon Boys when they hit the Southern touring circuits to promote their Sun releases in 1954. Top right: Elvis played a Memphis joint called the Eagles Nest in the summer of 1954, sometimes with Doug Poindexter's Starlight Wranglers. Left: Sam Phillips and Elvis enjoy the good life at Taylor's Fine Foods, the small restaurant next door to Sun.

BEST SINGLES
"Baby Let's Play House"

ELVIS' FOURTH SINGLE for Sun Records, recorded on February 5, 1955, and released in late April, became the first Elvis Presley effort to chart nationally. Backed by "I'm Left, You're Right, She's Gone" on the flip side, "Baby Let's Play House" stayed on *Billboard*'s country chart for ten weeks, reaching number ten.

Rhythm-and-blues singer Arthur Gunter had written and recorded the song in 1954, basing it on country singer Eddy Arnold's 1951 hit, "I Want to Play House with You." Being a rythmn-and-blues reworking of a country-western song, "Baby Let's Play House" was perfect for Elvis' rockabilly repertoire. Gunter himself had been influenced by rockabilly artists, and he made a good model for Elvis, who had purchased a copy of Gunter's version the previous December at the House of Records in Memphis. Elvis made the song his own with the inclusion of the syncopated phrasing "babe-babe-baby" in the verse. He also tinkered with the lyrics, changing "You may have religion" to "You may drive a pink Cadillac"—a humorous foretelling of the car that he would come to be identified with. Sam Phillips added drums to the recording session for the song, marking the first time drums were used on a Presley single. As the song received national exposure, it was called a country song in trade publications, and few connected it with the relatively unknown rythmn-and-blues artist who had inspired Elvis.

Elvis added "Baby Let's Play House" and "I'm Left, You're Right, She's Gone" to his act in the spring of 1955. About this time, his popularity was rapidly increasing because of his appearances on the *Louisiana Hayride* radio show and because of touring across the South with ever-larger country-western shows. Elvis sang "Baby Let's Play House" on his second appearance on *Stage Show* on February 4, 1956, just as his sensual performing style was beginning to create a national controversy. If his hip-swinging performance on *Stage Show* raised eyebrows, then the lyrics to "Baby Let's Play House" added to the provocative connotation. Basically a proposition, the song is a plea from the singer to his girlfriend to return to him because he wants to "play house" with her, a slang term for an unmarried couple living or sleeping together. Despite the singer's plea, he takes a confrontational stance, telling his girl, "I'd rather see you dead than with another man."

"Baby Let's Play House" (Sun 217) charted nationally on Billboard's *country list, peaking at number ten.*

SUN RECORDS

Aside from 3764 Elvis Presley Boulevard, 706 Union Avenue is probably the most famous address in Memphis. There, Sam Phillips opened the doors to Sun Records in February 1952, along with the Memphis Recording Service. Phillips had been recording such blues artists as Howlin' Wolf, B.B. King, Little Walter, Ike Turner, Little Junior Parker, and Bobby Blue Bland since 1950, but he leased those recordings to other labels, including Chess Records and RPM Records. Until Sun was established, there was no major place in the South for artists to record. After Phillips established Sun, he could release his artists on his own label.

Many know that the legendary producer recorded blues and R&B performers, but less familiar are the country singers that he began recording in 1953. He started out with the Ripley Cotton Choppers, then moved on to Doug Poindexter, Slim Rhodes, and Warren Smith.

After Elvis experienced success on the Sun label, others who would become rockabilly legends signed with Phillips, including Jerry Lee Lewis, Carl Perkins, Johnny Cash, Roy Orbison, Charlie Rich, Conway Twitty, and Charlie Feathers. Phillips sold Sun in 1969.

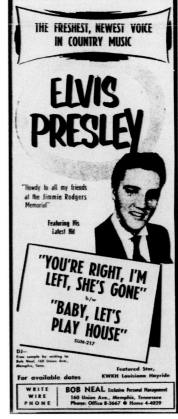

Top: *An ad promotes Elvis' fourth single for Sun.* Above: *The little studio at 706 Union Avenue in Memphis became home to some big names in rockabilly.* Left: *Elvis played several small towns in Texas in July 1955.*

BEST SINGLES
"Heartbreak Hotel"

"I WALK A LONELY STREET." So I read the suicide note of an anonymous soul who ended his life in a Miami hotel. *The Miami Herald* ran a photo of his corpse on the front page with the headline, "Do You Know This Man?" The story went on to explain that the man had been discovered with no identification. Police found only the note in one of his pockets. In Gainesville, songwriter-musician Tommy Durden thought the line in the note resonated the blues and would make a great lyric in a song. He sought the opinion of his friend Mae Boren Axton, who was a local songwriter, TV personality, and publicist. Axton had once done some work for Colonel Tom Parker, and she suggested that they write the song for Elvis Presley. As the story goes, she had once told Elvis that she was going to write his first million seller. After Mae decided that "down at the end of Lonely Street" one would naturally find a "Heartbreak Hotel," the rest of the song was composed by the team within the hour. Glen Reeves, a local singer, recorded a demo record of the

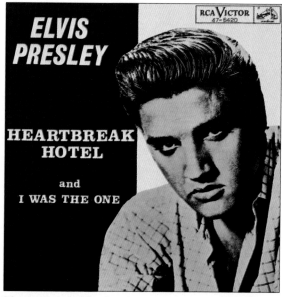

Elvis' voice combined with an exaggerated echo effect perfectly conveyed the despair in the lyrics of "Heartbreak Hotel" (RCA 47-6420).

song in a style that suggested Elvis Presley. Axton flew to Nashville in November 1955 to introduce the song to Elvis, who was in Music City to attend a convention for country music disc jockeys. Elvis loved the song, supposedly exclaiming, "Hot Dog, Mae!" as he played it about ten times in a row.

"Heartbreak Hotel" became the first record Elvis released on his new label, RCA. In December 1955, RCA had reissued Elvis' "Mystery Train," originally released on the Sun label, but the reissue did not sell particularly well. Elvis entered RCA's Nashville studios on January 10, 1956, to record new material. "Heartbreak Hotel" was the second song Elvis recorded that day.

Axton had asked Reeves to emulate Elvis' style on the demo, and Elvis copied the vocal intonations of Reeves for his recording. This story shows that Elvis' style was familiar enough to be recognized as his at the time. It also illustrates Elvis' pattern when recording a demo. He copied the interpre-

MAE, KEN, AND MRS. ED WOOD

Elvis recorded hundreds of songs written by a variety of composers during his career, so it is not surprising that some of those songwriters might fall under the heading "peculiar." Mae Boren Axton, the coauthor of "Heartbreak Hotel," was an English teacher who worked around the periphery of show business while living in Florida. She had worked as a publicist for the Hank Snow All-Star Jamboree, which had also employed Colonel Tom Parker. Axton was the

sister of Oklahoma senator David Boren and the mother of singer/actor Hoyt Axton. After Elvis died, she contributed to the liner notes of Ronnie McDowell's *The King Is Gone*.

Academy Award-winning composer Ken Darby wrote and arranged "Love Me Tender" for Elvis' first film. Early in his career, Darby made a unique contribution to American movie culture when he fulfilled an unusual assignment for the film *The Wizard of Oz*. He was responsible for

creating the distinctive sound of the Munchkin's voices.

Dolores Fuller cowrote 12 songs for Elvis, including "Rock-a-Hula Baby," "Do the Clam," and "Barefoot Ballad." Fuller was the wife of Ed Wood, Jr., a now famous director of horror and exploitation films who worked on the fringes of the industry during the 1950s and 1960s. She appeared in his 1954 film *Jail Bait*.

tation of the demo singer whenever he recorded his version of a song.

At Sun Records, Elvis had been backed by Scotty Moore on guitar and Bill Black on bass. Later a drummer was added—a position eventually filled by D.J. Fontana on a permanent basis. At RCA, Elvis' combo was joined by Chet Atkins on rhythm guitar and Floyd Cramer on piano, along with a gospel trio consisting of Ben and Brock Speer of the Speer Family and Gordon Stoker of the Jordanaires. "Heartbreak Hotel" borrowed the echo sound that was associated with Elvis' Sun releases, perhaps even exaggerating it. The effect is eerie, downright ghostly, particularly during the opening lines to each verse when Elvis sings without accompaniment. His voice is penetrating, and the sound is despondent, perfectly capturing the alienation of disaffected youth.

The song was released as a single on January 27, 1956, backed by "I Was the One." The next day Elvis appeared on Tommy and Jimmy Dorsey's television variety series, *Stage Show*, but he did not sing "Heartbreak Hotel" until his third appearance on the show, February 11. He sang it on two subsequent *Stage Show* appearances and on his first appearance on *The Milton Berle Show* on April 3. The television exposure undoubtedly helped propel the song to the number-one slot on *Billboard*'s best-seller and juke box charts, where it stayed for eight weeks. The song also reached number one on the country chart and number three on the R&B chart. It became Elvis' first million seller, just as Axton had predicted.

Top: *Elvis worked hard in his first session at RCA's Nashville studios.* Bottom: *Legendary guitarist Chet Atkins played rhythm guitar on Elvis' first RCA recordings.*

BEST SINGLES
"Hound Dog"

AFTER HE ROCKED *The Milton Berle Show* with his bump-and-grind rendition of "Hound Dog," this gritty R&B tune became indelibly linked with Elvis Presley. Yet, he was not the first to record a hit version of it, nor did he sing the original lyrics.

The song was written by Jerry Leiber and Mike Stoller in 1952 for blues singer Willie Mae "Big Mama" Thornton at the request of Johnny Otis, a hustling bandleader, producer, composer, and R&B deejay. Otis invited the team to watch Thornton rehearse in his garage-turned-studio. After watching the mighty singer belt out a few numbers, Leiber and Stoller composed "Hound Dog"—a song about a gigolo—in about ten minutes. Thornton growled the saucy lyrics to a hard-driving blues beat, and "Hound Dog" sold over half a million copies, climbed to number one on the R&B charts, and became a top-selling record in the R&B market during 1953. Memphis disc jockey Rufus Thomas recorded an answer song called "Bear Cat," which was released on Sam Phillips' Sun label.

Several performers covered "Hound Dog," including country artists Tommy Duncan, Betsy Gay, Jack Turner, and Billy Starr, and lounge act Freddie Bell and the Bellboys. Bell enlivened the tempo and tampered with the lyrics in a humorous way, adding the line, "You ain't never caught a rabbit, and you ain't no friend of mine." Elvis caught the Bellboys' act in April 1956 when he was booked into the New Frontier Hotel in Las Vegas. Though Elvis and his combo flopped in Vegas, he brought back a little souvenir in the form of Bell's comedic version of "Hound Dog."

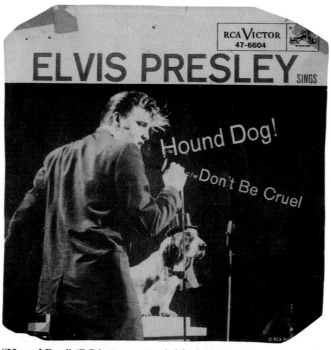

"Hound Dog" (RCA 47-6604) solidified Elvis' image as a notorious rock 'n' roller after he performed it on television.

Part of the reason Elvis' version became so famous was undoubtedly due to television. Elvis introduced the song to a national audience on *The Milton Berle Show* on June 5, 1956, and the attention generated by that controversial performance resulted in a booking on *The Steve Allen Show,* where Elvis gamely sang the song to a basset hound. By the time Elvis sang "Hound Dog" on *The Ed Sullivan Show,* the song was associated with controversy. Elvis teased Sullivan's studio audience, who were primed for fireworks from the young singer, by starting and then stopping the song after the first note.

A male singer belting out the opening line to "Hound Dog" seems odd because the song was clearly written for a female voice, and Elvis' decision to add "Hound Dog" to his repertoire has been interpreted variously by rock music historians. Some insist that Elvis must have been familiar with the Thornton version because he was an R&B enthusiast, and they speculate that he recorded Bell's version because he recognized its humor. Detractors suggest that he appropriated the blues tune without realizing its roots. It seems likely, however, that Elvis did know of Thornton's record. Though Elvis' recorded version was a rock 'n' roll interpretation patterned after Bell's, his rendition on the Berle show owes something to the growling, bump-and-grind vernacular of Thornton's bluesy "Hound Dog."

Pressured by producer Steve Sholes to record the tune, Elvis finally captured "Hound Dog" after about 30 takes in RCA's New York studios. Backed by "Don't Be Cruel," the record became the biggest two-sided hit single in history.

The summer of 1956 proved to be "Hound Dog" days for Elvis as the song climbed to the top of the charts. **Top left:** *The execs at RCA, particularly Steve Sholes (right), pressured Elvis to record the offbeat rhythm-and-blues tune that made the singer a household name.* **Above:** *The sheet music for "Hound Dog" featured a photo of Elvis in rehearsal for* **The Steve Allen Show.** **Left:** *Famed rock 'n' roll songwriters Leiber and Stoller were barely in their twenties when they penned "Hound Dog" in 1952 for blues singer Willie Mae "Big Mama" Thornton.*

BEST SINGLES
"Don't Be Cruel"

"HOUND DOG" and "Don't Be Cruel" became a double-sided hit that climbed to number one and retained that position for 11 weeks—longer than any other single release of the rock 'n' roll era. It also reached number one on the country-western and rhythm-and-blues charts.

As the sheet music indicates, Elvis received a cocredit for "Don't Be Cruel," though he never wrote any part of it.

"Don't Be Cruel" was written by rhythm-and-blues singer-songwriter Otis Blackwell, though Elvis was given a cowriting credit. Blackwell had sold the song to a music publisher, Shalimar Music, for $25 on Christmas Eve 1955. Elvis' parent publisher, Hill and Range, had acquired the song, and the demo was one from a stack that the hot new singer listened to during an RCA recording session in July 1956. When Elvis wanted to record the song, Blackwell was told that he would have to cut a deal and share the writer's credit with him, though Elvis did not contribute anything to writing the song. Blackwell was uneasy about the deal, but he realized he stood to make a great deal of money from royalties—even at half-interest—if Elvis recorded the song. This would not be the last time that Elvis received a writing credit on a song he did not originally compose.

During the recording session, Elvis rehearsed the song a couple of times with his regular backup musicians, a piano player hired by RCA, and the Jordanaires. Then, the group worked on the song, finessing it as they went through almost 30 takes.

Though Elvis liked to tickle the ivories to warm up before a session, he seldom played the piano on any of his recordings. Shorty Long played piano on "Don't Be Cruel."

All the musicians contributed something in their own way. D.J. Fontana used Elvis' leather-covered guitar as a makeshift drum to capture a snare effect by laying it across his lap and hitting the back with a mallet. Their efforts resulted in one of Elvis' most beloved songs and one of his personal favorites. Total sales for any Presley single are often difficult to calculate, but by March 1992, "Don't Be Cruel"/"Hound Dog" had been awarded triple platinum status by the RIAA.

BEST SINGLES
"All Shook Up"

OTIS BLACKWELL, who had written "Don't Be Cruel," also penned the number-one hit "All Shook Up." In retrospect, the tune tends to be overshadowed by Elvis' other major recordings from 1957, but "All Shook Up" racked up some interesting statistics in its time. The song remained at the top of *Billboard*'s pop chart for nine weeks, and it stayed on the chart for 30 weeks—the longest of any Elvis single. At year's end, "All Shook Up" was named the number-one single for 1957. Elvis also had the number-one single for 1956, "Heartbreak Hotel," making him the first singer of the rock era to top the year-end charts for two consecutive years.

Blackwell's inspiration for the title "All Shook Up" came from a mundane incident straight out of everyday life, though the story has undoubtedly been enhanced through repeated tellings. While working for Shalimar Music as a songwriter, Blackwell was sitting in the office trying to come up with a new powerhouse tune. Al Stanton, one of the owners of the music publishing company, dropped in while downing a bottle of soda. He shook up the bottle so that the contents foamed and fizzed, casually remarking, "Why don't you write a song called 'All Shook Up?'" A couple of days later, Blackwell surprised Stanton with a draft of the song.

Contrary to some reports, Blackwell did

The flip side to "All Shook Up" (RCA 47-6870) was "That's When Your Heartaches Begin"—one of the songs that Elvis recorded when he first walked into Sam Phillips' Memphis Recording Service in 1953.

Otis Blackwell wrote a song based on a chance conversation, resulting in the hit "All Shook Up."

not compose the tune specifically for Elvis as a follow-up to "Don't Be Cruel." Two other singers, David Hill and Vicki Young, recorded "All Shook Up" before him. Elvis recorded the tune in Hollywood at Radio Recorders in January 1957. In his version, Elvis overdubbed himself slapping the back of his guitar, which is a pleasant reminder of his Sun Studio sound.

Again, Blackwell reluctantly agreed to share a writing credit with Elvis, or else Elvis' management (including Colonel Parker and music publishers Hill and Range) would not have allowed him to record the tune.

BEST SINGLES
"Jailhouse Rock"

PENNED BY THE LEGENDARY Jerry Leiber and Mike Stoller, "Jailhouse Rock" became another number-one record for Elvis. It entered the British charts at number one, making it the first single ever to do so. The rock 'n' roll songwriting duo was commissioned to write most of the songs for the movie *Jailhouse Rock*, though they were less than enthusiastic about the assignment.

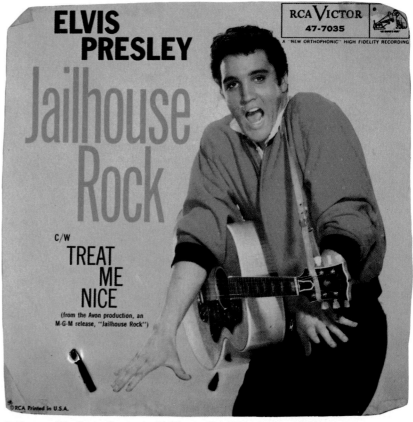

Elvis clowns around during a recording session for the Jailhouse Rock *soundtrack.*

Prior to *Jailhouse Rock,* Elvis had recorded a handful of songs from Leiber and Stoller, including "Hound Dog," "Love Me," and a couple of tunes from *Loving You.* The two songwriters were not impressed with Elvis' interpretation of their material. Leiber and Stoller tended to write hard-driving, R&B-flavored tunes with satiric or tongue-in-cheek lyrics that could be understood at more than one level. Elvis, on the other hand, performed most of his material straight, as when he recorded the duo's "Love Me," which they had originally intended as a lampoon of country-western music. Leiber and Stoller also felt that Elvis' foray into R&B territory was a fluke, and they were suspicious of his interest in blues and rhythm and blues.

The three met during the April 1957 recording session for "Jailhouse Rock," and Leiber and Stoller quickly changed their minds about Elvis once they realized he knew his music and that he was a workhorse in the studio. The pair took over the recording sessions, serving as unofficial producers of "Jailhouse Rock," "Treat Me Nice," "(You're So Square) Baby, I Don't Care," and other tunes. Their collaboration with Elvis and his musicians on "Jailhouse Rock" resulted in

Leiber and Stoller, who wrote "Jailhouse Rock" and "Treat Me Nice" (RCA 47-7035), served as unofficial producers on the two songs.

the singer's hardest-rocking movie song. As D.J. Fontana once noted about his drum playing on the record, "I tried to think of someone on a chain gang smashing rocks."

The short period of time that Leiber and Stoller worked with Elvis proved beneficial to both sides. The irony and ambiguity in the lyrics of "Jailhouse Rock" gave Elvis one of his most clever rockers while the singer's sincere and energetic delivery prevented the song from becoming too much of a burlesque—a tendency with some of Leiber and Stoller's songs written for the Coasters. The songwriters hung with Elvis long enough to contribute to the *King Creole* soundtrack, among other projects, but eventually they ran afoul of Elvis' management for trying to introduce him to new challenges.

BEST SINGLES
"It's Now or Never"

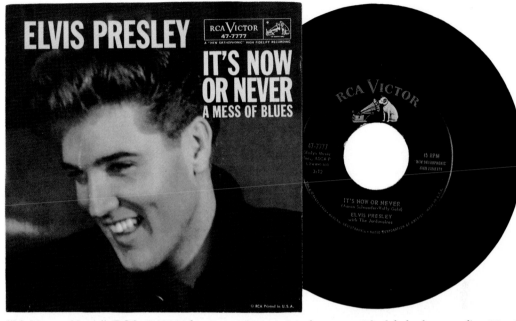

WHO COULD HAVE guessed that a reworked version of the 1901 Italian opera-style classic "O Sole Mio" with a cha-cha arrangement would become the King of Rock 'n' Roll's biggest-selling single? But then, in 1956, when Elvis was skewered by most newspapers in the country for thrusting his hips to the bluesy beat of "Hound Dog," no one would have guessed that he would become a press favorite in just four short years. Elvis won the hearts and minds of the mainstream press and general public by quietly serving his country in the army. This helped soften his image as a dangerous rock 'n' roller. Further distancing himself from that image, Elvis began to move away from rock 'n' roll when he returned to recording in 1960. "It's Now or Never" was an important single release

"It's Now or Never" (RCA 47-7777) became an international success, with global sales exceeding 20 million copies. It entered the English charts at number one and remained there for eight weeks.

Elvis returned from the army without sideburns, another attempt to soften his image as a notorious rock 'n' roller.

for Elvis in that regard. It received airplay on conservative radio stations that previously wouldn't have touched a Presley record, thus exposing Elvis to a wider, adult audience.

Yet Elvis did not record the song just to gain a broader audience. "O Sole Mio" was written by G. Capurro and Eduardo di Capua at the turn of the century, but it had been made popular much later by Mario Lanza.

Elvis was a fan of Lanza and undoubtedly heard the opera singer's recording, but he had also heard the English version of the song, "There's No Tomorrow" by Tony Martin. While still in the army, Elvis asked his music publisher, Freddie Bienstock of Hill and Range (a part of RCA), to find someone to write new lyrics for the song. The only songwriters available at Hill and Range to do it were Aaron Schroeder and Wally Gold, who jumped at the chance because they knew the royalties on an Elvis Presley song would be enormous. They composed the lyrics in less than half an hour. A singer named David Hill (aka David Hess) recorded the demo with a cha-cha arrangement, and Elvis loved it. He was challenged by the operatic style, and he was attracted to the drama of it.

"It's Now or Never" charted for 20 weeks, holding the number-one slot for five weeks. Worldwide sales of the tune, according to *The Guiness Book of Recorded Sound*, eventually exceeded 20 million copies.

BEST SINGLES
"Can't Help Falling in Love"

WRITTEN SPECIFICALLY for *Blue Hawaii* by George Weiss, Hugo Peretti, and Luigi Creatore, "Can't Help Falling in Love" is remembered as the ballad Elvis closed his concerts with during the 1970s. In the film, Elvis' character sings it to the grandmother of his girlfriend for her birthday, but that context has long since been forgotten. Because Elvis sang it so many times in concert, it is more fitting to suggest that the song belongs to the fans. It speaks to the way the fans felt about Elvis, and it was his love song to them.

Just as "It's Now or Never" was based on "O Sole Mio," "Can't Help Falling in Love" was adapted from an 18th century melody called "Plaisir d'Amour" by Italian composer

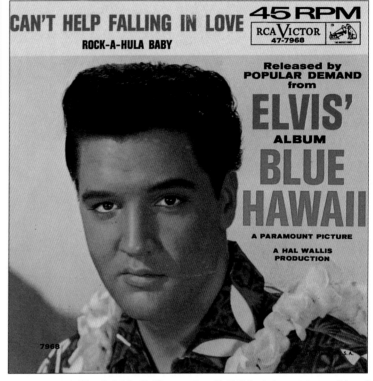

In retrospect, "Can't Help Falling in Love" (RCA 47-7968) is considered Elvis' love song to the fans.

Giovanni Martini. A handful of songs from Elvis' career were based on classic compositions or melodies, and he rose to the occasion by offering earnest, tender, or passionate interpretations of them.

The single hit the charts in December 1961. It peaked at number two on *Billboard*'s Hot 100 listing, and it remained on the charts for 14 weeks. The RIAA certified a gold record for "Can't Help Falling in Love" in March 1962, and a platinum record exactly 30 years later.

Record collectors should note that the movie version of "Can't Help Falling in Love" was not the one released as a single or on the album. Two takes of the movie version were recorded along with one take of the single release. The movie version of "Can't Help Falling in Love" was not released until after Elvis' death.

Both Al Martino and Andy Williams recorded "Can't Help Falling in Love" in 1970, which may have influenced Elvis to revive it in concert.

BEST SINGLES
"If I Can Dream"

COLONEL TOM PARKER had originally wanted Elvis' 1968 television special for NBC-TV to be a Christmas program, in which "his boy" sang an hour's worth of holiday classics. The producers, however, had something more challenging in mind. And for once, the Colonel did not get his way. Even with the change in format for the program, however, the Colonel still expected Elvis to close the show singing "Silent Night." Supposedly, Elvis was filmed singing the Christmas carol just to appease Parker, but things still didn't turn out the way the Colonel had planned.

The program, which was simply titled *Elvis*, closed with the moving contemporary spiritual "If I Can Dream." The song was written at the last minute at the request of the show's producer, Steve Binder. The musical director for *Elvis*, W. Earl Brown, wrote the song as a response to the assassinations of Robert Kennedy and Martin Luther King. It was intended as a statement of hope for the future of America. Elvis loved "If I Can Dream," and he gave it everything he had.

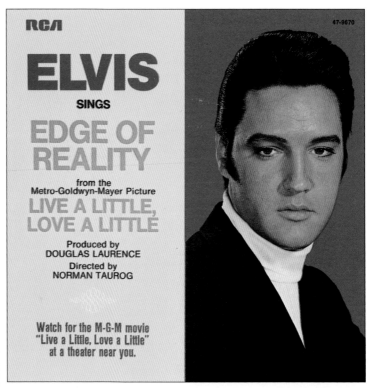

"If I Can Dream" was the flip side to the forgettable "Edge of Reality" (RCA 47-9670), but some record sleeves gave no indication of that.

The instrumental track was recorded on June 20 or 21, 1968. Elvis sang the song in front of the string section of the orchestra while the instrumental part was being recorded. Though his vocals were not to be used on the final version, he still sang it with all the passion the song inspired, even dropping down on his knee at one point. The effect left the string section with their mouths open. Later, Elvis rerecorded the vocals in a darkened studio, and once again, he performed the song rather than merely recording it.

The single was released in November, just prior to the telecast of the special. In perhaps one of RCA's worst marketing decisions, the flip side contained "Edge of Reality," a poor tune from one of Elvis' worst films, *Live a Little, Love a Little*. Despite this, "If I Can Dream" climbed to the number 12 position on the charts and earned Elvis another gold record.

Elvis sang "If I Can Dream" as the finale of his 1968 special. A sticker on some record sleeves reads, "As Featured on His NBC-TV Special."

BEST SINGLES
"Suspicious Minds"

ELVIS' LAST NUMBER-ONE SINGLE, "Suspicious Minds," offers an example of the large-scale sound that defined his later style. At four minutes and 22 seconds, it is his longest number-one song, and in his Las Vegas shows, he stretched it into a powerhouse, showstopping piece that ran eight minutes. Elvis had introduced the song in Vegas on July 26, 1969, when he made his first live performance in eight years at the International Hotel. It was not released as a single until the following September. It entered *Billboard*'s Hot 100 chart, peaking at the number-one position seven weeks later.

The song had originally been recorded at American Sound Studios on January 23, 1969, though it was held for release until a later date. "Suspicious Minds" featured backing vocals by Jeannie Green and Ronnie Milsap, a singer-songwriter who later became a prominent country-western star. To help achieve the large-scale sound, Elvis' Las Vegas band was over-dubbed on the single at a Vegas recording studio in August. Also, the end of the song was spliced on for a second time. This overdubbing and remixing was supervised by Elvis' producer, Felton Jarvis.

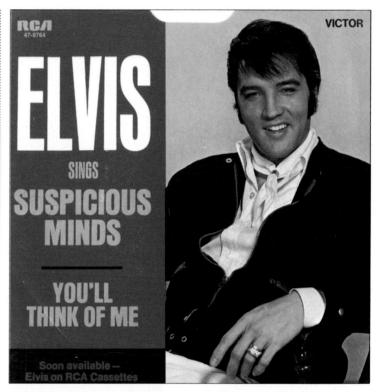

In a 1987 telephone poll by USA Today, *"Suspicious Minds" (RCA 47-9764) was named "favorite Elvis song."*

Elvis introduced "Suspicious Minds" during his live-performance come-back at the International Hotel in the summer of 1969.

After the two recording sessions at American Sound Studios in January and February of 1969, Elvis never recorded there again. Part of the reason was undoubtedly due to a clash over the rights to the songs that producer Chips Moman had suggested for Elvis, including "Suspicious Minds." RCA and Hill and Range, which oversaw Elvis' own publishing companies, wanted a substantial cut of the songs to which Moman owned the rights. If Moman refused, there was pressure to let those songs slip through the sessions without being recorded. Some quality material was not recorded by Elvis because of the haggling over song rights by Hill and Range. Moman did not want to budge on "Suspicious Minds," and he threatened to cancel the session if Freddie Bienstock of Hill and Range did not back off. Fortunately, Elvis did record "Suspicious Minds," but the tension over song rights took its toll.

BEST SINGLES
"Burning Love"

THE HIGHLIGHT of Elvis' studio sessions in Hollywood during March 1972 was the recording of "Burning Love." By this point, Elvis and his band were masters of this type of large-scale, fast-rocking number, and his interpretation of the song typifies his 1970s sound.

Band member James Burton provided the driving guitar lick for "Burning Love" in concert...

Dennis Linde composed "Burning Love" especially for Elvis, and the songwriter played guitar on the recording. It was Linde who dubbed in the raucous guitar lick on the bridges of the song. He had occasionally served as a bass guitarist in Elvis' recording band during the 1970s.

"Burning Love" became a worldwide hit for Elvis in 1972, and it quickly charted on *Billboard*'s Hot 100.

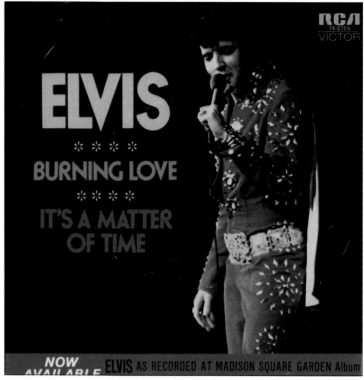

...though songwriter Dennis Linde had played the guitar for the "Burning Love" single (RCA 74-0769).

The Sweet Inspirations backed Elvis in concert during the 1970s. At one time, Cissy Houston (left), mother of Whitney Houston, was a member of the group.

Peaking at number two, it just missed becoming a number-one record. Chuck Berry's "My Ding-a-Ling" kept "Burning Love" from hitting the top of the charts. The record was certified gold by the RIAA in October 1972, and it was certified platinum in March 1992.

Unfortunately, Elvis did not follow up on the excitement generated by the rocking "Burning Love." His next single release was a ballad, "Separate Ways," backed by "Always on My Mind," which reached only number 20 on the Hot 100 chart. In addition, RCA buried "Burning Love" and its flip side, "It's a Matter of Time," on an album of old movie tracks creatively titled *Burning Love and Hits from His Movies, Volume 2*. In terms of Elvis' career, this hit song seems to have gotten lost amidst bad marketing decisions.

BEST SONGWRITERS

OTIS BLACKWELL

Respected singer-songwriter Otis Blackwell composed many rock 'n' roll standards in the 1950s and 1960s. Born in Brooklyn in 1932, Blackwell grew up admiring country-western singer and actor Tex Ritter. Otis became a staff writer for Shalimar Music in early 1956 after he sold six songs to that company for $25 each, including "Don't Be Cruel." Blackwell had been standing in front of the Brill Building (home to rock 'n' roll music publishing) in New York City on Christmas Eve when an arranger asked him if he had any songs to sell. He then took Otis to meet Shalimar's owners, who purchased the songs and hired him after the holidays. Elvis recorded ten Blackwell compositions including "Fever" (written with Eddie Cooley), "All Shook Up," "Paralyzed," and "Return to Sender" (cowritten with Winfield Scott). Among Blackwell's other rock 'n' roll classics are Jerry Lee Lewis' "Great Balls of Fire" and "Breathless." Blackwell sang on the demos of his songs for Elvis and Jerry Lee and imitated their styles, but Blackwell and Elvis never met.

MAC DAVIS

Dubbed the "the Song Painter" by Glen Campbell, Mac Davis is well known for composing songs that use concrete imagery to paint a picture or tell a story. In the 1970s, Davis teamed with Billy Strange, and Elvis recorded several Davis-Strange compositions. The pair provided Elvis with the theme song to *Charro!*, the tune "Nothingville" from the television special *Elvis*, a reflective ballad titled "Memories," and a couple of light pieces called "Clean Up Your Own Back Yard" and "A Little Less Conversa- tion." Alone, Davis wrote two of Elvis' biggest hits of the 1970s, the socially conscious "In the Ghetto" and the sentimental ballad "Don't Cry Daddy." During the late 1960s and 1970s, Davis' compositions were recorded by major artists, including Lou Rawls, Bobby Goldsboro, Glen Campbell, Kenny Rogers, Andy Williams, Sammy Davis, Jr., and Dolly Parton. Davis ventured into acting in the 1970s and costarred in a handful of major Hollywood movies, including *North Dallas Forty* and *Cheaper to Keep Her*.

LEIBER AND STOLLER

Jerry Leiber and Mike Stoller adapted aspects of rhythm and blues and blues when writing for rock 'n' roll performers. Their integration of these musical genres in the 1950s expanded the commercial possibilities of rock 'n' roll. The pair met in Los Angeles in 1950 when they were just 17 years old. Stoller the musician and Leiber the songwriter found they shared an interest in blues and R&B, so they spent the summer writing songs in those styles. Lester Sill, sales manager for Modern Records, took them under his wing and introduced them to performers and industry reps. Despite their youth, the pair fared well because the prominent Tin Pan Alley songwriters of the day thought rock 'n' roll was beneath them. Leiber and Stoller are noted for structuring their songs like playlets. That is, they tell a story—usually with wit or satire—within the three-minute length of a popular song. Elvis recorded about two dozen Leiber and Stoller tunes, including "Hound Dog" and "Jailhouse Rock."

DOC POMUS AND MORT SHUMAN

Brooklyn-born Doc Pomus (pictured) and native New Yorker Mort Shuman teamed to write 15 songs for Elvis, including some that were used for his movie soundtracks. The unforgettable title song for *Viva Las Vegas* was composed by Pomus and Shuman especially for the film. Other movie songs included earlier Pomus-Shuman compositions that were then recycled for the soundtracks. Pomus cowrote a few other soundtrack tunes with other songwriters, including "Girl Happy," "I Feel That I've Known You Forever," and "She's Not You." The team's best work was for Elvis' nonsoundtrack recordings, including the million-selling "Little Sister." Other significant Pomus-Shuman compositions include "Surrender," based on the Italian ballad "Come Back to Sorrento," and "Suspicion." Pomus and Shuman also penned several rock classics for other artists, including "This Magic Moment" and "Save the Last Dance for Me" by the Drifters and "A Teenager in Love" by Dion and the Belmonts.

BEST SONGWRITERS

JERRY REED

Born in Atlanta, Georgia, on March 20, 1937, country singer-songwriter Jerry Reed Hubbard composed four songs recorded by Elvis. Though this is only a handful in comparison to other songwriters who wrote for Elvis, two of the tunes included "Guitar Man" and "U.S. Male." These songs were recorded just prior to the surge of creativity generated by the television special *Elvis.* The songs represented a move away from the soundtrack recordings and toward better-quality material with a contemporary feel. Reed also played guitar for Elvis on "Guitar Man." Reed was one of several Southern musicians who had been influenced by Elvis and later ended up working with him. In 1967, Reed recorded "Tupelo Mississippi Flash," an Elvis novelty record that was a comic tribute to his idol. Reed's career as a performer accelerated in the 1970s. He profited from his rowdy good-old-boy image when a vogue for things Southern hit Hollywood. He costarred with Burt Reynolds in four films, including the popular *Smokey and the Bandit.*

BEN WEISMAN

Born in 1921 in Providence, Rhode Island, Ben Weisman wrote or cowrote more than 50 songs for Elvis—more than any other songwriter. Weisman began his prolific association with Elvis with "First in Line," which was recorded in 1956. He was often teamed with Fred Wise, but he also composed with Aaron Schroeder and Randy Starr. Many of Weisman's compositions were written for Elvis' movie soundtracks, so they were intended to fit into the storyline or advance the plot. Most were in the smooth, pop-flavored style that defined Elvis' soundtrack recordings. Within those limitations, Weisman sometimes came up with some memorable tunes. Some of his best include "Crawfish" from *King Creole,* the title tune from *Follow That Dream,* "Rock-a-Hula Baby" from *Blue Hawaii,* "I Slipped, I Stumbled, I Fell" from *Wild in the Country,* and "Got a Lot o' Livin' to Do" from *Loving You.* In his later career, Weisman had a recurring role on the CBS soap opera *The Young and the Restless* as a pianist in the Club Allegro.

Best Reinvented Songs by Elvis

"That's All Right" was written and recorded by Arthur "Big Boy" Crudup *(above)* as a country blues tune in 1947 and reworked by Elvis in 1955. His faster-paced, rockabilly interpretation became his first single release.

"Hound Dog" was written by Jerry Leiber and Mike Stoller for blues singer Big Mama Thornton in 1953. The original lyrics contain a sexual connotation, and Thornton belted out her version in a gritty, slow blues style. Elvis' humorous interpretation was borrowed from Freddie Bell and the Bellboys.

Elvis recorded two versions of the Dave Bartholomew-Pearl King blues tune "One Night of Sin," which had been a hit for Smiley Lewis in 1956. On January 24, 1957, he recorded Lewis' version, and a month later he rerecorded the song as "One Night" using cleaned-up lyrics. In Lewis' risqué original, the singer is praying for "One night of sin," while in Elvis' more hopeful rendition, he is hoping for "One night with you...."

Tin Pan Alley songwriters Lou Handman and Roy Turk composed "Are You Lonesome Tonight?" ("To-night" on original record sleeve) in 1926, and it was originally recorded by Al Jolson the following year. Supposedly the only song Colonel Tom Parker ever urged Elvis to record, "Are You Lonesome Tonight?" was released by Elvis in 1960 and was nominated for three Grammys.

"Bridge Over Troubled Water" was composed by Paul Simon and Art Garfunkel and recorded by the folk-rock duo in 1970, becoming a number-one hit for them. Elvis recorded his version, which had a larger sound and a more dramatic vocal rendering, during the filming of *Elvis—That's the Way It Is*.

Eddy Arnold, "the Tennessee Plowboy," had a hit record with the soft-sounding ballad "I Really Don't Want to Know" in 1954, just as Elvis was barnstorming across the South with his rockabilly style. Composed by Howard Barnes and Don Robertson, the song was released by Elvis in 1970 with another country tune, "There Goes My Everything," on the flip side. These songs represent Elvis' rediscovery of contemporary country music during the 1970s.

Originally arranged and recorded by country singer Mickey Newbury, "An American Trilogy" is a medley of "Dixie," "The Battle Hymn of the Republic," and "All My Trials." The integration of two Civil War songs (one a Southern anthem, the other a Northern anthem) with a traditional spiritual suggests the curiously Southern tradition of blending diverse cultural elements. Elvis' 1972 version of the piece offered an operatic interpretation that matched the breadth of the song's meaning.

Elvis sang James Taylor's 1970 composition "Steamroller Blues" in concert during the early 1970s, but his gritty rendition during the *Aloha from Hawaii* television special stopped the show. The version from the special was released as a single in April 1973.

In 1968, country singer Marty Robbins wrote "You Gave Me a Mountain," a wrenching ballad about life's hardships. Though pop star Frankie Laine was the first to release it, Elvis began singing the song in concert during the early 1970s and released it in 1973. Elvis' interpretation is generally considered autobiographical in that it paralleled his breakup with Priscilla Presley.

"My Way," an anthem of independence and individuality, was written by Paul Anka *(above, right)* for Frank Sinatra and originally recorded by him in 1969. Elvis sang "My Way" on the *Aloha from Hawaii* television special and in concert during the 1970s. A recording of this song by Elvis was released shortly after he died, making it almost a biographical statement.

BEST CONCERTS

OVERTON PARK SHELL

Memphis, Tennessee
July 30, 1954

On a hot summer night, Elvis made his first billed appearance at the Overton Park Shell. The headliner was Slim Whitman, a country singer who incorporated yodeling into his style. Also on the bill were Billy Walker, Curly Harris, Sugarfoot Collins, Tinker Fry, and Sonny Harville. The newspaper ads touting the event misspelled Elvis' name as "Ellis Presley." Elvis' first single, "That's All Right" backed by "Blue Moon of Kentucky," had been released just 11 days earlier, and most have speculated that he sang both sides of his new single that night. Elvis was clearly nervous for the first show, and he moved constantly while he was singing. The girls in the audience began to scream and make noise. After it was over, Elvis asked bandmember Scotty Moore what they were "hollering'" at, and Moore replied, "It was your leg, man. It was the way you were shakin' your left leg."

FLORIDA THEATER

Jacksonville, Florida
August 10–11, 1956

The controversy over Elvis' sensual performing style reached a fevered pitch during his 1956 summer tour. When Elvis played Jacksonville, Florida, in mid-August, he sold out all three shows both nights at the Florida Theater. Reacting to the publicity surrounding Elvis the Pelvis, Juvenile Court Judge Marion W. Gooding attended the first show, in which Elvis moved to his music as usual. Gooding met with Elvis and Colonel Tom Parker afterward and warned the young singer to "quieten" his act. The police attended to film the show to ensure that Elvis obeyed the Judge's directive. In an atypical public display of sarcasm, Elvis reacted to the directive by wiggling only his little finger during the performance. *Life* magazine centered their August 27 article on Elvis around the Jacksonville incident, sensationalizing the stories about the Judge's threats and the tales about the crazed fans who tore off Elvis' clothes after one of his shows.

MISSISSIPPI-ALABAMA FAIR AND DAIRY SHOW

**Tupelo, Mississippi
September 26, 1956**

Despite the controversy surrounding his career, Elvis returned as a hometown hero to Tupelo, Mississippi, on September 26, 1956. Elvis Presley Day was proclaimed in the tiny town of Tupelo by Mayor James Ballard, and a scroll was awarded to Elvis from Mississippi Governor J.P. Calamine. Elvis performed two shows that day at the Mississippi-Alabama Fair and Dairy Show, where he once crooned "Old Shep" as a child while competing in the fair's talent show. The delirious hometown crowd, overheated by Elvis as much as by the 100-degree temperatures, was held back by 100 National Guardsmen assigned for crowd control. During the afternoon show, Elvis had to stop singing to get the audience to calm down. Elvis was accompanied throughout the day by proud parents Vernon and Gladys.

LOUISIANA HAYRIDE

**Shreveport, Louisiana
December 16, 1956**

At the end of his first year as a national sensation, Elvis performed for the last time on the *Louisiana Hayride*, a live show broadcast from the Shreveport Municipal Auditorium over radio station KWKH. Elvis was under contract to perform on the show every Saturday night, and exposure from the broadcasts and the tours as part of the Hayride cast had helped make him a major sensation in the South by the spring of 1955. When Elvis began playing large venues across the South, though, the contract hindered him financially. He agreed to pay $400 for each missed performance until his contract expired in November 1956. Elvis appreciated what the Hayride had done for his career and appeared there as often as he could in 1956. His last show, a benefit for the Shreveport YMCA, was moved to the Hirsch Youth Center. A frenzied crowd of 10,000 watched Elvis sing his hits dressed in a kelly green coat, blue pants, and white bucks.

BEST CONCERTS

MAPLE LEAF GARDENS

Toronto, Canada
April 2, 1957

Elvis played an afternoon and evening show at the Maple Leaf Gardens in Toronto on April 2, 1957. The following day, he performed a matinee and evening show in Ottawa. On August 31, he played one show at Empire Stadium in Vancouver, British Columbia *(pictured)*. These five shows in three days represent the only performances by Elvis outside the United States. The Toronto appearances were part of a ten-day tour booked by Australian promoter Lee Gordon. For this tour, Elvis had the famous clothier Nudie of Hollywood custom-make a gold suit. The suit generated as much commentary by reporters and critics as the singer's performances. During the evening show in Toronto, Elvis split the inseam of his gold pants, and he never wore the entire gold outfit again. The Toronto shows went smoothly compared to those in other cities that year, partly because 90 police officers were assigned to crowd control.

PAN PACIFIC AUDITORIUM

Los Angeles, California
October 28–29, 1957

Anticipating a huge, unmanageable crowd for Elvis' performances, security for the Pan Pacific Auditorium removed the first 20 rows of seats and stationed two dozen police officers around the front of the stage. Despite the precautions, the audience was loud and anxious as they sat through 60 minutes of dismal entertainment before Elvis dashed onstage. When the crowd of 9,200 saw Elvis, they roared so loudly that they were heard two blocks away. Elvis belted out 18 tunes during his hour onstage, but the fans demanded an encore so he launched into "Hound Dog." The show raised eyebrows, particularly when Elvis rolled around on the floor with a giant replica of the RCA dog, and he was ordered to clean up his act by Deputy Chief of Police Dick Simmons. The next evening, the police filmed the show, which Elvis found amusing. During one point, he formed a halo over his head and offered his wrists for handcuffs.

BLOCH ARENA

**Pearl Harbor, Hawaii
March 25, 1961**

During the 1960s, Elvis and his management team focused exclusively on his film career. One of the consequences of that decision was to curtail live performances. Elvis sang before an audience only twice in 1961. The last time was at a benefit concert for the USS *Arizona* Memorial Fund held at Bloch Arena. A press conference for reporters, photographers, and a hand-picked group of 27 high-school reporters was held at the hotel where he was staying. Tickets for that night's show were $10, $5, $3.50, and $3, which was more expensive than usual. The benefit raised more than $62,000 for the memorial to the *Arizona*, which had been sunk during the Japanese attack on Pearl Harbor. Elvis and Colonel Tom Parker bought 50 seats for patients at Tripler Hospital. On March 30, the Hawaiian legislature passed Resolution #105 to officially express their gratitude to Elvis. The day after Elvis died, the Navy laid a wreath at the USS *Arizona* Memorial in his honor.

INTERNATIONAL HOTEL

**Las Vegas, Nevada
July 31–August 28, 1969**

After the benefit for the USS *Arizona* at Bloch Arena at Pearl Harbor, Elvis did not perform before a live audience for more than eight years. Invigorated by his 1968 television special, *Elvis,* and his first major album in years, *From Elvis in Memphis,* he accepted an offer to perform in the new 2,000-seat showroom of the International Hotel in Las Vegas (later the Hilton). Barbra Streisand had opened the room the previous month, and Elvis attended her closing night. Elvis had rehearsed for a month with his new band, and despite a few glitches, the audience of celebrities and reporters responded to his opening night with a standing ovation. In his new act, Elvis performed a medley of his greatest hits but also included new material from his recent recording sessions. Reviews of his nearly sold-out engagement were positive. Total attendence exceeded 101,509, which was a Vegas record, as was the $1,522,635 box-office take.

BEST CONCERTS

ASTRODOME

Houston, Texas
February 27–March 1, 1970

Elvis' Las Vegas engagements in August 1969 and February 1970 represented his return to live performances, but his three-day gig at the Houston Astrodome launched his return to touring. The show was part of the Texas Livestock Show and Rodeo, and Elvis held two press conferences in conjunction with his engagement. At one, he acknowledged the importance of country music to his career and told reporters he was happy that it had gained in popularity. Though significant in terms of his career, the Astrodome engagement was not his best work, mainly due to problems with the equipment and microphones. Local reviews were positive, but they noted that the Astrodome was not the best place to see any type of musical concert. It was an enormous arena that even Elvis found somewhat intimidating. Still, his six shows drew about 207,494 people.

MADISON SQUARE GARDEN

New York City, New York
June 9–11, 1972

Elvis Presley made entertainment history with his four-show engagement in Madison Square Garden. He was the first performer to sell out all of his shows in advance, grossing about $730,000. A total of 80,000 people attended his performances, including John Lennon, David Bowie, Bob Dylan, and George Harrison. During the engagement, he wore sequined jumpsuits and gold-lined capes, which by 1972 was typical for his concert performances. The Sweet Inspirations, J.D. Sumner and the Stamps Quartet, and Elvis' touring band backed him. The act included a medley of his classic hits, during which he engaged in some self-parody to the delight of the audience. He also performed new material, including the very Southern "An American Trilogy," a song that mystified the New York critics. Remarkably, the engagement marked the first time Elvis had ever given a live concert in New York City.

BEST ELVIS TUNES BY OTHER ARTISTS

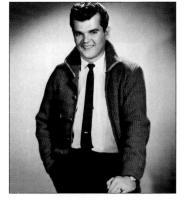

"The Girl of My Best Friend" was included on the 1960 album *Elvis Is Back.* Elvis sound-alike Ral Donner *(above)* became the second artist to cover the tune. He recorded a demo of it in 1960 with his backup group the Gents and then re-recorded it with the Starfires. Released in 1961, it made it into the top 20.

"Baby Let's Play House," originally cut by Elvis for Sun Records in 1955, was recorded by Elvis sound-alike Vince Everett in 1963.

"Suspicion," composed by Doc Pomus and Mort Shuman, was recorded by Elvis in 1962 as part of the album *Pot Luck.* Terry Stafford's 1964 version reached number three on the charts, prompting RCA to release Elvis' version as the B-side of "Kiss Me Quick."

"Such a Night" was originally recorded by Clyde McPhatter and the Drifters in 1954. Several others released the tune before Elvis cut it in 1960. Conway Twitty *(above)* recorded it in 1964, before he was considered a country singer. What connects Twitty's single to Elvis Presley is that he backed it with another Elvis song, "My Baby Left Me."

"All Shook Up," written by Otis Blackwell, was recorded by Elvis in March 1957. Rocker Suzi Quatro's version was released in 1974, and it reached number 85 on *Billboard*'s Hot 100 chart.

"Always on My Mind," written by Mark James, Wayne Carson, and Johnny Christopher, was recorded by Elvis in 1972. Ten years later, the song reached even greater success, topping the country chart and hitting

number five on the Hot 100 chart when it was remade by Willie Nelson *(above).*

"Little Sister" became one of Elvis' best recordings of the 1960s. In 1988, Dwight Yoakam had a country hit with it, and Yoakam's video for the song was nominated by the Country Music Association for Top Country Video.

The 1990 version of "It's Now or Never" by Paul McCartney *(above)* is as

much an homage to Elvis as it is a remake. Elvis' version, released in 1960, was his biggest-selling single of all time and a song that became indelibly linked with him. McCartney's version was featured on *The Last Temptation of Elvis,* an album of Elvis tunes recorded by contemporary rock artists.

"Viva Las Vegas," written in 1963 by Pomus and Shuman, was the title tune for one of Elvis' best films. In 1990, Bruce Springsteen *(above)* recorded a raucous version, which was included on *The Last Temptation of Elvis.*

"(You're the) Devil in Disguise," recorded in 1963 by Elvis, became a million-seller for him. Country singer Trisha Yearwood's classy 1992 version was included on the soundtrack of *Honeymoon in Vegas.*

BEST ELVIS-RELATED RECORDS

During the 1950s, the entertainment press frequently contrasted the notorious, hip-swiveling Elvis Presley with the clean-cut Pat Boone, although the two actually maintained a friendly acquaintance. With a wink toward the media-made rivalry, Boone released an album of Elvis songs done in a soft pop style, including "It's Now or Never" and "Hound Dog." Cleverly titled *Pat Boone Sings... Guess Who?*, the 1964 album featured Boone on the cover in a replica of Elvis' famous gold suit.

Released by Epic Records in 1964, *The Guitar That Changed the World!* offers

Elvis' long-time guitarist Scotty Moore performing songs such as "Heartbreak Hotel," "Hound Dog," and "Don't Be Cruel." The album showcases the driving rhythm of Moore's guitar style, which contributed so much to Elvis' music.

King Does the King's Things is a 1969 release by Albert King. With his blues-based interpretations of Elvis' classic hits, King's work demonstrates the powerful role that blues and R&B played throughout Elvis' entire musical career.

J.D. Sumner and the Stamps Quartet backed Elvis in con-

Albert King in the studio.

cert from 1972 to 1977, and Elvis, a fan of gospel music since childhood, would often sing sacred songs with them to warm up before concerts or recording sessions. *Elvis' Favorite Gospel Songs* features Sumner and the Stamps performing some of these same songs and also includes a musical tribute to Presley called "Elvis Has Left the Building."

Otis Blackwell authored many rock 'n' roll songs

now considered classics, including the Presley hits "All Shook Up," "Don't Be Cruel," and "Return to Sender." The 1976 album *Otis Blackwell: These Are My Songs!* offers a chance to hear Blackwell sing these and other songs he wrote that were made famous by performers such as Elvis, Brenda Lee, and Jerry Lee Lewis.

After Elvis died in 1977, a glut of tribute records flooded the market. A few were poignant or sincere, but many were maudlin or merely exploitative. The May 1978 release of *To Elvis: Love Still Burning* was an attempt to gather the best of these Elvis tribute recordings. The album became a significant collectors' item because it was the world's first commercially issued pic-

The famed Million Dollar Quartet (from left to right): *Jerry Lee Lewis, Carl Perkins, Elvis, and Johnny Cash.*

ture disc; the record disc itself was a smiling portrait of Elvis.

Released in 1990, *The Last Temptation of Elvis* consists of remakes of 26 Elvis songs, most of them movie tunes. Typically, Elvis' movie tunes are trashed by critics and other performers, so it is significant that this album focused on Presley's soundtrack recordings. Even more significant was the range of performers included on the album—from superstar Bruce Springsteen to progressive country singer Nanci Griffith to the gritty folk rock band the Pogues.

On December 4, 1956, Carl Perkins was recording at Sun Studios with Jerry Lee Lewis on piano and Johnny Cash in the control booth. Some time in the afternoon, Elvis walked in with Vegas dancer Marilyn Evans on his arm. Before long, the four legends were singing, and the engineer was recording them. A bootleg version of 17 of the 37 songs on the famous tape was released in 1980; in 1990, RCA released a legitimate version under the title *The Million Dollar Quartet.*

The film comedy *Honeymoon in Vegas* tells an offbeat love story set in gaudy, garish Las Vegas with its neon lights, noisy casinos, and... Elvis impersonators. The faux Elvises appear throughout the film but reach a high point with "the Flying Elvises," who skydive onto the Vegas Strip as part of their act. The clever movie soundtrack consists completely of Elvis songs remade or reworked by prominent pop, country, and rock performers: Willie Nelson sings a unique arrangement of "Blue Hawaii,"

Travis Tritt belts out a wicked "Burning Love," Billy Joel checks into the "Heartbreak Hotel," and Vince Gill's delicate voice is perfect for "That's All Right."

In October 1994, the estate of Elvis Presley organized a live musical tribute to Elvis at the Pyramid in Memphis, Tennessee. About 20,000 fans attended, and the concert aired on cable television. Performers from all parts of the entertainment industry appeared, including Chet Atkins, Dwight Yoakam, Michael Bolton, Carl Perkins, Tony Bennett, and Aaron Neville, attesting to the influence and impact of Elvis Presley on all types of popular music. The 15-song album *It's Now or Never: The Tribute to Elvis* represents the musical highlights of the program.

Movies

*E*LVIS' FILM CAREER began with promise, but he left Hollywood in the late 1960s disillusioned with the formulaic musical comedies he had been limited to making. Still, no Presley film ever lost money, and many remain popular with fans and family audiences. As a whole, his acting represents a significant part of his image . . . regardless of whether he played a rebellious youth or a singing race-car driver.

BEST MOVIES
Loving You

ELVIS PRESLEY was not simply the star of *Loving You;* in a sense, he was also the subject. The film served as a vehicle built around Elvis' image and designed to showcase his rock 'n' roll music and explosive performing style. The storyline, costuming, and music incorporated specific characteristics strongly associated with the real-life Elvis Presley and then manipulated them to suit specific ends. The ultimate effect was a reshaping of Elvis' rebel image into one more recognizable and therefore more acceptable to mainstream audiences.

Lizabeth Scott portrays an ambitious manager who exploits the sexual attractiveness of her star talent, Deke Rivers (Elvis)

music, Deke runs away. Glenda realizes her mistake in exploiting the more volatile side of his music and arranges for the canceled show to go on. She even manages to get it televised nationally to prove that Deke's music is legitimate and does not incite young people to juvenile delinquency. The success of the telecast opens the door to national stardom for Deke.

Many of the parallels in *Loving You* to Elvis' own life and path to stardom are obvious, even to viewers today. Specific parts of the storyline, most notably the singer with a hot new sound, the association with juvenile delinquency, the exaggerations of the press, the effect of Deke's music on women in the audience, and the power of television to propel Deke's career, are directly patterned after what had happened to Elvis in 1956, the year before the film was released. *Loving You* also took advantage of more-personal references to Elvis, which would have been obvious to most audience members of the time—fans and nonfans alike. For example, the attention paid to Elvis' hair by the press and public early in his career amounted to an almost fetishistic fixation. Columnists, reporters, and celebrities condemned Elvis' ducktail hairstyle and long sideburns at every turn, while both male and female fans emulated this look. In *Loving You,* Deke is harassed for his long hair and sideburns. In the scene where Deke sings "Mean Woman Blues," a local punk taunts the singer by referring to him repeatedly as "Sideburns," a key word that echoed the criticisms of Elvis' own hairstyle.

Facts about Elvis' life, as gleaned from publicity articles, also became fodder for the script of *Loving You.* For instance, the

Released in 1957, *Loving You* was the first Elvis Presley film by Hal Wallis, the veteran Hollywood producer who had signed the notorious young singer to a movie contract the year before. Elvis plays Deke Rivers, a young, working-class Southerner who is known locally for his "boogie-woogie" singing style. Coaxed by his buddy into singing with professional country performers Tex Warner and the Rough Ridin' Ramblers at a local picnic, Rivers astounds the young girls in the crowd with his hot new sound and his sensual performing style. Glenda Markle, the shrewd public-relations person for the Ramblers, recognizes Deke's potential to tap the youth market and hires him as part of the show. While Deke, a naive young man, does not seem to grasp the sexual effect he has on women, Glenda exploits his sexual attractiveness in various publicity stunts. Deke's popularity soars, and a booking agent offers the singer a one-man concert—which is canceled after one of Glenda's publicity stunts backfires. Deke is burdened with a reputation as a troublemaker, while his music is criticized by the older generation for being unwholesome. Depressed by the unwarranted attacks on his reputation and his

The script for Loving You *was loosely based on Elvis' real-life career experiences, and references to Elvis were included in the film.* Top left: *Elvis' backup musicians D.J. Fontana and Scotty Moore (far right) played band members.* Top right: *Before the film began, director Hal Kanter traveled with Elvis to get an idea of what his life was like.* Bottom right: *Deke fights with a local boy who had taunted him with the name "Sideburns." Elvis was frequently criticized for his own side-whiskers.* Bottom left: *Deke cuts loose in a raucous performance.*

film makes a clever and effective reference to Elvis' taste in automobiles, particularly Cadillacs. Glenda plans a massive publicity stunt for Deke when she buys him a large white convertible with a red interior. She gives the press a false story concerning the car, telling them that a wealthy, elderly woman gave Deke the car because she was touched by his talent. The huge car becomes not only a part of the storyline but also a symbol of the lies and half-truths in the publicity surrounding Deke's meteoric rise to popularity. Later, the film shows several fans writing messages on the car with lipstick while it's

parked behind a theater where Deke is to perform. The scene is never discussed or referred to later in the movie. This makes clear reference to similar incidents that occurred when Elvis was touring in 1956. One of Presley's cars was vandalized by fans in Jacksonville, Florida, when they wrote love notes on it in lipstick, scratched phone numbers into the paint with fingernail files, and broke into the car and stole some of his personal effects. Later in the tour, fans in Miami festooned one of his Lincolns in a similar

In the film, Deke is given a white convertible, which echoed Elvis' own taste in big, flashy cars.

manner. A famous photograph of the lipstick-laden Lincoln was featured in *Life* magazine in August 1956, and the story was told and enhanced by the press in article after article.

These parallels between Deke and Elvis were clearly intentional. To insure that the film captured the flavor of Elvis' life as a popular performer as well as the excitement elicited by his performing style, Hal Wallis sent director-coscriptwriter Hal Kanter to observe Elvis as he made his final appearance on the *Louisiana Hayride* in Shreveport, Louisiana, on December 16, 1956. Influenced by what he saw while observing Elvis for a few days in Memphis and in Shreveport, Kanter not only helped shape a script that closely followed the young singer's life, but he also wrote an article for *Variety* about his experiences. Ironically titling it "Inside Paradise," Kanter offered one of the first accounts of the negative side to Elvis' enormous popularity. He stressed Elvis' need for protection from the huge crowds that formed wherever he appeared and lamented his lack of privacy. Kanter also remarked on the "electric excitement" generated by Elvis at the *Hayride* as well as the "mass hysteria" of the crowd. The most interesting aspect of Kanter's article was the fact that he never mentioned Elvis' name. By using certain phrases—phrases commonly used to describe Elvis and his career—Kanter identified the subject of his article without ever using the name Elvis Presley. Words such as "controversy;" phrases such as "a body as loose, as unadorned and as unpredictable as a whip;" and stories about the purchasing of Cadillacs and motorcycles

HAL B. WALLIS

Hal Wallis, a respected veteran of the film industry, worked in Hollywood from the silent era through the 1970s. He began as a publicity man for Warner Bros., working his way up to executive producer in charge of production by 1933. There he produced several classics, including *Little Caesar, Sergeant York*, and *The Maltese Falcon*. In 1944, he became an independent producer, releasing his films through Paramount and later Universal. As an independent, Wallis had a reputation for fostering new talent and was dubbed "the Discoverer." Among those whose screen careers he helped were Kirk Douglas, the team of Dean Martin and Jerry Lewis, Shirley MacLaine, and Elvis Presley.

Of the nine films that Wallis produced starring Elvis, his personal favorite was *King Creole*. He once said that one of the biggest regrets in his career was that he was not able to follow through on his idea for a western starring John Wayne as an old gunfighter with Elvis as his protégé. Wallis died in 1986.

In the same way that Elvis made a national splash on network television, the character Deke Rivers uses the medium to advance his career.

were unmistakable references to Elvis for any reader at the time. Kanter's film *Loving You* worked in much the same way as the article. By using familiar imagery and phrases associated with Elvis, Kanter made a movie about Presley without using his name.

Even with the similarities to Elvis' life, the storyline of *Loving You* is a familiar one about a talented, hard-working performer who wants to make it in show business. Hollywood musicals had been using this storyline since 1927 when popular singer Al Jolson starred in *The Jazz Singer*, the first feature-length synchronized-sound film. By remolding elements of Elvis' life and career as a familiar show business success story, *Loving You* helped older audience members understand that Deke Rivers (read Elvis Presley) was not just the rebellious rock 'n' roller that the press claimed him to be. He was actually a misunderstood youth with a new sound for a new generation—like other performers had been in previous generations. Just as Glenda tells the community leaders in the film that Deke's music is as fun and innocent as the Charleston was in the 1920s, so the producers of *Loving You* were telling 1950s America to relax—the Deke Rivers/Elvis Presley story was really just a modern-day version of the Al Jolson story.

CAST AND CREDITS

Paramount Pictures
Produced by Hal B. Wallis
Directed by Hal Kanter
Screenplay by Herbert Baker and Hal Kanter
Based on a story by Mary Agnes Thompson
Photographed in VistaVision and Technicolor by Charles Lang, Jr.
Music by Walter Scharf
Released July 30, 1957

Deke Rivers . . . . Elvis Presley
Glenda Markle . . . . Lizabeth Scott
Walter (Tex) Warner . . . . Wendell Corey
Susan Jessup. . . . . Dolores Hart
Carl Meade. . . . . James Gleason
Jim Tallman . . . . Ralph Dumke
Teddy . . . . Skip Young
Skeeter . . . . Paul Smith
Wayne . . . . Ken Becker
Daisy Bricker . . . . Jana Lund
Sally. . . . . Yvonne Lime
Eddie (bass player). . . . . Bill Black
Musician (drummer). . . . . D.J. Fontana
Musician (guitar player) . . . . Scotty Moore
Bit. . . . . Barbara Hearn

BEST MOVIES
Jailhouse Rock

KING CREOLE boasts a powerful cast and a skilled director, and *Blue Hawaii* features slick production values, but the gritty, low-budget *Jailhouse Rock* remains Elvis Presley's best film. If Elvis the rock 'n' roll rebel liberated a generation from the values, tastes, and ideals of their parents, then *Jailhouse Rock* is the only Presley film that speaks directly to the feral, sensual, and unruly nature of rock 'n' roll music.

Elvis' musicals, including *Jailhouse Rock,* belong to that genre known as the teenpic or the teen musical, in which rock 'n' roll performers were showcased in musical vehicles designed to cash in on the immense popularity of the youth-oriented music. From *Rock Around the Clock,* featuring real-life rocker Bill Haley, to *Rock, Pretty Baby,* starring actors pantomiming to ersatz rock tunes, producers and studios pandered to the teenage audience by combining teen fashion, teen jargon, and teen idols with a healthy dose of generational conflict.

Costar Judy Tyler was killed in a car crash just after production wrapped on Jailhouse Rock. *Elvis could never bring himself to watch the film.*

of view, the film's treatment of rock music differs from other teenpics. For example, rock 'n' roll is an established, accepted style of music when the story begins, and there is no organized resistance to it by authority figures. In general, the attitude toward the music in the script is both knowing and respectful, serving to validate rock 'n' roll as a popular art form—an important consideration to teenagers of the era.

One scene does acknowledge the conflict in musical tastes between the generations. Vince and Peggy drop in on a cocktail party hosted by Peggy's parents. Mr. Van Alden is a college professor, so his friends and associates are depicted as upper-middle-class professionals. Bored and out of place, Vince is standing beside a group talk-

Released in 1957, *Jailhouse Rock* offers more than a superficial rundown of the latest fads and fashions, however, and it excludes the standard clash between generations. The plot features an insider's look at the rock 'n' roll record business (as interpreted by Hollywood) through the character of Peggy Van Alden, a record exploitation "man" who helps ex-con Vince Everett (Elvis' character) launch a singing career. Because the audience sees the business through Peggy's point

ing about music. A woman exclaims, "Some day they'll make the cycle back to pure old Dixieland. I say atonality is just a passing phase in jazz music. What do you think, Mr. Everett?" Vince snarls, "Lady, I don't know what the hell you're talking about!" The scene curtly draws a line between the two types of music by generation and by class, and it concludes without the two sides attempting to reconcile, which was atypical for teenpics of this era. Instead, the jazz fans come off as snobbish and dull, while Vince's ultimate success with records, television, and movies validates his style of music. For once, rock 'n' roll bests another type of music and its proponents without any character having to explain or defend rock 'n' roll's existence.

As Vince Everett, Elvis swaggers through the film with a chip on his shoulder, playing up the notorious side of his real-life image. Top left: *Elvis' controversial performing style formed the basis of the choreography in the "Jailhouse Rock" production number.* Top right: *Tough-minded businesswoman Peggy Van Alden and streetwise Vince make a formidable pair when they negotiate with a slick lawyer to manage Vince's financial affairs.* Middle right: *Vince realizes the heated effect he has on women when he reads his fan mail.* Bottom: *Vince meets record exploitation "man" Peggy Van Alden in a seedy strip joint when she comes to check the play numbers on the juke box.*

The heart of *Jailhouse Rock* is the character of Vince Everett, who swaggers and prowls through the film with attitude and magnetism. Despite his Hollywood-style conversion in the final moments, it is Vince's impudence and haughty defiance that stay with the viewer long after the final fadeout. The character embodies the rebellious spirit and sexuality of rock 'n' roll, in much the same way that Elvis did in his career. This close identification between real-life performer and fictional character is not a detriment; indeed, it is the film's strength.

Several scenes and shots illustrate the similarities between the performing styles of Elvis and Vince and help audiences make the connection. Of particular interest is a scene in which Vince spends time in a recording studio searching for a

THE HAIRCUT

The scene in which the prison barber shaves off Elvis' infamous ducktail made fans weep and parents cheer. Over the years, much speculation existed as to whether it was Elvis' real hair that was cut or a wig. A glance at the production schedule as reprinted in Jim Hannaford's *Inside Jailhouse Rock* reveals the truth: Two wigs were used to represent Elvis' atrocious prison 'do. The schedule indicates that Elvis had to film three scenes in one week—one with the butch haircut, one with the hair partially grown back, and one with his regular style. Obviously, his real hair could not have grown back in that short span of time. In later years, makeup artist William Tuttle revealed that a series of plaster casts of Elvis' head allowed them to make wigs that fit so well that they were nearly impossible to detect.

singing style. Listening to himself croon "Don't Leave Me Now," he realizes that he lacks a personal style. After rocking the tune just a bit, Vince discovers how "to make the song fit him." The scene echoes Elvis' own efforts to work through a personal style at Sun Records way back in the summer of 1954, which was an oft-repeated tale in Elvis' publicity. To make the connection between Vince and Elvis even stronger, the musicians used in the scene were Elvis' own backup band, Scotty Moore, Bill Black, and D.J. Fontana.

Stills from the "Jailhouse Rock" production number try to capture Elvis' rebel image.

Also, Vince's costume in this scene duplicates Elvis' unique style of clothing. With his baggy black pants held in place by a thin belt and his tight-fitting shirt with turned-up collar and rolled-up sleeves, Vince sports the type of ultrahip attire Elvis purchased at Lansky's clothing store on Beale Street in Memphis. Similarly, Vince's hairstyle is a slightly cleaned-up version of Elvis' notorious ducktail and sideburns. Costuming and hairstyle might seem like minor details now, but to fans and audiences of the era, the similarities would have been obvious and meaningful.

Most of the songs were written especially for the film by Jerry Leiber and Mike Stoller, with Stoller making a brief appearance as a studio pianist during the scene in which Vince records "Don't Leave Me Now." The participation of these famous rock 'n' roll scribes in the making of the film adds an authenticity to it, as does the elaborate choreography for the title tune. Elvis participated in choreographing "Jailhouse Rock," with the steps based on his controversial performing style.

Thus, Elvis' image defined the role of Vince Everett as much as Vince perpetuated Elvis' image as a rebellious rock 'n' roller. For MGM and the producers, this guaranteed a sizable audience of Elvis fans; for audiences of the era, it added credibility and authenticity to the film. For contemporary audiences, it captures Elvis in his most popular incarnation—the young rebel who not only changed the course of popular music but gave a generation an identity and an attitude.

Top: *The final scene represents a typical Hollywood happy ending. An accident involving damaged vocal chords makes Vince realize how fortunate he is to have loving friends and a successful career. The defiant, arrogant rock 'n' roller is transformed into a humble, penitent young man in the final few moments of the film. Despite the ending, most viewers remember Vince Everett as a swaggering rebel.* Right: *Dozens of publicity photos were generated for* Jailhouse Rock, *including this one of Judy Tyler and Elvis amusing themselves between set-ups. Behind-the-scenes publicity shots from later Elvis films are extremely rare.*

CAST AND CREDITS

Metro-Goldwyn-Mayer
Produced by Pandro S. Berman
Directed by Richard Thorpe
Screenplay by Guy Trosper
Based on a story by Ned Young
Photographed in CinemaScope by Robert Bronner
Music by Jeff Alexander
Most songs by Mike Stoller and Jerry Leiber
Released October 17, 1957

Vince Everett . . . . Elvis Presley
Peggy Van Alden. . . . . Judy Tyler
Hunk Houghton. . . . . Mickey Shaughnessy
Mr. Shores . . . . Vaughn Taylor
Sherry Wilson . . . . Jennifer Holden
Teddy Talbot . . . . Dean Jones
Laury Jackson . . . . Anne Neyland
Warden. . . . . Hugh Sanders

BEST MOVIES
King Creole

A MUSICAL DRAMA with a cast of Hollywood's most respected character actors, *King Creole* was directed by veteran Michael Curtiz and produced by Hal Wallis for Paramount Pictures. Though not a classic, it is a well-crafted example of a typical Hollywood film from the era when the studio system still dominated the industry. In this production, which was less of a vehicle designed around Elvis than the majority of his movies were, the young actor held his own with a cast of talented professionals. *King Creole* now stands as a testament to Elvis' acting potential, which was never fully realized in the succession of teen musicals made for him in the 1960s.

In 1956, when Elvis began his acting career, Hollywood was undergoing changes that

As Danny Fisher, Elvis is always "lookin' for trouble" in the musical drama King Creole.

permanently altered the industry and affected the way a movie was produced. The old studio system, in which a major studio would control the entire production of a film from its conception to its theatrical exhibition, was fading away to be gradually replaced by a system in which small independent production companies made movies for the major studios, who then distributed them. Under the old studio system, eight major studios accounted for 80 percent of the films released in Hollywood. Each of these studios employed on a permanent basis the personnel needed to produce and distribute a film— a staff of writers, a pool of directors, an editing department, a costume designer and assistants, a marketing department, a distribution company, and so on. Each studio also had under

contract a wide variety of actors, including movie stars, character actors, and bit players. When not appearing in films, performers attended acting, dance, and voice lessons to perfect their craft. The studio system, which developed during the 1920s and faded away by the early 1960s, ran like a well-oiled machine—it was efficient and proficient. The studio system cultivated the skilled crew members and actors needed to make a movie, and Hollywood was characterized by a level of technical expertise and talent that no other film industry could match.

Though Hollywood was in the process of changing during the 1950s, many films were still produced under the old studio system, and the industry was still dominated by those skilled professionals trained under it. Most of Elvis' 1950s films fall into this category, but *King Creole* provides the best example of the craftsmanship that the studio system signified—behind the camera and in front of it. It's obvious from Elvis' performance that he benefitted from the expertise of the cast and crew.

Elvis would work with a number of talented character actors and veteran movie stars throughout his career, but he would rarely have the supporting cast of the caliber of *King Creole*. Some of the cast members were at the peak of their careers; some were established supporting players who had been a part of Hollywood for several years; some were relative unknowns at the start of lucrative careers.

Elvis worked with a cast of top Hollywood talent in **King Creole.** *Top left: Fresh-faced Dolores Hart played the story's "nice girl." Top right: Walter Matthau began his film career playing villains like Maxie Fields. Middle: Carolyn Jones' striking appearance and offbeat portrayals made her a sought-after supporting player during the 1950s. Bottom right: Vic Morrow added depth and grit to his stereotypical juvenile delinquent character. Bottom left: The career of well-respected character actor Dean Jagger spanned 50 years.*

Dolores Hart may have won Elvis' hand in the final reel of *King Creole*, but the real female lead was Carolyn Jones, who starred as Ronnie, the bargirl with the heart of gold. Jones is best known for playing Morticia Addams in the 1960s television series *The Addams Family*, but during the 1950s, she excelled in a variety of offbeat film roles that used her distinctive looks and sophisticated manner. The year that *King Creole* was released, Jones starred in *Bachelor Party*, a film about contemporary social values written by Paddy Chayefsky, and garnered an Oscar nomination for her six-minute performance as a Greenwich Village bohemian. Struck by Elvis' youthful naiveté during the short time they spent working on *King Creole*, she suggested that to improve his craft, he should take acting lessons—advice that he never heeded.

Of Elvis' male costars, Walter Matthau would later become a bona fide movie star, winning an Oscar for his supporting role in *The Fortune Cookie*. Matthau began as a stage actor, and by the mid-1950s, he was playing heavies in Hollywood movies. As a trained actor, Matthau had a more studied approach to his craft than Elvis, who lacked the polished subtleties of a professional. The potential for Matthau's formal style of acting to clash with Elvis's instinctual approach occurred to Michael Curtiz, who directed Matthau to hold back and let

Several sequences from **King Creole** *were shot on location, including the climactic scene at Lake Pontchartrain.*

Elvis emote. The strategy worked, with Matthau's low-key performance suited to his role as a deadly gangster and Elvis' more emotive performance appropriate for his role as a hot-headed teenager in over his head. Despite Elvis' lack of training, Matthau admired the young actor's ability to portray a character by being himself but staying within the confines of the story.

Dean Jagger and Vic Morrow played characters who had become staples of youth-oriented dramas by 1957. Jagger portrayed Elvis' weak-willed father, who was similar to the father character in *Rebel Without a Cause*. The highly respected Jagger, a veteran of the big screen since 1929, was a versatile character performer who won an Oscar as best supporting actor in the war drama *Twelve O'Clock High*. Morrow portrayed a version of the tough juvenile delinquent he had played in his film debut, *Blackboard Jungle*. His intense, edgy interpretation of *Jungle's* tough hood in a black jacket helped turn that character into an icon of disenfranchised youth. It also typecast Morrow as a heavy for most of his career. Other notable character actors in *King Creole* included Paul Stewart as the owner of a nightclub and Ned Glass as a hotel clerk.

LILIANE MONTEVECCHI

Liliane Montevecchi appeared in a small role in *King Creole* as Forty Nina, a dancer at the nightclub where Elvis' character works. Her big scene included a production number called "Banana," in which her character per-  forms in a skimpy banana-covered costume. The Italian-born actress made headlines in the entertainment press with her observations on her famous costar: "When they tell me I am to do picture with that man, I am devastated. I think of him only as the belly dancer, the big sexy pot...[But] he is like little boy, very sweet. So am nice to him, only I do not want to get too close. He is too much complexes, young spoiled." After *King Creole*, Montevecchi continued her career as a professional dancer, appearing onstage as late as 1991 in the Broadway musical *Grand Hotel* as Greta Garbo.

Two veterans of the Golden Age of Hollywood, director Michael Curtiz (left) *and producer Hal Wallis* (middle), *offered Elvis the benefits of their experience during filming.*

Those working behind the camera proved just as noteworthy as the cast, particularly Hungarian-born director Michael Curtiz. Curtiz's career represents the strengths and virtues of the studio system. A contract director for Warner Bros. during the 1930s and 1940s, he was at home in any genre and worked with every notable movie star, including Humphrey Bogart, Joan Crawford, Errol Flynn, Cary Grant, Bette Davis, and many others. Best known as the director of the classic *Casablanca*, for which he won an Oscar, Curtiz was also responsible for *The Adventures of Robin Hood, Mildred Pierce, Life with Father,* and *Yankee Doodle Dandy.* His experiences with so many famous stars gave him a gift for directing actors of all temperaments, though he was infamous for intimidating and berating his cast. When Elvis arrived on the set of *King Creole*, he seemed a prime candidate for Curtiz's harsh tactics because of his fame and fortune, but Elvis was so cooperative and eager that Curtiz was disarmed. Curtiz stated, ". . . this is a lovely boy, and he's going to be a wonderful actor."

Curtiz's sure-handed direction was matched by the atmospheric cinematography of Russell Harlan, another veteran of the studio system who excelled in the black-and-white photography that dominated Hollywood's Golden Age. Harlan's work included *Red River, The Thing, Blackboard Jungle, Rio Bravo,* and *To Kill a Mockingbird.*

King Creole was adapted from a Harold Robbins' novel called *A Stone for Danny Fisher.* The rights to the novel had been purchased by producer Hal Wallis in February 1955. The storyline involved a young boxer in New York City whose career is threatened when he becomes involved with mobsters. Wallis owned the property before he signed Elvis to a three-film contract in 1956, and according to Hollywood lore, such actors as Ben Gazzara and James Dean were considered for the role of Danny Fisher. Thus, the film was not originally conceived as a vehicle for Elvis, though major changes were made in the basic story to accommodate Elvis' talents. For example, Danny Fisher became a young singer with a new sound, and the action was transplanted to New Orleans.

Surrounded by Oscar-caliber talent and skilled craftsmen trained in the slick professionalism of the studio system, Elvis offered a vivid performance in *King Creole* that garnered the best reviews of his career. It would be the last time that he adjusted completely to the demands of the project rather than having the project completely adjusted to fit his image.

CAST AND CREDITS

Paramount Pictures
Produced by Hal Wallis
Directed by Michael Curtiz
Screenplay by Herbert Baker and Michael Vincente Gazzo
Photographed by Russell Harlan
Music by Walter Scharf
Released July 2, 1958

Danny Fisher . . . . Elvis Presley
Ronnie . . . . Carolyn Jones
Nellie . . . . Dolores Hart
Mr. Fisher . . . . Dean Jagger
Maxie Fields . . . . Walter Matthau
Mimi Fisher . . . . Jan Shepard
Charlie LaGrand . . . . Paul Stewart
Shark . . . . Vic Morrow
Forty Nina . . . . Liliane Montevecchi

BEST MOVIES
Blue Hawaii

"**E**XCITING ROMANCE... Dances... Music in the World's Lushest Paradise of Song!" "Elvis Presley Guides You Through a Paradise of Song!" So blared the promotion for *Blue Hawaii*, Elvis' most financially successful film. Its lush location footage, large selection of songs, and colorful supporting cast accounted for its popularity, success, and good reputation, and that success and popularity determined the course of Elvis' movie career thereafter. With *Blue Hawaii*, a formula was established for Presley vehicles that was followed almost exclusively.

The exotic locale was a key element in the promotion of *Blue Hawaii* and in its success. It provided more than just beautiful cinematography.

Just as the posters for Blue Hawaii *promised, the movie delivered music and dances on the beaches of an exotic paradise. Elvis and his costars get into the island spirit by "Slicin' Sand."*

As a tropical paradise, it was the perfect setting for romance, and it represented an escape from the mundane everyday world of most viewers. Even the title reinforced the locale, reminding audiences of the beautiful paradise that had become America's fiftieth state amidst much fanfare in 1960. The entertainment industry had taken advantage of the public interest in Hawaii's admittance to the union with the release of *Blue Hawaii* and *Gidget Goes Hawaiian* on the big screen in 1961 and the series *Hawaiian Eye* on the small screen in 1959.

Exotic locales and vacation settings—and the romance and escape that went with them—became an essential ingredient in the formula for Elvis' later movies. Elvis returned to Hawaii to make *Girls! Girls! Girls!* and *Paradise, Hawaiian Style*, while *Follow That Dream*, *Girl Happy*, *Easy Come, Easy Go*, and

Clambake are set in Florida. The titles of *Fun in Acapulco*, *It Happened at the World's Fair*, and *Viva Las Vegas* let the viewers know immediately where the action is, while *Harum Scarum* and *Double Trouble* offer adventures on distant continents. Exotic and vacation settings became such a well-known element in Elvis' movies that he dubbed them "Presley travelogues."

Any viewer familiar with Elvis' movies recognizes the prevalence of unique and exotic locations, but not all realize the extent to which these settings affect the whole film. For example, Elvis' characters were independent spirits who worked as race-car drivers, pilots, tour guides, entertainers, or boat captains—atypical occupations, to say the least. Yet these occupations seem almost appropriate given the exotic setting. In a way, the settings determined the occupations of Elvis' charac-

The inviting locales were so prominent in the film that the state of Hawaii practically became a character. **Top left:** Elvis played budding tour guide Chad Gates, which offered an excuse for showing off the scenery. **Top right:** Angela Lansbury played Chad's mother, Mrs. Sarah Lee Gates. The Gates family owns a pineapple factory, which provides another interesting location for the film. **Middle right:** Chad sings "Can't Help Falling in Love" to his girlfriend's grandmother, a native of the Islands. **Above and right:** The beautiful blue waters of Hawaii gave the film its name.

ters, which indirectly helped define them as free souls who reject the conventional, nine-to-five lifestyle. In addition, exotic and vacation settings convey the idea of escaping to paradise for romantic escapades. For decades, travel brochures have used this very notion to entice tourists to distant lands. As soon as viewers recognized the setting of an Elvis film as exotic, unique, or a haven for fun-seeking vacationers, the stage was set for romance. And romance was the main attraction in an Elvis Presley vehicle. The plot may center around a quest or an adventure, but it parallels the pursuit of a beautiful woman by Elvis' carefree hero. The story concludes when the goal is completed or the quest fulfilled, which is represented by the union of Elvis' character with his leading lady. The complete closure of the film in terms of fulfilling the goal and winning the girl is generally indicated by the final musical number in which the couple are united via song and/or dance.

With *Blue Hawaii*, this pattern was firmly established. Here, Elvis plays Chad Gates, an ambitious young man just out of the army who refuses to go into the family business. By the end of the film, after several misadventures, he has established his own tour-guide service. The fact that he is a success is

Chad the tour guide shows a school group around the Islands.

indicated by his marriage to his girlfriend, Maile, because he refused to marry her until he had proven himself. "Hawaiian Wedding Song," which concludes *Blue Hawaii*, is part of their wedding ceremony and serves to announce their union. The fulfillment of Chad's dream and the winning of Maile are neatly tied together in this final number.

"Hawaiian Wedding Song" provides an excellent example of how Elvis' music changed from his pre-army movies to the Presley travelogues. In this song, Elvis does not sing on a stage setting; he sings *to* someone who shares the spotlight with him, and the song advances the story. Most of the production numbers in the film are presented in a similar fashion, which was the exact opposite of the musical numbers in his pre-army films. *Blue Hawaii* established the formula for the presentation of the songs in Elvis' movies thereafter. In Elvis' postarmy vehicles, the songs are integrated into the storyline, meaning they help advance the story or they relate something about the characters to the viewers. In this type of

NORMAN TAUROG

Norman Taurog *(pictured, on left)* was responsible for nine Elvis Presley features—more than any other director. Elvis always favored Taurog, probably because of his kind nature and lack of ego. After particularly difficult scenes, the fatherly director would pass out candy bars to his cast and crew. Taurog was known primarily for lightweight vehicles and comedies, a specialty that dated all the way back to 1919 when his directorial career was launched with a series starring silent comedian Larry Semon. The consummate studio director, Taurog directed many major stars in over 70 films across six decades. He won an Oscar in 1931 for *Skippy*, a vehicle for child star Jackie Cooper, and he was nominated again in 1938 for the classic *Boys Town*. Taurog, who died in 1981, said of Elvis, "I was always proud of his work, even if I wasn't proud of the scripts. I always felt that he never reached his peak."

In the end, Chad has achieved his goal and won the girl, which is conveyed through the closing musical number, "Hawaiian Wedding Song."

In this rare candid taken on the set, Elvis enjoys a moment to himself between camera set-ups.

musical, characters tend to burst into song at any moment—on the beach, in a car, even on a horse. Elvis disliked this type of musical and was uncomfortable when his character sang in situations where people would not normally sing.

Because the musical numbers often tell part of the story, it is not unusual for them to include other characters. Most often, Elvis' characters sing to or dance with the leading ladies as a means of winning their love or to symbolize the couple's growing affection. Sometimes the film will feature Elvis singing to a child, a pet, or an elderly woman to help soften the vagabond nature of his characters. In *Blue Hawaii*, Chad gives Maile's grandmother a music box that plays "Can't Help Falling in Love," which Chad sings along to. The scene helps the audience understand that Chad is not the rash, immature young man that his parents believe him to be.

Elvis' performing style in *Blue Hawaii* and in his subsequent vehicles differs a great deal from that of his 1950s films. Gone are the sensual hip movements, leg swivels, pelvic thrusts, and dramatic hand gestures that drove the ladies wild in *Loving You.* Elvis still moved while he sang, but his style was noticeably toned down. This seemed an appropriate change if Elvis was singing to another character. The notorious performing style of his early career was not suitable for romantic situations or when singing to a child or grandmother. When he wasn't singing to someone else, or when he sang a tune with an upbeat tempo, a bevy of beautiful women often danced in the background. Thus, Elvis no longer needed to move provocatively because a chorus of women did it for him. After all, women dancing in a sexual or provocative way was a more conventional—and therefore more acceptable—sight in mainstream movies.

Elvis' toned-down style was less controversial and was considered more suited to family entertainment. His musical comedy vehicles were designed to attract the family audience. Elvis, Colonel Tom Parker, Hal Wallis, and Abe Lastfogel, who was Elvis' agent at William Morris, wanted to turn Elvis into a mature leading man for the movies. His new singing style and smoother pop-oriented music helped accomplish that. A version of this image had been introduced in *G.I. Blues,* but it was perfected in *Blue Hawaii,* which is arguably the best of Elvis' musical comedies.

Blue Hawaii was well crafted and shrewdly manufactured to suit Elvis' new image. It was also wildly successful. While it turned Elvis Presley into a highly paid star, it also limited the type of role he undertook thereafter, because it established the formula that his movies followed to the end of his Hollywood career. Much has been written about how Elvis' hopes of becoming a serious actor were foiled by the formula. His potential as an actor was a casualty of his success as a movie star. Because of this significance that it holds in Elvis' career, *Blue Hawaii* is a movie that is both revered and reviled.

CAST AND CREDITS

Paramount Pictures
Produced by Hal B. Wallis
Directed by Norman Taurog
Screenplay by Hal Kanter from a story by Allan Weiss
Photographed in Technicolor and Panavision by Charles Lang, Jr.
Music by Joseph J. Lilley
Released November 22, 1961

Chad Gates . . . . Elvis Presley
Maile Duval . . . . Joan Blackman
Sarah Lee Gates . . . . Angela Lansbury
Abigail Prentice . . . . Nancy Walters
Fred Gates . . . . Roland Winters
Jack Kelman . . . . John Archer
Mr. Chapman . . . . Howard McNear
Tucker Garvey . . . . Steve Brodie
Enid Garvey . . . . Iris Adrian
Waihila . . . . Hilo Hattie
Ellie Corbett . . . . Jennie Maxwell
Selena Emerson . . . . Pamela Kirk
Patsy Simon . . . . Darlene Tompkins
Beverly Martin . . . . Christian Kay
Carl Tanami . . . . Lani Kai
Ernie Gordon . . . . Jose Devega
Ito O'Hara . . . . Frank Atienza

BEST MOVIES
Viva Las Vegas

WHEN ELVIS returned to Hollywood in early July of 1963 to begin work on *Viva Las Vegas*, little did he realize he was about to meet his on-screen match. Ann-Margret was a starlet on the rise when she agreed to costar in Elvis' fifteenth film. A bona fide singer-dancer, Ann-Margret injected the musical production numbers in *Viva Las Vegas* with a vitality and professionalism that had been lacking in Elvis' films for some time. Elvis, who by this time was unhappy with his formulaic vehicles, rose to the occasion and matched her youthful eagerness with an enthusiasm he had not felt in a while. It surprised no one—neither friends, colleagues, nor the press—when the on-screen sparks between Elvis and Ann-Margret ignited a passionate relationship offscreen as well.

The pairing of Elvis and Ann-Margret resulted in a film filled with dynamic encounters.

a conventional musical comedy in the Broadway tradition, *Bye Bye Birdie* became popular among teenagers because it was about them, even if it was a spoof. Particularly appealing to youthful fans was Ann-Margret's performance of the title tune, which opened and closed the film. Her high-powered dancing style and her connection to teen culture via *Bye Bye Birdie* earned her a nickname— "the female Elvis Presley." After receiving such a nickname, and, after appearing in a film loosely based on his career, Ann-Margret seemed fated to team up with Elvis Presley for a movie.

Though Elvis' performing style had toned down considerably, he still sang up-tempo tunes in his movies, and he still moved to the beat. Combining Elvis and "the female Elvis" on the screen

Ann-Margret was considered a show-business sensation after appearing on the 1962 Academy Awards show in a knock-'em-dead song-and-dance number. However, she was not a hit among teenagers until her appearance in the musical film *Bye Bye Birdie*. Released in 1963, *Birdie* was a reflection of the impact rock 'n' roll music had made on popular culture. It spoofed the generation gap that had been widened by rock 'n' roll as well as the fan hysteria that surrounded this new form of popular music. The story involves the departure of a rock 'n' roll singing idol for the army, and any resemblance to the life and career of Elvis Presley was purely intentional. Though

meant that *Viva Las Vegas* was sure to highlight dancing. Two extended production numbers featured Elvis and Ann-Margret sizzling together on the dance floor. "C'mon Everybody" was performed in the gymnasium at the University of Nevada, where Ann-Margret's character, Rusty, practices dance routines with theater students. Rehearsing for the upcoming talent show at the Flamingo Hotel where she works, Rusty is clad in a black dance leotard and a tight cotton-knit shirt. "What'd I Say" features the couple dancing in a raucous nightclub scene while Elvis belts out the old Ray Charles tune. In addition to dancing together, each character also had the opportunity to

Dance dominated Viva Las Vegas. *Top left:* Ann-Margret landed her part after her high-energy role in Bye Bye Birdie. *Top right:* Elvis and his red-haired costar communicate via dance in "C'mon Everybody." *Bottom right: A new dance called the Climb was introduced in the film. Bottom left: Elvis was even precisely choreographed for his solo rendition of "Viva Las Vegas."*

perform solo in a dance-dominated musical number. Rusty sings and dances to "Appreciation" at the Flamingo's talent contest. Lucky chooses "Viva Las Vegas" for the contest, with Vegas showgirls providing most of the dancing for that musical number.

Not surprisingly, MGM's publicity department exploited the dancing in its promotion for the film. Shots of Elvis and Ann-Margret dancing while performing "C'mon Everybody" were used for the film's poster and ads, which was recognizable because of Ann-Margret's black leotard costume. Hyping the similarities between the two in terms of their rock 'n' roll performing styles, the poster declared, "It's that 'Go-Go' Guy and that 'Bye Bye' Girl." Some ads included references to current dance crazes by calling the film, "the new musical that's wild as the Wobble, bouncy as the Chicken-back and modern as the Monkey."

There were other efforts to exploit the film's rock 'n' roll dancing as well. In the nightclub scene just prior to Elvis'

WHAT MIGHT HAVE BEEN

During the years that Elvis was an actor in Hollywood, he had several opportunities to star in films that were not "Presley travelogues," but these opportunities fell through. Often, the Colonel refused to agree to a film that did not follow the formula or did not showcase Elvis to his best advantage. He turned down the 1956 rock 'n' roll spoof *The Girl Can't Help It,* because the money wasn't good enough and because Elvis had to share the screen with other notable rock n' roll acts. In the 1970s, Barbra Streisand was rumored to have wanted Elvis for her remake of *A Star Is Born,* but supposedly the Colonel turned her down. Kris Kristofferson played the role. Other roles that Elvis turned down included Hank Williams in *Your Cheatin' Heart* (George Hamilton played Williams) and the singing cowboy in *The Fastest Guitar in the West* (Roy Orbison got the part). Rumors persist that he could have appeared in *Thunder Road, The Way to the Gold,* and *The Defiant Ones,* but these rumors could have been born of bitterness over Elvis' lost potential as an actor.

Other factors prevented Elvis from appearing in certain films, including the timing of projects and failed deals. Elvis was once set to play a James Bond-like superspy in a comedy adventure called *That Jack Valentine,* but the film was never produced. Other projects that fell through include a proposed musical starring Elvis opposite a classical artist and a comedy teaming Elvis with French legend Brigitte Bardot.

"What'd I Say" number, a group called the Forte Four perform "The Climb." Though the song had been recorded by the Coasters in 1962, the dance called the Climb was not introduced until *Viva Las Vegas.* The producers had the Climb created for the film because they were hoping to introduce a new dance craze. Elvis and Ann-Margret are doing the Climb as Elvis sings "What'd I Say." The press book that accompanied the film's release suggested that theater managers stage a dance contest in conjunction with a local dance studio. The five couples who best perform the Climb would win up to $200 plus a free dance course. The press book guaranteed that the Climb would "catch the fancy of the pace-setting teenager," because, as the ad copy proclaimed, "Those who have tried it agree that it makes the Twist look like the Minuet."

A 24-year-old dancer named David Winters choreographed *Viva Las Vegas.* His hip dance routines showcased Ann-Margret's controlled yet frenzied style of dancing while still taking into account Elvis' free-form way of moving to his songs. Ann-Margret was a professional dancer; Elvis simply moved to the rhythm and beat of his music. Under Winters' guidance, it was the similarities between the two performers that were emphasized, not their differences. During the 1960s, Winters gained a name for himself as a choreographer who created rock 'n' roll dances or choreographed to rock music. He went on to choreograph three more of Elvis' films as well as two television specials for Ann-Margret. His highest profile as a choreographer probably occurred as the dance director

Though fanzines hoped that Elvis and Ann-Margret would wed in real life, the couple tied the knot on-screen only.

for the rock 'n' roll television series *Hullabaloo*. Prior to *Viva Las Vegas*, Charles O'Curran had staged the musical numbers for most of Elvis' movies. O'Curran was a generation older than the rock 'n' roll crowd, and he was not a creator of dances or dance movements. He merely staged Elvis' movements and positioned the musicians around him to their best camera advantage. The employment of Winters in lieu of someone like O'Curran seemed preferable to the producers for several reasons. Winters was of the same generation as Elvis and Ann-Margret and attuned to rock 'n' roll music and movements. And, he was capable of creating rock 'n' roll dances for Elvis' movies, which tied them more closely to the fads and fashions of the day. Winters' work in some of Elvis' later movies seems dated in retrospect, but in *Viva Las Vegas*, his careful handling of Elvis and Ann-Margret makes their musical numbers exciting and memorable.

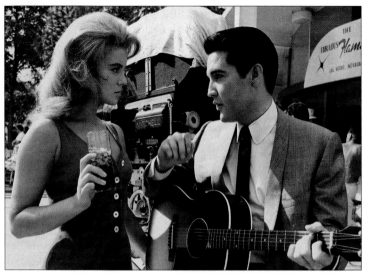
Viva Las Vegas *was a major success thanks to the chemistry between its two high-powered stars, though the publicity surrounding their romance certainly didn't hurt.*

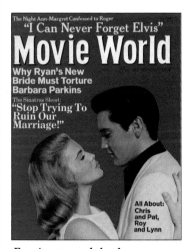
Fanzines touted the Ann-Margret/Elvis Presley affair as the romance of the year.

Dancing was not the only aspect of the film that was exploited by the publicity department of MGM. The romance between Elvis and Ann-Margret was promoted as heavily as the movie itself. Stories leaked out to the columnists detailing the off-set activities of the two stars while they were on location in Nevada. When the production returned to Hollywood to finish shooting, major newspapers featured stories about Elvis and Ann-Margret lunching together every day and retiring to his trailer between scenes. Even the press book teased, "The romantic sparks that emanate when they work together... seem equally prevalent in their private lives." Elsewhere the ads and promotion touted, "Here's the most inflammable combination since little boys and matches."

Whether it was the offscreen romance or Ann-Margret's talents that made *Viva Las Vegas* come alive, the film was a critical and popular success. It grossed $4.6 million at the box office, making it the fourteenth highest grosser of the year. Reviews were generally good. One critic was more perceptive than most when he remarked, "For once everybody in the cast of an Elvis Presley picture isn't overshadowed by the rock 'n'

roll hero." This was precisely what Colonel Tom Parker did not want to hear. Parker and others on Elvis' management team preferred that a Presley vehicle showcase Elvis Presley. After *Viva Las Vegas*, Elvis would never again woo a leading lady with the talent and charisma of Ann-Margret—either on or off the screen

CAST AND CREDITS

Metro-Goldwyn-Mayer
Produced by Jack Cummings and George Sidney
Directed by George Sidney
Screenplay by Sally Benson
Photographed in Metrocolor by Joseph Biroc
Music by George Stoll
Choreography by David Winters
Released June 17, 1964

Lucky Jackson	Elvis Presley
Rusty Martin	Ann-Margret
Count Elmo Mancini	Cesare Danova
Mr. Martin	William Demarest
Shorty Farnsworth	Nicky Blair
Jack Carter	Himself
Mr. Swanson	Robert B. Williams
Big Gus Olson	Bob Nash
Mr. Baker	Roy Engel
Mechanic	Barnaby Hale
Driver	Ford Dunhill
Master of Ceremonies	Eddie Quillan

BEST COSTARS

ANN-MARGRET

Dubbed "the female Elvis Presley" for her sensual, energetic dance style, Ann-Margret made a dynamic costar for Elvis in *Viva Las Vegas*. A trained singer and dancer, she followed a more conventional path to mainstream show business than Elvis did, starting her career as a nightclub performer in a singing combo. As the story goes, George Burns discovered her and put her in his Las Vegas show. A screen test followed, and she landed a small role in *Pocketful of Miracles* (1961). Her big breakthrough came when she performed a high-energy, provocative song-and-dance routine on the 1962 Academy Award telecast. The response resulted in an expansion of her role in *Bye Bye Birdie* (1963) and a multiple-picture deal with MGM. Trapped by her sex-kitten image for several years, she finally moved on to costar in *Carnal Knowledge* (1971) and *Tommy* (1975). Both performances resulted in Academy Award nominations and steered her toward dramatic films that emphasized her range as an actress.

BILL BIXBY

Born in San Francisco in 1934, Bill Bixby's first major success as an actor occurred in the 1960s television series *My Favorite Martian*. His role as eager, amiable Tim O'Hara, who shares his apartment with a space alien, made him recognizable to the family audience, which was the target of Elvis' later movies. From his TV experience, Bixby learned to play a character that was comically exaggerated yet still believable, a skill he brought to two of Elvis' films, *Clambake* and *Speedway*.

Bixby starred in other memorable TV series, including *The Courtship of Eddie's Father* and *The Incredible Hulk*, as well as such misfires as *The Magician* and *Goodnight Beantown*. By the 1990s, he had become a television director, experiencing his greatest success with the sitcom *Blossom*.

In the early 1990s, he hosted two television specials relating to Elvis—one claiming that Presley was alive and in hiding because of work he had done for the FBI, and the other disputing claims that Elvis was still alive. Bixby died in 1993.

DOLORES DEL RIO

Born Lolita Dolores Martinez Asunsolo Lopez Negrette in Durango, Mexico, Dolores Del Rio experienced several phases in her long film career. She was renowned for her dark beauty, which helped her conquer Hollywood during the silent era. After two decades in the American film industry working with such acclaimed directors as Raoul Walsh (*What Price Glory?*, 1926), King Vidor (*Bird of Paradise*, 1932), and Orson Welles (*Journey into Fear*, 1942), she returned to her native country to star in Mexican films.

Her work with director Emilio Fernandez during this period garnered her international acclaim. It was considered a triumph to land Del Rio, a major star of both the American and Mexican cinemas, for the role of Elvis' mother in *Flaming Star*. Directed by Don Siegel, the western was one of the few dramatic films that Elvis tackled, and it is generally well regarded, partly because of Del Rio's contributions. She made only one more Hollywood feature after that, John Ford's *Cheyenne Autumn* (1964).

RICHARD EGAN

Ruggedly handsome Richard Egan was a fixture in action films and melodramas during the 1950s as the virile leading man. In *Love Me Tender*, he starred as the oldest brother to Elvis' character. Offscreen, he played a similar role, guiding Elvis through his first screen appearance. Egan was well suited for the role of Elvis' unofficial instructor, as he had taught public speaking at Northwestern University before coming to Hollywood in 1949. Under contract to 20th Century Fox, he enjoyed a successful career in the waning days of the studio system. During the 1960s, he starred in the television series *Empire* and its spin-off, *Redigo*. His career ended on the small screen as a regular on the soap opera *Capitol*, which had a reputation for hiring former film stars.

Egan crossed paths with Elvis at least one more time after *Love Me Tender*. In 1972, he attended one of Elvis' shows in Las Vegas and began a standing ovation while Elvis was singing his closing number. Egan died in 1977, the same year as Elvis.

BEST COSTARS

DOLORES HART

If Ann-Margret and Tuesday Weld represented the sensual or provocative contemporary woman, then Dolores Hart was the girl next door. In keeping with her on-screen roles, Hart, according to Elvis, "was the nicest girl I've ever met." Born Dolores Hicks, Hart was seen by producer Hal Wallis in a school production of *Joan of Lorraine* just weeks before *Loving You* went into production. She was only 18 years old, and Wallis was charmed by her youthful innocence. She made her screen debut in *Loving You* and also played the good girl in *King Creole*, where her wholesome, blonde looks were contrasted with Carolyn Jones' sultry, dark-haired beauty.

After ten films, including the memorable teen flick *Where the Boys Are* (1961), Hart retired from screen acting to become a nun. Years later, mean-spirited rumors claimed that she joined a convent after being spurned by Elvis, but these tales are wholly unfounded. Now known as Mother Dolores, she is a member of the Benedictine Order.

ANGELA LANSBURY

Angela Lansbury earned celebrity in the 1980s and 1990s for her role as Jessica Fletcher on television's *Murder, She Wrote*. She also gained recognition among the younger set for a high-profile turn as the voice of Mrs. Potts in Disney's *Beauty and the Beast* (1992). Long before either of these roles, however, she was widely respected for her contributions to film and her Tony-winning performances on Broadway. Born in London in 1925, Lansbury began training for the stage at a very young age. Signed to a movie contract by MGM as a teenager, she costarred as a manipulative vixen in her first film, *Gaslight* (1944), and earned the first of three Oscar nominations. She continued in similar roles during her early career but moved on to specialize in portraying domineering women, often playing a character much older than herself. She played Laurence Harvey's mother in *The Manchurian Candidate* (1962), though she was only three years his senior. In *Blue Hawaii*, the 35-year-old Lansbury played the mother of Elvis' character.

WALTER MATTHAU

Born in the cold-water tenements of New York's Lower East Side, Walter Matthau became an accomplished stage actor before entering films. He began his career in summer stock and worked his way to small parts on Broadway and then to key supporting roles in high-profile plays. Desperately short of money, he agreed to a small role in a Hollywood western called *The Kentuckian* (1955) as the heavy who tricks star Burt Lancaster into a fight with whips. From this auspicious beginning, Matthau began a career as a character actor in the movies, most often as a villain. It was during this phase that he appeared in *King Creole* as ruthless gangster Maxie Fields. Contemporary audiences may be surprised to see Matthau as a cold-hearted villain because he has long been known for his comedic roles. Matthau's most popular screen work may be his comedies with friend Jack Lemmon, including *The Fortune Cookie* (1966), *The Odd Couple* (1968), *Grumpy Old Men* (1993), and *Grumpier Old Men* (1995).

JULIET PROWSE

Professional dancer Juliet Prowse arrived in Hollywood too late to star in the type of musicals that dominated the big screen in the 1940s and 1950s. By the 1960s, the musical genre was disappearing, partly due to expense and partly due to pop music being splintered by the rock 'n' roll revolution spearheaded by Elvis. In *G.I. Blues*, she played a nightclub dancer with all the right moves, but most new musicals were aimed primarily at the youth market and didn't have a place for Prowse's jazz-style dancing.

Born in Bombay, India, and raised in South Africa, Prowse appeared in her first Hollywood film, *Gentlemen Marry Brunettes*, in 1955. A supporting role in the big-budget musical *Can-Can* (1960) helped gain her industry recognition. Prowse was slated to costar with Elvis in *Blue Hawaii*, but her demands were considered extravagant, and she was replaced. After a short-lived television series called *Mona McCluskey* and a few more films, Prowse began appearing in Las Vegas, a venue that showcased her abilities as a dancer.

BEST COSTARS

NANCY SINATRA

On his return from the army in 1960, Elvis was scheduled to appear on *Welcome Home, Elvis,* a television special hosted by Frank Sinatra. Frank sent his daughter Nancy to the airport as Elvis' official greeter. The pair struck up a friendship that lasted for years and provided sparkling chemistry in *Speedway.* Her version of "Your Groovy Self" was included on the soundtrack album, marking the only time another artist sang a solo on a regular RCA Elvis album. In the mid-1960s, Nancy recorded four hit duets with singer-songwriter Lee Hazelwood, who also wrote her best-known hit, "These Boots Are Made for Walking." She earned her third gold record for a duet she sang with her father, "Something Stupid." She also spent a large part of the 1960s cavorting through teen musicals such as *Get Yourself a College Girl* (1964) and *The Ghost in the Invisible Bikini* (1966). During the mid-1990s, Nancy rode the crest of a nostalgia wave, singing her 1960s hits to a new generation and appearing in *Playboy* magazine.

BARBARA STANWYCK

Perhaps the biggest movie star ever to work with Elvis, Barbara Stanwyck brought a touch of the "old Hollywood" glamour and professionalism to *Roustabout.* Born Ruby Stevens in 1907, Stanwyck trained herself to be a dancer as a teenager. She began working in the chorus of the Ziegfeld Follies and other revues before making her screen debut in a silent film, *Broadway Nights* (1927). A disciplined and hard-working star, she brought her Hollywood career to a peak in the 1940s in such classics as *The Lady Eve* (1941), *Double Indemnity* (1945), and *Sorry, Wrong Number* (1948). Though nominated four times, she never won an Oscar but did receive an honorary Oscar in 1981 for her contributions to screen acting. Stanwyck conquered television with her image as the hard-edged, aggressive woman, winning Emmys for *The Barbara Stanwyck Show, The Big Valley,* and the acclaimed miniseries *The Thornbirds.* Stanwyck died in 1990.

TUESDAY WELD

Like Ann-Margret, Tuesday Weld became typecast as a fast-living, teenage sex kitten. Unlike Ann-Margret, Weld seemed to live the part off-screen as well. Born Susan Ker Weld, she entered modeling and became the sole support of her family at age three. She had a nervous breakdown by age nine, began drinking the next year, and attempted suicide by the time she was 12. The following year, she appeared in her first film, *Rock Rock Rock!* (1956). When she costarred with Elvis in *Wild in the Country* (1961), she was scarcely 18 years old but was already a Hollywood veteran who had survived numerous scandals and love affairs. Her life experiences and maturity added grit to her portrayal of Noreen, the poor girl whose only escape from poverty is her relentless wild streak. In the mid-1960s, Weld became something of a cult figure, boosted by her bone-chilling performance in *Pretty Poison* (1968). In 1988, her career intersected with Elvis once more in *Heartbreak Hotel*, a whimsical comedy about a boy who kidnaps Elvis as a gift for his mother.

GIG YOUNG

As the disillusioned, slightly corrupted fight promoter in Elvis' musical drama *Kid Galahad*, Gig Young offers a sympathetic portrait of an unscrupulous character, a variation on the type of role for which he was best known. Whether playing debonair cads, shallow playboys, or tragic losers, Young invested his characters with a depth and grace that prevented viewers from completely disliking them. Born Byron Elsworth Barr in 1913, the elegant actor stole his colorful stage name from a character in *The Gay Sisters* (1942), his first film. A versatile character actor who worked for several studios, Young was nominated for Academy Awards for *Come Fill the Cup* (1951) and *Teacher's Pet* (1958) and won the Oscar for his haunting portrayal of the sleazy emcee in *They Shoot Horses, Don't They?* (1969). In retrospect, Young's 1978 death adds a tragic connotation to the roles he gravitated toward. Found dead with his new bride in their apartment, Young apparently shot his wife and then committed suicide.

BEST MOVIE TUNES

"Love Me Tender" from *Love Me Tender*

"Teddy Bear" from *Loving You*

"Mean Woman Blues" from *Loving You*

"Got a Lot o' Livin' to Do" from *Loving You*

"Jailhouse Rock" from *Jailhouse Rock*

"(You're So Square) Baby, I Don't Care" from *Jailhouse Rock*

"Treat Me Nice" from *Jailhouse Rock*

"Don't Leave Me Now" from *Jailhouse Rock*

"Trouble" from *King Creole*

"New Orleans" from *King Creole*

"Hard Headed Woman" from *King Creole*

"G.I. Blues" from *G.I. Blues*

"Pocketful of Rainbows" from *G.I. Blues*

"Flaming Star" from *Flaming Star*

"I Slipped, I Stumbled, I Fell" from *Wild in the Country*

"Blue Hawaii" from *Blue Hawaii*

"Can't Help Falling in Love" from *Blue Hawaii*

"Rock-a-Hula Baby" from *Blue Hawaii*

"Follow That Dream" from *Follow That Dream*

"Angel" from *Follow that Dream*

"Return to Sender" from *Girls! Girls! Girls!*

"Girls! Girls! Girls!" from *Girls! Girls! Girls!*

"Bossa Nova Baby" from *Fun in Acapulco*

"Viva Las Vegas" from *Viva Las Vegas*

"What'd I Say" from *Viva Las Vegas*

"Little Egypt" from *Roustabout*

"Frankie and Johnny" from *Frankie and Johnny*

"Drums of the Islands" from *Paradise, Hawaiian Style*

"All That I Am" from *Spinout*

"Long Legged Girl (with the Short Dress On)" from *Double Trouble*

Elvis rocks with a tropical flair as he plays "Drums of the Island" (above) and belts out "Rock-a-Hula Baby" (right).

Top left: *A brooding, darkly clad Elvis rocks a sunny poolside party with his rendition of "(You're So Square) Baby, I Don't Care." Top right: Elvis and Ann-Margret shimmy to "What'd I Say." Bottom right: Dressed in one of the cutest costumes ever designed for him, Elvis just wants to be everyone's "Teddy Bear." Bottom left: Elvis gets down and dirty as he laments the "Mean Woman Blues."*

BEST DOCUMENTARIES
Elvis—That's the Way It Is

ELVIS'S 32ND FILM was not a narrative feature but a documentary showcasing his 1970 summer appearance at the International Hotel in Las Vegas. Elvis began rehearsals July 5 at the MGM studios in Hollywood, where he worked on his material for about a month. The show opened August 10. The MGM cameras not only recorded the rehearsals but also opening night, several performances throughout the engagement, and one show at Veterans Memorial Coliseum in Phoenix, Arizona. The film is structured so that the rehearsals and other scenes of preparation build to an extended climax of Elvis onstage. Performing in a simple, white jumpsuit accented with fringe instead of rhinestones and gems, Elvis is captured at the pinnacle of his career.

Filmmaker Denis Sanders captured the excitement of one of Elvis' Vegas concerts in the cinema verité *documentary* Elvis—That's the Way It Is.

"Blue Suede Shoes," he replaces the original lyrics in the chorus with "white suede shoes." Elvis emerges from this documentary as a person with a good sense of humor and a star who does not take himself that seriously.

Elvis—That's the Way It Is was directed by documentary filmmaker Denis Sanders and photographed by veteran cinematographer Lucien Ballard. Their skill and expertise are evident in the pacing, which gradually builds in intensity, and in the way they captured Elvis' grace and ease in his milieu. The film's main flaw is the series of interviews with fans interspersed throughout the documentary. A segment involving a fan convention in Luxembourg seems out of place, considering that the focus is supposed to be on Elvis in performance. Like those who later produced Elvis documentaries,

Unlike Elvis' musical comedies, *Elvis—That's the Way It Is* offers a realistic portrait of Elvis Presley as a singer and entertainer. During the rehearsal scenes, Elvis freely chats with bystanders, he explains the effects he's aiming for with his music, and he heckles the cameraman. Later, during the concert sequences, he jokes with the audiences. Between songs, he comments about his appearance on *The Ed Sullivan Show* when the cameras shot him only from the waist up. He mumbles that the incident had occurred a long time ago when he was "a little bitty boy, with little bitty sideburns, and a little bitty shaky leg." A short time later, during his rendition of

Sanders was perhaps so fascinated with the devotion of the fans that he felt compelled to convey the extreme level of their adoration.

Though not exhibited in as many theaters as Elvis' musical comedies, *Elvis—That's the Way It Is* filled a void for some fans during this time. After Elvis stopped making movies, fans accustomed to seeing him three times a year on the big screen felt deprived. The documentary allowed fans all over the country continued access to Elvis.

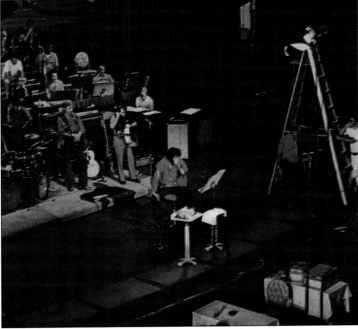

The documentary also included the rehearsals for the Vegas show. **Top left and above:** *Elvis directs his band and backup singers to create the musical effect he wants.* **Left:** *The film crew clearly enjoyed working with Elvis because he was a good sport who liked to joke with them.*

DENIS SANDERS

Trained at UCLA's film school, Denis Sanders, the director of *Elvis—That's the Way It Is*, had won Academy Awards for two previous documentaries, *A Time Out for War* (1954) and *Czechoslovakia, 1968* (1969). The former also won first prizes at the Venice and Edinburgh Film Festivals.

During the first part of his career, Sanders often collaborated with his brother, Terry. The two did make an effort to enter into feature filmmaking when they wrote the screenplay for *The Naked and the Dead* (1958). They worked on a few features together and then split, with Denis returning to the documentary arena. Sanders' professional background makes *Elvis—That's the Way It Is* a cut above the many Elvis-related documentaries that flooded the market after Elvis died.

CREDITS

Metro-Goldwyn-Mayer
Produced by Herbert F. Soklow
Directed by Denis Sanders
Photographed by Lucien Ballard
Edited by Henry Berman
Elvis' wardrobe by Bill Belew
Released November 11, 1970
Songs Include:
"Mystery Train"/"Tiger Man"
"Words"
"The Next Step Is Love"
"Polk Salad Annie"
"Crying Time"
"That's All Right"
"Little Sister"
"What'd I Say"
"Stranger in the Crowd"
"How the Web Was Woven"
"I Just Can't Help Believin'"
"You Don't Have to Say You Love Me"
"Bridge Over Troubled Water"
"You've Lost That Lovin' Feelin'"
"Mary in the Morning"
"I've Lost You"
"Patch It Up"
"Love Me Tender"
"Sweet Caroline"
"Get Back"
"Heartbreak Hotel"
"One Night"
"Blue Suede Shoes"
"All Shook Up"
"Suspicious Minds"
"Can't Help Falling in Love"

BEST DOCUMENTARIES
Elvis on Tour

THE SECOND DOCUMENTARY to capture Elvis in performance focused on his road show. *Elvis on Tour* followed the singer's 15-city tour in the spring of 1972. The tour started in Buffalo, New York, and came to a rousing conclusion in Albuquerque, New Mexico. Much of the tour centered in the South, where Elvis' popularity reached a peak in the 1970s.

In addition to the footage of Elvis in concert, the film attempted to reveal the real Elvis Presley backstage and off-guard. A camera followed the singer and his entourage, while Elvis was asked to comment on such topics as his music and his childhood. According to filmmakers Pierre Adidge and Robert Abel in the press kit for the film, "...after we filmed [Elvis] on tour and were allowed to shoot and record in places he had never allowed cameras in the past, we finally asked if he would mind talking about himself. He thought awhile and finally agreed." Despite a few humorous candid moments, however, these interviews did not reveal the real Elvis but only added to the myth that surrounded him; Elvis dropped no veils for the film-makers.

The most telling scene in the film is not one in which Elvis speaks—it is one in which he sings. Just before a concert, Elvis, his musicians, and backup singers are shown waiting to go onstage. A bit nervous, Elvis begins singing a gospel song to break the tension, and the others quickly join in. For the observant viewer, this bit of spontaneity offers some insight into Elvis Presley. His natural ability as a singer is readily apparent, as is his ability to rally and lead a musical entourage of rock musicians, a gospel quartet, and female backup singers. Most interesting is the role of gospel music. It is the thread that ties the diverse members of his musical troupe together, and therefore a basis of his music. While many biographers have stated this, this film sequence illustrates it.

Much of the success of the film was due to its creative use of filmmaking techniques, particularly a split-screen effect that helps convey the excitement of Elvis in concert by simultaneously showing multiple images of him performing. Split screen had been used in the rock documentary *Woodstock* as well as a few feature films of the era, including *The Boston Strangler*.

The documentary also made effective use of montage editing, a technique that rapidly presents a series of brief shots to compress the action or convey the passage of time. One such

Elvis on Tour made use of several filmmaking techniques that were in vogue during the early 1970s. This still from the film depicts the split-screen effect that was employed several times.

ELVIS: THE LOST PERFORMANCES

In 1986, MGM/UA began a routine inspection of their underground vaults, which are actually part of an old salt mine in Kansas. There, a pallet loaded with lard cans was discovered. The cans contained the camera-original negative cuts and outtakes from the documentaries *Elvis—That's the Way It Is* and *Elvis on Tour*. These outtakes were assembled into *Elvis: The Lost Performances*, an hour-long program consisting of concert performances filmed in Las Vegas in 1970 and in Virginia and North Carolina in 1972. The last ten minutes shows rehearsal footage from *Elvis—That's the Way It Is*. High-quality footage of Elvis singing in the prime of his career makes this of interest to fans. However, not every song performed by Elvis has the same spark or verve as those in the original documentaries, and the rehearsal scenes are neither revealing nor compelling. Despite its shortcomings, it makes a good companion piece to *Elvis—That's the Way It Is* and *Elvis on Tour*.

CREDITS

Metro-Goldwyn-Mayer
Produced and directed by
  Pierre Adidge and
  Robert Abel
Photographed by Robert
  Thomas
Edited by Ken Zemke
Montage supervised by
  Martin Scorsese
Elvis' wardrobe by Bill
  Belew
Released November 1, 1972
Songs Include:
"Johnny B. Goode"
"See See Rider"
"Polk Salad Annie"
"Separate Ways"
"Proud Mary"
"Never Been to Spain"
"Burning Love"
"That's All Right"
"Lead Me, Guide Me"

"Bosom of Abraham"
"Love Me Tender"
"Until It's Time for You to Go"
"Suspicious Minds"
"I, John"
"Bridge Over Troubled
  Water"
"Funny How Time Slips
  Away"
"An American Trilogy"
"Mystery Train"
"I Got a Woman"/"Amen"
"A Big Hunk o' Love"
"You Gave Me a Mountain"
"Lawdy Miss Clawdy"
"Can't Help Falling in Love"
"Memories"
"Lighthouse" sung by The
  Stamps
"Sweet Sweet Spirit" sung
  by The Stamps

Thin, healthy, and attractive in Elvis on Tour, *Elvis defies the stereotype that depicts him as overweight and overindulgent during this period.*

scene captured the hectic pace of Elvis' touring schedule through a montage sequence of cities visited during the tour. Another added a touch of humor via a collection of clips from his movies in which Elvis kisses a number of his costars. In charge of these montage sequences was a young filmmaker named Martin Scorsese.

Costing $600,000 to produce (not counting Elvis's fee of $1 million), *Elvis on Tour* recouped its production costs after only three days in the theaters. Documentaries are rarely major box-office draws, but this film proved to be a financial success. Critically acclaimed as well, *Elvis on Tour* won a Golden Globe as the Best Documentary of 1972. Elvis himself kept track of the awards ceremony the evening the Golden Globes were passed out, and he shouted with pride when the film was announced as the winner.

BEST DOCUMENTARIES
This Is Elvis

NOT LONG AFTER Elvis died, his life and career began to be chronicled, evaluated, and interpreted in biographies, musical retrospectives, rock 'n' roll histories, and films. The films took the form of both biographical features and documentaries. *This Is Elvis* is a clever mixture of both.

Produced, directed, and written by Andrew Solt and Malcolm Leo, *This Is Elvis* combines news footage, television performances, still photography, and re-created scenes with actors to tell the story of Elvis' life and career. The film opens with the shocking news of the legendary singer's death and then flashes back to his childhood years in Tupelo, Mississippi, where his story begins. Actors portray the young Elvis and his parents as those early years unfold on the screen. All in all, four dif-

In the docudrama This Is Elvis, *David Scott portrays Elvis at the start of his singing career.*

Paul Boensh III depicts Elvis at age ten; David Scott plays the budding young singer at 18; Dana Mackay is Elvis in the hospital scenes; and Elvis impersonator Johnny Harra portrays the King at age 42. *This Is Elvis* so cleverly weaves its elements that it is difficult to separate what has been re-created from actual documentation. Authentic photographs of Elvis are combined with simulated newsreel footage to illustrate the same event. The vigil at the hospital as Gladys Presley lay near death, for example, is represented through real photos of Elvis and Vernon waiting in the hospital corridor edited together with simulated newsreel footage of the same scene featuring David Scott as Elvis and Lawrence Koller as Vernon. The fake newsreel, shot in black and white, is complete

ferent actors portray Elvis at various points in his life, including his teen years when he performs in front of his high-school class for a talent show, his mature years when he is hospitalized for numerous ailments, and on the eve of his death at Graceland. Other events and phases of his career are depicted through news footage, home movies, concert material, and still photography. A voice-over narration by Elvis' friends and relatives (or actors playing those friends and relatives) ties it together and guides the viewer through the years. Released in 1981, *This Is Elvis* was one of the first serious, if biased, examinations of Elvis' life.

with scratches to create the illusion of a worn-out newsreel from another era.

The narration is a complex weaving of actors' voices and the actual voices of Elvis' friends and family. Elvis' voice is provided by Ral Donner, making him the fifth "actor" to portray Elvis in the film. Joe Esposito and Linda Thompson provide the voices for their parts of the narration, but Thompson was portrayed on the

Ral Donner

together with shots of his funeral procession winding through the streets of Memphis. Elvis is performing "An American Trilogy," and as he sings the final words, "His truth goes marching on," he drops to one knee and uses his arms to spread out his cape as though it were a set of angel wings. The filmmakers depict the moment in slow motion, a spellbinding touch that enhances the importance of the gesture. Intercut with footage of Elvis' funeral procession, the image takes on a divine connotation.

A brooding young Elvis dominates the critically acclaimed design for the soundtrack album and movie poster.

This Is Elvis does not reveal the man behind the myth; instead, it offers the myth that has been wrapped around the man.

Real-life Elvis impersonator Johnny Harra played Presley at age 42.

screen by Cheryl Needham. Elvis' colorful Uncle Vester played himself on-screen, as did Graceland employees Pauline Nicholson, Mary Jenkins, and Nancy Rooks.

The film and its makers have been criticized for manipulating the material and for combining the real with the re-created to reinforce the existing legends and stories about Elvis Presley without uncovering the truth or offering insight. Yet no documentary is without bias, and presenting any objective view of Elvis is difficult because the profusion of material that exists about him tends to obscure rather than reveal. If Solt and Leo were not interested in giving us the real Elvis Presley, they have succeeded in re-creating the myth in a lively and moving interpretation.

A telling example of the film's power is the concluding sequence, which depicts a triumphant Elvis in concert edited

CAST AND CREDITS

Warner Bros.
Produced, directed, and written by Malcolm Leo and
  Andrew Solt
Photographed by Gil Hubbs
Edited by Bud Friedgen
Original music score by Walter Sharf
Consultants were Jerry Schilling and Joe Esposito
Technical Adviser was Colonel Tom Parker
Released April 10, 1981

Elvis (age ten) . . . . Paul Boensh III
Elvis (age 18) . . . . David Scott
Elvis in the hospital. . . . . Dana Mackay
Elvis (age 42) . . . . Johnny Harra
Vernon Presley . . . . Lawrence Koller
Gladys Presley . . . . Debbie Edge
Priscilla Beaulieu Presley . . . . Rhonda Lyn
Dewey Phillips . . . . Larry Raspberry
Bluesman. . . . . Furry Lewis
Minnie Mae Presley . . . . Liz Robinson
Sam Phillips . . . . Knox Phillips
Linda Thompson . . . . Cheryl Needham
Ginger Alden . . . . Andrea Cyrill
Bill Black . . . . Jerry Phillips
Scotty Moore . . . . Emory Smith

BEST DOCUMENTARIES
Elvis '56

PERHAPS THE BEST documentary on Elvis Presley, this made-for-cable production spotlights Elvis' career in the pivotal year of 1956, when the hot young singer blew up from the South with the force of a hurricane and changed the face of popular music forever. The documentary begins in January 1956 when Elvis started recording for RCA Records and concludes in January 1957 when he made his third and final appearance on *The Ed Sullivan Show*. In between, it offers in-depth coverage of Elvis' other major television appearances on *Stage Show*, *The Milton Berle Show*, and *The Steve Allen Show*. It also details his failure in Las Vegas, examines the controversy created by his erotic version of "Hound Dog" on Berle's show, and chronicles the change in his lifestyle as a result of his sudden fame. A conventional-style documentary, *Elvis '56* combines television clips of Elvis' performances, news footage, photographs, and audio interviews to illustrate that momentous year. A well-written text spoken by Levon Helm of the rock group the Band serves as the narration.

Most of the photographs used in *Elvis '56* were shot by Alfred Wertheimer, who snapped close to 4,000 photos of Elvis just as the young singer was breaking big. In his many candids, Wertheimer captured an energetic, charismatic, drop-dead handsome Elvis enjoying the exciting life that was opening up to him. In other photos, Elvis is shown combing his hair or eating at a diner. Though vivid, Wertheimer's photo-

In 1956, Elvis burst onto the national scene amidst controversy and fanfare, making it a pivotal year in the life of the young Southern boy.

graphic style offers the realism of a documentary. His work was a perfect choice to convey what Elvis's life was like during this period.

The key to this documentary is its attempt to place Elvis in the context of the times, which helps illustrate why he became so popular and controversial at the same time. More than just a nostalgic journey to another time and place, it offers an overview of the 1950s that captures the complacency of the era and illustrates why Elvis was thought to be so dangerous. He represented a different type of popular idol and sang a different brand of music, one that was openly and unabashedly influenced by rhythm and blues and country-western. Both of these types of music were indigenous to the South and not part of the Tin Pan Alley tradition that spawned the mainstream popular music of the day. In addition, he drew heavily on the musical sound and outrageous performing styles of black artists in an era when segregation was still openly practiced.

Many viewed Elvis as lacking the proper decorum of other pop singers and saw his material as raw and sensual. The documentary clearly shows this perception by contrasting a clip of Perry Como singing "Hot Diggety Dog Diggety" to a clip of Elvis performing "Baby Let's Play House." Como's bland pop song with the trite lyrics withers beside Elvis' sensual performing style and the sexual connotation of the song. *Elvis '56* effectively illustrates for fans and nonfans alike the impact of Elvis Presley on mainstream America.

Top left and right: *It is easy to understand the controversy surrounding Elvis when Perry Como's low-key style is compared to Elvis' frenetic stage moves.* Above: *Elvis '56 also chronicles Elvis' one failure of that year—his shows at the New Frontier in Las Vegas, where the crowds consisted of older, middle-class patrons. In this photo, Elvis and his band enjoy some sun before a show.*

CREDITS

An Elvis '56 and Light Year Production
Produced and directed by Alan Raymond and Susan Raymond
Written by Martin Torgoff, Alan Raymond, and Susan Raymond
Edited by Bruce Follmer
Released 1987

THE VARIETY SERIES

Elvis '56 makes the point that Elvis' many performances on the small screen in 1956 stood out—way out—next to the variety acts that were typical for mainstream television of the period. Those who remember television only after the Beatles appeared on *The Ed Sullivan Show* in 1964 may not fully grasp what the fuss was about.

In 1956, Elvis appeared on *Stage Show*, *The Milton Berle Show*, *The Steve Allen Show*, and *The Ed Sullivan Show*, which were all variety series. Variety shows of the time featured a different group of performers each week, ranging from pop singers to animal acts to ballet dancers. The one thing these acts had in common was their identity as mainstream entertainment, meaning they had evolved from the acts that had played the vaudeville, variety, and musical circuits since the turn of the century. Elvis brought a new sound and performing style that had evolved from the country-western music and rhythm-and-blues performers of the South. Elvis' differences from the other acts becomes obvious by looking at his six appearances on Tommy and Jimmy Dorsey's *Stage Show*. The hosts and guest stars who eventually appeared with Elvis included jazz singers Sarah Vaughan and Ella Fitzgerald, comedians Joe E. Lewis and Henny Youngman, a chimp act called Tippy and Cobina, an acrobatic team known as the Tokayers, and an 11-year-old organist named Glenn Derringer. In comparison to these acts—which were considered suitable for family audiences—Elvis' new, high-powered music and sexual performing style seemed alien. He defied the familiar style of performance associated with popular singers of the day. In addition, his hip attire and slicked-back ducktail haircut made the young singer stand out further.

BEST DOCUMENTARIES
Elvis in Hollywood: The '50's

ELVIS' CAREER in the movies is rarely treated with any depth—let alone respect. In most biographies and documentaries, his movies are criticized and his decade in Hollywood blamed for a creative decline in his career. The only part of his movie output to escape sharp criticism are those films he starred in before going into the army, and still discussions of this period of his film career generally lack detail and depth.

Elvis in Hollywood: The '50's offers a thorough, though not insightful, examination of his movie career prior to his stint in the army. Consisting of interviews, film and news footage, photographs, and a voice-over narration, this video documentary begins with a look at Elvis' initial path to stardom as the most

Behind the scenes on the set of Jailhouse Rock, *life-long movie fan Elvis Presley snaps some candids of his costars in action.*

controversial singer of the era. Though some attention is paid to Elvis' introduction to moviemaking, the bulk of *Elvis in Hollywood* examines the four films he made between 1956 and 1958. Such information as preproduction details, behind-the-scenes anecdotes, Elvis' preparations as an actor, and critical response for each film unfolds in a well-organized format at a lively pace.

One of the strengths of the documentary is its attempt to set Elvis' movie experience in a context or perspective. Instead of the familiar abbreviated version of Elvis' conquest of Hollywood through sheer charisma and charm, *Elvis in Hollywood* offers details about why Elvis' popularity as a

singer attracted the attention of Hollywood and of producer Hal Wallis, who signed him to a movie contract. For example, various people interviewed attest to Wallis' reactions to Elvis and what he thought the singer's appeal was. Also, information on what the film industry was like during the 1950s, including vintage film clips of Hollywood, helps to convey how Elvis fit into the industry scene. Through interviews and narration, the film reveals the process of becoming a movie star. Many don't realize that Elvis took two screen tests for Hal Wallis. The first, in which he had to lip-synch to "Blue Suede Shoes," appears in its entirety. The charisma that Wallis saw is evident in this color screen test, though Elvis is clearly ill at ease with the procedure of lip-synching. The second screen test has been lost, but photographs of Elvis performing a scene from *The Rainmaker* show him attempting to channel his energy into another form of artistic expression—acting.

The documentary is also set apart by its choice of people that were interviewed. Such familiar faces as Scotty Moore and George Klein relate what they remember about Elvis' experiences in Hollywood, but more revealing are the interviews with Hollywood notables. Actresses and various behind-the-scenes personnel recall how Elvis responded to the challenge of acting on the big screen. For example, Hal Kanter, who directed *Loving You*, talks about how that film was patterned after Elvis' own life. Jan Shepard, who costarred in *King*

Elvis in Hollywood *examines the young singer's early film career.* Top left: *Elvis confers with director Michael Curtiz and costar Dean Jagger on the set of* King Creole. Left: *Director Hal Kanter* (far left) *reviews a scene from* Loving You *with Wendell Corey and Elvis as producer Hal Wallis* (far right) *looks on.* Above: *Director Robert Webb discusses a scene with Richard Egan and Elvis on the set of* Love Me Tender.

Creole, discloses director Michael Curtiz's thoughts about Elvis' acting ability. Makeup artist William Tuttle recalls the famous haircut scene from *Jailhouse Rock.* Though it has become common knowledge that it was a wig that was cut for the scene—not Elvis' actual hair—Tuttle discusses how he made that wig look so real. In addition to the information about Elvis, these Hollywood notables provide an inside look at moviemaking in the 1950s.

Though Elvis did not become the serious actor he would have liked, he was a bona fide movie star. Yet, because of the typically negative viewpoint about Elvis' movies, thoughtful evaluations of any period of his movie career are few and far between. *Elvis in Hollywood* provides a well-rounded look at his early film career.

CREDITS

Goldman/Taylor
    Entertainment Co. in
    association with Elvis
    Presley Enterprises
Producer: Jerry Schilling
Director: Frank Martin
Editor: Ellen R. Rennell
Released 1993

JERRY SCHILLING

Jerry Schilling, who produced *Elvis in Hollywood,* worked as a bodyguard for Elvis and was part of that group of employees and companions known as the Memphis Mafia. Schilling first met Elvis in 1954 and was employed by the singer from 1964 to 1976. He accompanied Elvis to Washington, D.C., in December 1970 when Elvis visited President Richard Nixon. Having attended Arkansas State University, Schilling had a reputation for being the most educated of the Mafia. After he left Elvis' employ, Schilling made a living at various jobs in the entertainment industry. He managed the Sweet Inspirations and the Beach Boys, and he worked as a film editor for Paramount Pictures. Schilling has worked on several Elvis-related projects since Elvis' death in 1977. He served as a consultant for *This Is Elvis,* as a technical adviser on the TV miniseries *Elvis and Me,* and as an executive producer with Priscilla Presley on the television series *Elvis.* He now works as a consultant for Elvis Presley Enterprises.

BEST LINES OF DIALOGUE

Clint (Elvis): Whoa!... Brett... Vance... They told us you were dead!

Elvis' first words on the big screen
LOVE ME TENDER

Peggy: How dare you think that such cheap tactics would work with me.

Vince (Elvis): That ain't tactics honey. That's just the beast in me!

JAILHOUSE ROCK

Sherry: You didn't say a thing about my outfit.

Vince (Elvis): Flippy... real flippy!

JAILHOUSE ROCK

Sherry: I'm coming all unglued.

after kissing Vince (Elvis)
JAILHOUSE ROCK

Danny (Elvis): When they swing at you, Pa, it's not enough to duck. You gotta swing back.

KING CREOLE

Mrs. Sarah Lee Gates: My baby's home from the Big House.

after son Chad (Elvis) is released from a night in jail
BLUE HAWAII

Maile (soaking wet): I bought this dress to welcome you home. It's the first time I've worn it.

Chad (Elvis): You know something? On you, wet is my favorite color.

BLUE HAWAII

Alicia: Did anyone ever tell you you were very handsome?

Toby (Elvis): Only girls.

FOLLOW THAT DREAM

Sherry unglued in Jailhouse Rock.

"Whoa!" Love Me Tender.

WHAT'S IN A NAME?

Hollywood films commonly change their titles during production, but Elvis' musical comedies were notorious for doing this, often at the very last minute. Sometimes the change represented an improvement, as when *Hawaii Beach Boy* was given the much more romantic title *Blue Hawaii*. Usually, however, the final titles were little better than the originals. *Flaming Star* was at various times *Flaming Lance*, *Flaming Heart*, and *Black Star*. *In My Harem* became *Harem Holiday*, which turned into *Harem Scarum* and then finally *Harum Scarum*, with that all-important misspelling so that the first word could match the second. The memorable *Kiss My Firm But Pliant Lips* was changed to the forgettable *Live a Little, Love a Little*. *A Girl in Every Port* became *Welcome Aboard*, which became *Gumbo Ya-Ya*, which then became *Girls! Girls! Girls!* Perhaps the worst series of titles belonged to *Spinout* because they were mostly meaningless clichés. Those considered included *Jim Dandy*, *After Midnight*, *Always at Midnight*, *Never Say No*, and *Never Say Yes*. To complicate matters, its British release title was *California Holiday*.

Toby: I like girls alright, except when they start to bother me.

Alicia: Young virile man like you, I should think you'd love to be bothered.

Toby: The botherin' part is alright, but I ain't gonna marry no girl and build no house just so I can be bothered regular.

FOLLOW THAT DREAM

Rusty (Ann-Margret): I'd like you to check my motor. It whistles.

Lucky (Elvis): I don't blame it.

VIVA LAS VEGAS

Charlie (Elvis): You could get a little closer. You know, I give off a lot of body heat.

ROUSTABOUT

Greg "Rick" Richards (Elvis): Last one out of the water is a papaya picker.

PARADISE, HAWAIIAN STYLE

Jill (to Elvis): You've no idea what your singing does to me.

DOUBLE TROUBLE

Joe Lightcloud (Elvis): Man, that's what I call one hell of a fight.

Elvis' first profanity in a comedy
STAY AWAY, JOE

Bernice: I'll bet you're a marvelous lover.

Greg (Elvis): I'm representing the United States in the Olympics.

LIVE A LITTLE, LOVE A LITTLE

One hell of a fight from Stay Away, Joe.

Greg (Elvis) invents an Olympic event in Live a Little, Love a Little.

AUTHOR! AUTHOR!

Little is written about the dozens of writers who penned scripts for Elvis' movies. Of these, Hal Kanter remains the most prestigious. Kanter, who occasionally directed, began writing screenplays in the early 1950s, specializing in comedy. In 1989, he received the distinguished Paddy Chayefsky Laurel Award from the Writers' Guild. In addition to cowriting and directing *Loving You* and writing *Blue Hawaii* for Elvis, he wrote vehicles for Bob Hope and the team of Jerry Lewis and Dean Martin.

Former newspaper reporter Allan Weiss worked on the most Elvis movies. In the early 1960s, he had an idea for a book, which he called *Hawaii Beach Boy*. His book idea became a movie story, which was then made into a screenplay for *Blue Hawaii* by Kanter. Sometimes teaming with veteran scripter Edward Anholt, Weiss also wrote the stories and/or screenplays for *Girls! Girls! Girls!; Fun in Acapulco; Roustabout; Paradise, Hawaiian Style;* and *Easy Come, Easy Go.*

Respected screenwriter Charles Lederer, who specialized in comedy, contributed *Follow that Dream* to Elvis' body of films. Lederer began his career by cowriting the dialogue for the classic 1931 comedy *The Front Page.* He also wrote plays and occasionally directed films.

BEST MOVIE TRIVIA

Elvis was inducted into the Los Angeles Indian Tribal Council by Native American Wah-Nee-Ota after portraying the son of an Indian and a white settler in *Flaming Star.*

The white suit that Elvis wore in *Clambake (above)* was cut into small pieces and packaged with the album *Elvis: The Other Sides— Worldwide Gold Award Hits, Volume 2.* This was a puzzling choice for a promotional offering for more than one reason: The suit was reportedly worth about $10,000— an expensive costume to cut into pieces; *Clambake* was released in 1967, but the album was issued in 1971, so the offer did nothing to promote the movie; and none of the movie-related songs included on the album came from *Clambake.*

Raquel Welch launched her screen career in 1964 with bit roles in *A House Is Not a Home* and Elvis' *Roustabout.* Though she became a potent sex symbol in the 1960s, she played a clean-cut college student in *Roustabout.*

Currently active in Republican politics, Maureen Reagan, daughter of Ronald Reagan, was featured in *Kissin' Cousins.* She appeared in a nonspeaking bit role as one of the man-crazy Kittyhawks, though she is sometimes erroneously identified as Lorraine, leader of the Kittyhawks.

Elvis received his first screen kiss in his second feature film, *Loving You (above).* Actress Jana Lund bestowed the legendary kiss, which was the one act that made her minor screen career memorable. Other films she appeared in included the teen flicks *Don't Knock the Rock, High School Hellcats,* and *Hot Rod Girl.* Her last screen appearance was in *Married Too Young* in 1962.

In *It Happened at the World's Fair,* a young Kurt Russell appeared in a bit role as a bratty boy who kicks Elvis' character in the shins. Thirteen years later, Russell starred as Elvis Presley in the critically acclaimed television film *Elvis (above).*

Elvis's father, Vernon Presley, appeared in cameos in two of his son's films, *Loving You* and *Live a Little, Love a Little.* Elvis's mother, Gladys Presley, also appeared in *Loving You.*

Contrary to popular belief, Colonel Tom Parker was not credited as technical adviser on all of Elvis' movies. Nine movies did not credit the Colonel: *Wild in the Country; Viva Las Vegas; Frankie and Johnny; Stay Away, Joe; Speedway; Live a Little, Love a Little; Charro!; The Trouble with Girls;* and *Change of Habit.*

Character names in Hollywood films have to be cleared through a studio's legal department. Neither "Vince Mathews" nor "Vince Edwards" were approved for the main character in *Jailhouse Rock,* so MGM's legal department suggested "Vince Delwyn," "Vince Jackwood," or "Vince Ledway." Fortunately, the writers came up with "Vince Everett."

The first Elvis Presley film to be shown on national television was *Love Me Tender,* which was broadcast on December 11, 1963. Those who missed Elvis on the little screen could see him in the theaters in *Fun in Acapulco,* which had opened on November 27.

Millie Perkins costarred as one of Elvis' three love interests in *Wild in the Country (above),* released in 1961. Thirty years later, Perkins played Elvis' mother in the television series *Elvis.*

According to some sources, the song "It's a Wonderful World" from *Roustabout* was considered for an Academy Award nomination. Despite the rumors, the song by Sid Tepper and Roy C. Bennett was not nominated. However, it remains the only Elvis movie tune to ever be considered.

David Winters, who choreographed several Elvis films as well as the television series *Hullabaloo*, was asked to invent a dance for *Girl Happy (above)*. Winters came up with the Clam, which was introduced in the song "Do the Clam." Unfortunately, the Clam did not catch on like other 1960s dance crazes such as the Pony, the Monkey, or the Jerk.

The Clam was not the only dance that was spotlighted in an Elvis Presley film. The Forte Four sing "The Climb" in *Viva Las Vegas*, with Elvis and Ann-Margret performing the steps to a dance of the same name. In *Blue Hawaii*, Elvis introduced a dance called Slicin' Sand with a song by the same name, but like the Clam, the dance did not catch on.

Allied Artists was experiencing financial difficulty when they signed Elvis for *Tickle Me (above)*. They gave him a $750,000 salary plus 50 percent of the film's profits. Considering Elvis' box-office track record, the studio expected the film to do well, and it did. *Tickle Me* became the third highest grossing film in the studio's history, and Elvis is credited with rescuing Allied Artists from bankruptcy at the time.

Elvis made 31 feature films between 1956 and 1969, averaging nearly three releases per year. The years 1964–1968 represent a frenzied peak in terms of Elvis'

output. For example, in early 1968, he had four films in production at MGM: *Stay Away, Joe* was being scored for an Easter release; the final touches were being made to *Speedway*, which had a summer release; MGM was prepping *Live a Little, Love a Little;* and plans were being made for a fourth film. This is remarkable considering that Elvis worked for several studios, usually alternating films by studio.

While filming *Live a Little, Love a Little (above)*, Elvis was actually knocked over by a couple of senior citizens who were excited about getting an autograph—except they were not after Elvis' signature! It seems they were pushing him out of the way in order to get to Rudy Vallee, a legendary singer from the 1920s. Vallee had a supporting role in the film.

Elvis' films were not as universally panned as many so often assume. However, when his films were criticized, reviewers rarely held

back, often aiming their pointed pens directly at Elvis. For example, *Time* magazine's review of *Spinout (above)* included this commentary about a new hairstyle Elvis wore in the film: "[Elvis] now sports a glossy something on his summit that adds at least five inches to his altitude and looks like a swatch of hot buttered yak wool."

The Great Dane that appears in *Live a Little, Love a Little (above)* was Elvis' dog in real life. The dog's name was Brutus, but in the film he is called Albert.

PERSONAL ELVIS

ELVIS LEFT BEHIND no autobiography, and he only reluctantly revealed any of his deepest thoughts or feelings in a public forum. The following lists attempt to offer clues that might provide some insight into the private side of Elvis, and readers are free to use the information to sketch a rough portrait of Elvis the man . . . though a truly complete canvas can never be painted.

BEST SIGHTS AT GRACELAND
Music Gates

WHEN 21-YEAR-OLD Elvis Presley purchased Graceland in 1957, the music gates were not a part of the property. Designed for Elvis by Abe Saucer and custom-built by John Dillars, Jr., of Memphis Doors, Inc., they were added later that year. Today, many visitors pass through the gates on their way up the main drive or they gaze between the bars to catch a glimpse of the mansion without realizing that they are a significant, even symbolic, part of Elvis lore.

While Elvis was alive, fans often gathered at the gates, hoping to see him as he drove through. To this day, countless snapshots circulate among fans that show Elvis driving through the gates—sometimes smiling, sometimes waving. At times, Elvis rode one of his horses or his golf cart down to the gates to greet the fans personally and sign autographs. These visits to the gates became a way for Elvis to meet with fans in a controlled situation.

Circa 1957. By this time, Elvis was on the inside looking out.

Fans also enjoyed chatting with the guards stationed in the small guardhouse just inside the gates. Elvis' family members were often employed as guards, including his uncle Vester Presley, who worked as head guard for over 20 years, beginning in 1957. Sometimes Vester entertained the fans and tourists with stories of his famous nephew, or he obligingly posed with them for a photo or two.

Meeting at the gates became a bonding experience for many fans, who struck up acquaintanceships and even close friendships over the years. The gates continue to serve this role each year during Tribute Week, when fans from all over the world gather in Memphis to commemorate Elvis' death.

Each side of the wrought-iron gates features a caricature of Elvis playing the guitar.

The gates afforded Elvis and his family some distance from the intrusions of the outside world, but the sculpted iron also restricted their access to that world. Some might interpret the photos of Elvis looking through the bars of the music gates from the inside as suggesting the prison that fame made of his life. While the story of the gates certainly attests to Elvis's intimate relationship with his public, it also reminds us of the price he paid for his immense celebrity.

BEST SIGHTS AT GRACELAND
TCB Logo

A HUGE WHITE lightning bolt outlined in yellow blazes across the wall of the TV Room on the lower floor of Graceland. The bolt is rendered abstractly or graphically, as opposed to realistically, which seems appropriate for a symbol. The lightning bolt represents a part of Elvis' trademark and motto—"Takin' Care of Business in a Flash."

Most often, the motto "Takin' Care of Business" is represented by the initials TCB pierced by a lightning bolt. This is the version rendered on the tail of the *Lisa Marie* jetplane, on Elvis' tombstone, and on the necklaces given to Elvis' closest cohorts. The famous ring worn by Elvis features the letters TCB framed by two lightning bolts. For the wall of the TV Room, the initials have been excluded in favor of a simple design that recalls the bright colors and bold patterns of the early 1970s—a design style then known as supergraphics.

A slang phrase from the late 1960s, "Takin' Care of Business" was adopted by Elvis around 1970 as a slogan for him and his organization. Many stories, embellished

Elvis' trademark—the initials TCB with a lightning bolt—adorned almost everything, from the wall of his home ...

to personal pieces of jewelry ...

to his airplane, the **Lisa Marie.**

over time, have been handed down by members of his entourage—the Memphis Mafia—explaining why the lightning bolt was added. Some say the bolt was inspired by the insignia used by Elvis' army battalion; others claim it was simply representative of the phrase "in a flash." The most far-fetched version explains that the West Coast Mafia used a lightning bolt as a symbol, and since Elvis and his clan were dubbed the Memphis Mafia, the bolt seemed appropriate. The design for the logo may have been worked out by Priscilla and Elvis during a plane trip, though others have claimed authorship of the logo.

Soon after the inception of TCB, TLC (Tender Loving Care) was developed for the wives of the Memphis Mafia members. Eventually, TCB and TLC became slogans and symbols that bound together Elvis' inner circle ever more tightly. Though a true sign of camaraderie, this bonding contributed to the sense of isolation and insulation needed to maintain such a constant, close-knit set of companions.

BEST SIGHTS AT GRACELAND
Hall of Gold

THE HALL of Gold, located in the Trophy Room just behind the Graceland mansion, contains the many gold records, awards, and honors that Elvis received as a performing artist. When the mansion was opened to the public in 1982, these records and awards (many gold-plated, or at least gold-painted) were moved into cases lining this 80-foot hallway to create the illusion of a "hall of gold." At the entrance to the hallway sits a huge color television and stereo console that was

The magnitude of Elvis' impact as a recording artist becomes immediately apparent when viewing the Hall of Gold.

given to Elvis in 1960 by RCA as a reward for selling over 50 million records. Though now a quaint relic from the past, the television was quite a luxury item at the time and represents RCA's attempts to take care of their hottest artist.

The gold and platinum records on display are those that Elvis received during his lifetime. The sheer number of them makes for an impressive sight and immediately conveys the magnitude of Elvis' recording career. Countries from all over the world honored Elvis with awards, though he performed outside the United States only briefly when he appeared in three Canadian cities in 1957. A

The gold trophy from RCA's division in South Africa.

huge trophy from RCA's division in South Africa, featuring a gold record on top and four golden gazelles leaping from the base, celebrates Elvis' many million-selling records in that country from 1956 to 1960. Other trophies from Japan, Norway, Australia, Germany, Sweden, France, and Belgium acknowledge his international popularity and influence.

The Hall also contains honors from many music magazines. *New Musical Express* honored Elvis with a special crystal and gold trophy for repeatedly being named Top World Singer and Top World Entertainer. There were also awards from *Billboard* and *Cash Box*, and *Photoplay* gave him a gold medal to acknowledge his popularity as an actor.

While the 160 gold and platinum records in the Hall of Gold make an astounding visual impact, most of them were the originals presented during Elvis' lifetime, so the Hall does not represent the most up-to-date tallies of his gold and platinum record status. The new display of gold and platinum records in the old racquetball court is a more accurate accounting of his record sales status.

BEST SIGHTS AT GRACELAND
Gold Belt from the International Hotel

AT 10:00 PM ON July 31, 1969, Elvis bounded onto the stage of the International Hotel and captivated an audience of celebrities and reporters with his first stage performance in eight years. Twice a night for the next four weeks, he drove the Vegas audiences into a state of frenzy. Reviews of his show are filled with references to standing ovations and mesmerized audience members who stomped their feet or stood on their chairs cheering for more. The brand-new Showroom at the International was supposed to seat 2,000, but on the weekends during Elvis' engagement, seating was increased to accomodate 3,500. At the end of his engagement, total attendance exceeded 101,500 and gross receipts topped

Elvis did not consider the gold belt to be a mere trophy, and he proudly wore it onstage and for special occasions.

An exec from the International awards Elvis his gold belt.

$1,522,635. Both of these figures set records in Las Vegas.

As a reward for his spectacular, record-breaking engagement, the management of the International presented Elvis with an enormous belt made of gold over sterling silver. The buckle is inscribed "Worlds Championship Attendance Record." Below that is "Las Vegas Nevada," and below that is "International Hotel." The date "1969" is inscribed in the top corners. The articulated belt features animal designs that are reminiscent of the signs of the zodiac. Later, Elvis had a jeweler add real diamonds, rubies, sapphires, and other gems and stones. The belt is currently on display in the Trophy Room at Graceland, but Elvis did not consider the belt to be just a trophy. He sometimes wore it as part of his onstage ensembles, including during his Madison Square Garden engagement in 1972.

The gold belt is ostentatious, larger-than-life, a real showstopper; some might call it garish. Upon first glance, it seems too immense to have any real value, yet it remains awe-inspiring in its magnitude … just like the Las Vegas period of Elvis' career.

The belt is now on display at Graceland.

BEST SIGHTS AT GRACELAND
Firearms Collection

ELVIS OWNED an extensive collection of firearms. He simply enjoyed buying, carrying, and collecting guns. When he died in 1977, he owned 37 firearms, including rifles, pistols, machine guns, and that old Southern cliché—a sawed-off shotgun.

Currently on display in the Trophy Room, Elvis' gun collection features several unique pieces that command attention. A Colt Python .357 pistol is personalized with Elvis's TCB logo

Elvis' interest in firearms dates back to his youth, though it is often wrongly attributed to his depressed, drug-induced state from the 1970s.

in gold just behind the chamber. An engraved filigree design with gold accents adds a further decorative touch to the pistol, which cost Elvis $1,900 in 1970. One of Elvis' personal favorites was a turquoise-handled Colt .45 marked by Elvis' initials: An "E" is engraved on one side of the handle, and a "P" on the other. He also owned a pearl-handled derringer, a

20-gauge shotgun and .22 rifle combination, a .44 Ruger Blackhawk revolver, a Thompson submachine gun, a Walther PPK pistol, and even an M-16.

Elvis examines part of his firearms collection.

Elvis' interest in guns remains a controversial aspect of his persona. Detractors like to recount the stories of his irresponsibility with guns, most of which have been exaggerated through retelling in countless books. Many of these stories originated in biographies by ex-employees and associates who had an axe to grind, so some of their "memories of Elvis" are dubious at best. Elvis once shot the screen out of a television set because Robert Goulet was singing. This has been exaggerated over time into a version in which Elvis shot out the screen every time he saw Robert Goulet, or any singer he didn't like, on TV.

Despite the hyperbole, Elvis was not a mere fan of firearms; he was a fanatic. Occasionally plagued by death threats during the 1970s, he took to wearing a derringer strapped to his leg *while* he was performing. When he attended a private showing of a James Bond movie, he liked to carry his Walther PPK because that was the weapon issued to 007. As he grew more despondent

"TCB" appeared on several of Elvis' guns, including this Smith & Wesson.

in the last few years of his life, his misadventures with guns increased, casting a dark shadow over a troubled man.

BEST SIGHTS AT GRACELAND
Badge Collection

INTERSPERSED with Elvis' collection of firearms in the Trophy Room at Graceland is his assortment of law enforcement badges. The integration of the two sets of collectibles casts a negative connotation on the badges, which is probably not intentional. Still some writers play armchair psychiatrist and use the badge and firearms collections as evidence for attributing an authority complex to Elvis.

Elvis appreciated and respected law officers and security personel, particularly after they began to protect him from frenzied crowds while touring during the 1950s. When he began collecting badges, word spread quickly, and various local police departments and security agencies made him an honorary member of their law enforcement fraternities. From the police department of Prince George's County, Maryland, to the sheriff's department of Los Angeles, Elvis was honored with badges from all over the country. Another celebrity collector of badges, Dan Ackroyd, was amazed at the breadth of Elvis' collection, remarking that he had never seen one so varied.

One of the more interesting stories related to Elvis' badge collection involved a trip to the seat of America's government. In December 1970, Elvis boarded a commercial flight bound for

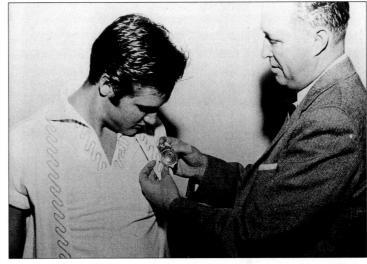

As this photo reveals, Elvis began his badge collection during the 1950s.

Washington, D.C. He then flew from D.C. to Los Angeles, where he picked up friend Jerry Schilling. The pair returned to D.C. and were joined by bodyguard Sonny West. Elvis went to the nation's capital to drop in on one of the city's prominent residents—President Richard M. Nixon. Though Elvis told Nixon that he had come because he was concerned about the youth of the country, he also mentioned that he was interested in getting a federal narcotics bureau badge. He had first asked Bureau of Narcotics Deputy Director John Finlator for a badge. Finlator didn't feel it was appropriate, so Elvis went over his head. During his impromptu visit to the White House, Elvis presented Nixon with a WWII Colt .45 and asked the President for the badge he coveted. When Nixon came through with the badge, Elvis was so thrilled he gave the president a bear hug.

Elvis visited President Richard Nixon after Bureau of Narcotics Deputy Director John Finlator turned down Elvis' request for a badge.

Elvis coveted this badge from the U.S. Bureau of Narcotics.

BEST SIGHTS AT GRACELAND
Wedding Dress and Suit

ON MAY 1, 1967, at the Aladdin Hotel in Las Vegas, Elvis Aron Presley and Priscilla Ann Beaulieu were married in a simple ceremony performed by Nevada Supreme Court Justice David Zenoff. Memphis Mafia stalwarts Joe Esposito and Marty Lacker served as Elvis' best men, while Priscilla's sister, Michelle, acted as her maid of honor.

Elvis' wedding garb seems surprisingly subdued considering his always-ostentatious personal taste in clothing. The black brocade jacket and matching vest is made from a paisley fabric. Paisley prints, which were fashionable during the 1960s, were often loud and colorful, but the all-black fabric of Elvis' suit tempers the large pattern. Plain black trousers completed the wedding attire.

Priscilla's gown was not designed especially for her. As a matter of fact, it was purchased off the rack shortly after Elvis proposed to her. The reasons for her choice of gown had as

The newlyweds smile for the press at their breakfast reception at the Aladdin Hotel in Las Vegas.

much to do with the need for secrecy as it did with her personal tastes. If word had leaked out while wedding arrangements were being made, the press and fans might have interfered and turned a personal event into a public spectacle. Elvis and Priscilla even devised a back up plan for eloping as an additional precaution.

Priscilla did talk with a couple of seamstresses about designs, but she didn't trust them enough to tell them it was for her wedding dress. Disguised in dark glasses and a hat, Priscilla searched several exclusive shops in Memphis and Los Angeles for her dress, usually with Charlie Hodge posing as her fiancé. The story of Priscilla's wedding gown is yet another indication of the price that Elvis and his family paid for his celebrity.

Priscilla found her gown in an out-of-the-way shop in L.A. It was a simple design made of white silk organza, trimmed in seed pearls. A six-foot train was the most extravagant feature on the dress. Her tulle veil was held in place by a tiara.

The couple donned their wedding ensembles a second time when a second reception was held at Graceland for relatives, friends, and staff members who did not attend the ceremony in Las Vegas.

Elvis and Priscilla's tiered wedding cake measured five-and-a-half feet tall.

BEST SIGHTS AT GRACELAND
Elvis' Record Collection

MUCH OF ELVIS' record collection is currently housed in an exhibit called Sincerely Elvis, which is located in the visitors plaza across the street from the Graceland mansion. Graceland owns and maintains the visitors plaza, which is just a few feet away from the Automobile Museum. The record collection attests to the diversity of Elvis' personal tastes in music, which in turn speaks volumes about the many influences on his musical style throughout his career.

Elvis began collecting records as a teenager. In his oversized jackets, shiny black pants with the pink stripe, and ducktail haircut, he breezed into such colorful establishments as Ruben Cherry's House of Records to buy rhythm-and-blues singles. His knowledge of R&B performers and

In a rare quiet moment, a youthful Elvis relaxes at home by spinning a platter on his portable record player.

their music was based on radio programs broadcast over WHBQ and WDIA and on his extensive record collection, which included singles by Arthur "Big Boy" Crudup, Arthur Gunter, and many others. Some of these are now used to fill Elvis' home jukebox located in the TV Room in the Graceland mansion.

Anyone who knows Elvis' music will not be surprised that his collection included country and gospel albums. He owned albums by the legendary Hank Williams as well as by smooth country stylists Ray Price and Eddy Arnold. His gospel favorites included the Stamps Quartet, the Jordanaires, Mahalia Jackson, the Imperials, and the Blackwood Brothers.

Surveying his collection of such diverse albums as Duke Ellington's *Piano in the Foreground,* Tom Jones' *Live in Las Vegas,* Ray Charles' *A Man and His Music,* and the Clovers' *Dance Party* offers rare insight into Elvis Presley the man. A part of his collection is not music at all: Elvis had a fondness for comedy albums, reflecting his wonderful sense of humor. He laughed along with the recordings of Jonathan Winters as well as *The First Family,* a popular album during the 1960s that lampooned President John F. Kennedy and his family as they adjusted to life in the White House.

BEST SIGHTS AT GRACELAND
RCA Display of Gold and Platinum Records

AN ACCURATE accounting of Elvis' gold and platinum records did not occur until 1992. Part of the reason for this oversight had to do with the timing of Elvis' career. The organization responsible for officially tabulating record sales to award gold and platinum records is the Recording Industry Association of America (RIAA). However, record companies must report sales figures and request the awarding of gold and platinum certification. The RIAA was not formed until 1958—two years after Elvis exploded on the national scene as a prominent figure in the music industry. RCA had awarded Elvis in-house gold records from 1956 to 1958, but they never requested retroactive certification by the RIAA. In addition, they rarely requested additional certification whenever Elvis' records went gold more than once.

This etched-glass sculpture commemorates Elvis' recording career.

When BMG took over RCA in 1986, they felt Elvis deserved an accurate accounting of his record sales status. Fortunately, Graceland had just purchased Colonel Tom Parker's files, photography, and memorabilia, and BMG used the Colonel's well-organized records to locate the correct sales figures for Elvis' records.

On August 12, 1992, RCA, the RIAA, Elvis Presley Enterprises, the press, and 90 Elvis fan club presidents attended an unveiling ceremony at Graceland. In the ceremony, the RIAA presented the new certifications of Elvis' records and re-awarded those that had been certified in the past.

An astounding 111 of Elvis' recordings have been certified gold, platinum, or multiplatinum.

Altogether, 110 Elvis Presley titles were certified gold, platinum, or multiplatinum, marking the largest presentation of gold and platinum records in history. Then, RCA presented a nine-foot etched-glass sculpture to commemorate Elvis "as the greatest recording artist of all time."

The elegant display of gold and platinum records and the glass sculpture from RCA are located in the racquetball court at Graceland. The display serves as a reminder of Elvis' impact on the recording industry: As of 1996, 111 of Elvis' albums and singles have been certified gold, platinum, or multiplatinum—more than any other artist in music history.

BEST SIGHTS AT GRACELAND
Meditation Garden

MEDITATION Garden is the final resting place for Elvis and his immediate family. His mother, Gladys Love Smith Presley, his father, Vernon Elvis Presley, and his grandmother, Minnie Mae Presley, are buried next to

Peaceful Meditation Garden.

Elvis in this small garden that was originally intended as a tranquil retreat for the residents of Graceland. Elvis was fascinated by Eastern philosophies and religions during the 1960s, and he had Meditation Garden built as a place for contemplation, despite its close proximity to the swimming pool.

Elvis was originally interred in a mausoleum at Forest Hill Cemetery in Memphis, but a few weeks after his burial, a group of men were arrested for trying to steal his body for ransom. Vernon received special permission to remove the bodies of his son and first wife to the grounds at Graceland. Gladys' original monument was also moved and placed at the edge of Meditation Garden. Vernon was buried there in 1979, and Minnie Mae followed in 1980. A ground plaque in memory of Elvis' twin brother, Jessie Garon, is located nearby.

In memory of Jessie Garon, Elvis Aron's twin.

If Meditation Garden became more than the serene site that Elvis had intended, then it is also more than his final resting place. Fans solemnly walk around the graves, silently pondering the impact of Elvis on their lives. They leave handmade or special-ordered floral arrangements in every possible design, which Graceland dutifully exhibits for a select period of time.

Like visitors to the Vietnam War Memorial, some leave behind hand-written notes expressing their thoughts or carefully composed tributes that few will ever read.

Not long after Graceland was opened to the public, a fan visited Meditation Garden and left behind a little wooden cross with a note pinned to it. The note expressed the kind of facile sentiment that the media finds so easy to ridicule. But only the most hardened would not be moved by the sincerity of its author, a sincerity that is indicative of many Elvis fans. The note read:

> "From the womb of your loving mother
> To the hearts of your loving fans
> To the arms of our Savior Jesus
> With whom you do now stand."

Vernon Presley wrote the epitaph inscribed on the bronze plaque that sits atop the grave of his famous son.

Best Vehicles

The pink Cadillac Fleetwood *(above)* that Elvis bought for his mother is the car he is most remembered for. Customized for Elvis, the 1955 sedan has become synonymous with the spirit of rock 'n' roll.

The first motorcycle that Elvis owned was a 1956 Harley KH *(below)*. It is currently on display at the Harley-Davidson Motor Company Museum and Archives in Milwaukee, Wisconsin.

When Elvis wanted his new 1956 Cadillac Eldorado *(above)* painted purple, he squashed a handful of grapes on the fender and asked the customizing firm to match the color. Upon delivery, the firm sprinkled grape drink into the carpet so it would even smell purple.

Elvis kept his 1956 white Continental Mark II, made before Continentals were a part of Lincoln, for 20 years. It was once trashed by overzealous fans; Elvis court-ed Natalie Wood in it; and Priscilla drove it to school in the 1960s.

Car customizer George Barris converted a 1960 Cadillac Sedan Limousine *(below)* into a tricked-out roadhog for Elvis. Coated with ten layers of diamond-dust gold pearl paint, the car featured gold-plated bumpers and hubcaps. The interior included a record player, telephones, television, and shoe buffer.

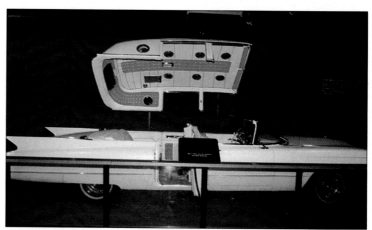

1973 Stutz Blackhawk III *(below, left)* with a red leather interior and gold-plated trim and a 1971 Blackhawk Coupe *(below, right)*. Elvis drove the 1973 Stutz the night before he died, making it the last car he ever drove.

According to stepbrother David Stanley, Elvis' favorite car to drive was a 1975 Dino Ferrari 308 GT4 Coupe

(above). The hot sports car supposedly could reach 165 mph.

Purchased by Elvis in 1975, the Convair 880 aircraft was customized at a cost of $800,000 and named the *Lisa Marie*. It features gold wash basins, a conference room, a lounge, and a bed complete with seatbelt.

A life-long fan of Harley-Davidson motorcycles, Elvis purchased many over the years, including a 1966 Harley Electra Glide full dresser *(above)*. The King of Rock 'n' Roll rode the king of motorcycles.

Purchased by Elvis in 1960 for less than $2,000,

the pink Willys Jeep *(below)* was used by the Graceland guards. Fans were often allowed to sit in it, and guards occasionally took a lucky fan for a ride when Elvis was away.

Elvis owned three neoclassic Stutz automobiles during his life, including a black

ELVIS' PROUDEST ACHIEVEMENTS

ELVIS PRESLEY YOUTH FOUNDATION

When Elvis was a toddler in Tupelo, Mississippi, he and his family were evicted from their two-room home by landlord Orville Bean. On September 26, 1956—almost 20 years later—Elvis returned to Tupelo as America's latest singing sensation. He performed two benefit shows at the Mississippi-Alabama Fair and Dairy Show and donated the proceeds to the city to purchase his birthplace and the surrounding land from Bean. The surrounding land was to become a park with a swimming pool, baseball diamond, tennis courts, and other recreation facilities. The Elvis Presley Youth Foundation was established to handle the financial arrangements and construction of the Elvis Presley Center. After construction of the Youth Center, the Foundation provided scholarships for underprivileged students. It still receives a portion of the income generated by the Presley estate.

CREATIVE ACCOMPLISHMENTS

Elvis was particularly proud of some of his achievements in the recording studio and on the big screen. Of his 31 feature films, he was most gratified at his performance in *King Creole*. Under the direction of veteran Michael Curtiz and supported by a talented cast of Hollywood notables, Elvis worked hard to express a range of emotions. The good reviews for his performance attested to his efforts. In other arenas, Elvis was creatively inspired by the positive results of the television special *Elvis (pictured)*, and he expressed pride in his work on the recording sessions for *From Elvis in Memphis*. Elvis was also proud that the documentary made about his concert tours, *Elvis on Tour*, won a Golden Globe. Elvis rarely disclosed his personal thoughts on any subject, particularly to outsiders. He left no personal account that revealed his opinions on his life or career. Biographies by associates and family members divulge some insight into what Elvis thought about his own work, but much of what he felt has been lost forever.

GRAMMY AWARDS

Despite his immeasurable impact on 20th century popular music, Elvis won only three Grammy Awards during his lifetime. The Grammy is the most prestigious award in the music industry, but it was particularly coveted during Elvis' lifetime because there were far fewer music awards at the time. In 1967, Elvis won a Grammy for Best Sacred Performance on the album *How Great Thou Art*. Five years later, he won for Best Inspirational Performance for *He Touched Me*, and in 1974, he won Best

Inspirational Performance for the song "How Great Thou Art" from the album *Elvis Recorded Live on Stage in Memphis*. Because gospel music played such an important role in his life, he was especially gratified that he won for his inspirational recordings. In addition to his three awards, Elvis was nominated for Grammys ten times during his career. Also, the cover for *For LP Fans Only* was nominated for best album cover in 1959. To date, he has received two posthumous nominations.

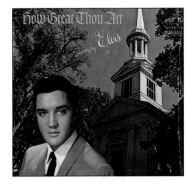

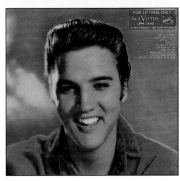

OUTSTANDING YOUNG MAN OF AMERICA

On January 16, 1971, Elvis Presley was named one of the Ten Outstanding Young Men of America by the Junior Chamber of Congress (Jaycees), a nationally based community group devoted to civic duty. Each year, the Jaycees nominate young men, usually under the age of 30, who are praiseworthy in their fields. A panel of distinguished judges makes the final selection of ten. The judges, who included former President Lyndon B. Johnson, chose Elvis not only

because he was the greatest entertainer of his time but also because of his many acts of philanthropy and charity. The other nine honored that year included Boston councilman Thomas Atkins, White House aide Ron Ziegler, Medal of Honor winner Capt. William Bucha, media magnate Jim Goetz, cancer researcher Dr. George Todaro, and volunteer programs founder Thomas Coll. Visitors who see the Jaycees award at Graceland cannot help but notice the scuff and scratch marks. Elvis carried the statue with him on every tour and trip until he died.

ELVIS' PROUDEST ACHIEVEMENTS

GRACELAND

Elvis was proud of his home, Graceland, but not because of its grandeur or value. When Elvis first experienced success as a singer, he used his newfound fortune to improve the quality of life for his parents. Always struggling in poverty, the Presleys never had a permanent home and scrambled for menial jobs to survive. As soon as Elvis realized that his singing career was solid, he told his father, Vernon, to quit his job as a laborer. In May 1956, Elvis paid $40,000 for the first real home his family ever knew—a ranch-style house on Audubon Drive in the suburbs of Memphis. He bought two Mixmaster mixers for Gladys so she would not have to walk across the kitchen so much. In March 1957, Elvis purchased Graceland on the outskirts of Memphis to protect his family's privacy and to give his mother her dream home. Elvis was gratified that he could share the fruits of his success with his parents, because he could return to them the sense of security that they had always given him throughout his youth.

RAISING LISA MARIE

Lisa Marie Presley was born on February 1, 1968, which was nine months to the day after Elvis and Priscilla were married. In virtually every biography by those who knew him, Elvis is painted as the proud, doting father. After Elvis and Priscilla were divorced, Lisa Marie lived with her mother in Los Angeles, where she was shielded from the press and the fans. On her frequent visits to Graceland, she was indulged by her father. For her birthday, Elvis arranged lavish celebrations or rented the amusement park Libertyland for her and her friends. He bought her a golf cart and a pony, which he let her ride through the front door of Graceland.

Elvis' enthusiasm for Lisa Marie, his only child, is best seen through her eyes. In a 1988 interview for *Life*, she recalled the time they spent together, "He was always up to something, shooting off firecrackers or guns, running around, driving golf carts or snowmobiles. . . . He called me Buttonhead or Yisa. . . ."

ELVIS' FAVORITES

Elvis commissioned a life-size oil portrait of himself by Ralph Cowan (*above*) in 1969 and was quite pleased with the results. The portrait presents a dreamlike interpretation of a bold, youthful Elvis that appears mythic in retrospect.

When it was time to eat, Elvis preferred Southern-style home cooking, such as pork chops with mashed potatoes smothered in brown gravy, fried peanut butter and banana sandwiches, beef roast and string beans, and fried bacon.

Of all the directors Elvis worked with in his 31 feature films, his favorite was soft-spoken Norman Taurog. Taurog directed nine of Elvis' musical comedies.

Elvis bought hundreds of guitars during his career, but a 1956 Gibson J200 with a personalized leather cover (*above*) was one of his favorites. It appears in the poster for *Loving You* and was also used in the 1968 television special.

The diversity of singers that Elvis called his favorites reveals a music fan with eclectic tastes. He loved to listen to Dean Martin, Jackie Wilson (*above*), Billy Eckstein, the Blackwood Brothers, Roy Hamilton, and Mahalia Jackson.

Among the films Elvis enjoyed repeatedly were *Patton*, *Dr. Strangelove*, and *The Party*. His favorite actors changed over time but included James Dean, Marlon Brando, and Peter Sellers. He also enjoyed the performers from *Monty Python's Flying Circus*.

Elvis became seriously interested in horses in the mid-1960s and favored a palomino quarter horse named Rising Sun (*above*), who lived in a barn called "the house of Rising Sun." The horse died in 1986 and was buried facing the rising sun.

Elvis' most cherished books were on religious or mystical subjects, including *The Prophet* by Kahlil Gibran, *The Face of Jesus* by Frank O. Adams, and the Bible. His favorite passage: "It is easier for a camel to go through the eye of a needle, than for a rich man to enter the Kingdom of Heaven" (Matthew 19:24).

Elvis maintained that the best sport was football. His favorite professional team was the Cleveland Browns. In both Memphis and Hollywood, he organized his friends and associates into teams to play on Sundays (*above*).

Bubbly Shelley Fabares (*below*) was supposedly Elvis' favorite costar. She appeared in *Girl Happy*, *Clambake*, and *Spinout*. A child actress, Fabares got her start on the TV sitcom *The Donna Reed Show*. She eventually returned to a career on the small screen.

Best Quotes by Elvis

"Why buy a cow when you can get milk through the fence?"

when asked if he would marry "Teeners' Hero," Time, May 14, 1956

"The colored folks been singing it and playing it just like I'm doin' now, man, for more years than I know. They played it like that in the shanties and juke joints and nobody paid it no mind 'til I goose it up. I got it from them. Down in Tupelo, Mississippi, I used to hear old Arthur Crudup bang his box the way I do now, and I said if I ever got to the place I could feel all old Arthur felt, I'd be a music man like nobody ever saw."

Charlotte Observer, June 26, 1956

"I lose myself in my singing. Maybe it's my early training singing gospel hymns. I'm limp as a rag, worn out when a show's over."

Tacoma New Tribune, September 2, 1957

"My fans want my shirt. They can have my shirt. They put it on my back."
"A Predicament Called Presley," *Illustrated, September 7, 1957*

Wally George: "When will you write more songs?"

Elvis: "That's all a hoax. I can't even read music."

George: "What about your guitar?"

Elvis: "Can't play it—use it as a brace."

George: "What do you think of rock 'n' roll?"

Elvis: "It's the greatest ever, mainly because it's all I can do."

"Off the Record," *Los Angeles Times,* **November 2, 1957**

"She was the most wonderful mother anyone could ever have. She was always so kind and good."
"Services To Be Held Today for Elvis Presley's Mother," *Memphis Press-Scimitar,* **August 15, 1958**

"Can't play it—use it as a brace."

Getting milk through the fence.

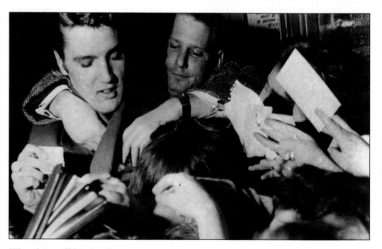

The shirt off his back.

"I lose myself in my singing."

"Is it another of those highness deals?"
upon preparing to meet a group of Scandanavian princesses
Life, May 1960

"I don't regard money or position as important. But I can never forget the longing to be someone. I guess if you are poor, you always think bigger and want more than those who have everything when they are born."
"Forever Elvis," Time,
May 7, 1965

". . . the trouble is, when a fellow is by himself and starts thinking, the sad things are always stronger in his memory than the happy things."
"Elvis," Tropic, April 28, 1968

"I get tired of playing a guy who gets into a fight, then starts singing to the guy he's just beat up."
commenting on his movie career
"Return of the Pelvis,"
Newsweek, August 11, 1969

"I learned very early in life that, 'without a song, the day would never end; without a song, a man ain't got a friend; without a song, the road would never bend—without a song.' So I keep singing a song. . . ."
accepting the Jaycees'
Outstanding Young Man of
America Award, 1971

"My daddy knew a lot of guitar players, and most of them didn't work, so he said, 'You should make your mind up to either be a guitar player or an electrician, but I never saw a guitar player that was worth a damn.'"
from the documentary
Elvis on Tour, 1972

Q: "Elvis, are you satisfied with your image?"

Elvis: "Well, sir, it's very hard to live up to an image."
press conference prior to Madison Square Garden concert,
June 9, 1972

"Since I was two years old, all I knew was gospel music. That music became such a part of my life it was as natural as dancing. A way to escape from the problems. And my way of release."
reprinted in Elvis in His Own Words, 1977

"[Clothes] say things about you that you can't, sometimes."
reprinted in The World According to Elvis, 1992

"Don't criticize what you don't understand, son, you never walked in that man's shoes."
reprinted in The World According to Elvis, 1992

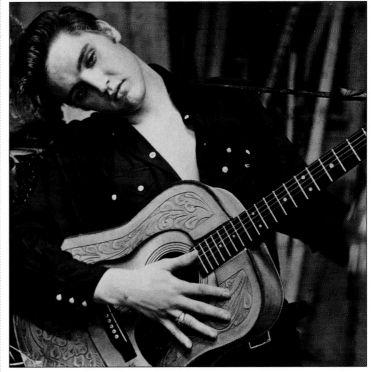

One guitar player that was worth a damn.

PUBLIC ELVIS

*F*ROM "ELVIS THE PELVIS" to "fat super-star," from "an American tragedy" to "an American myth," the image of Elvis Presley conveyed by the media over the years was always extreme, sometimes contra-dictory, and occasionally false. Rather than an accurate portrait of a popular entertainer, the public depiction of Elvis tends to be a reflection of America . . . but through a cracked mirror.

BEST CONTROVERSIES ABOUT ELVIS
Elvis the Pelvis

ELVIS PRESLEY WAS INTRODUCED to a national audience in 1956 at a time when rock 'n' roll was under fire in the press. The controversy centered on whether or not this new style of music, associated predominantly with teenagers, lead to juvenile sex and crime. From April 1956 until the end of that summer, a wave of articles discussing the link between

rock 'n' roll and juvenile delinquency appeared in such popular magazines as *Time, Newsweek, Life, Look, New York Times Magazine,* and *America.* At the same time, these nationally based magazines featured articles on Elvis that detailed the effect his sensual (read sexual) performing style had on teenage girls. It did not take a great leap for journalists, reviewers, parents, and others to relate Elvis' personal appearance and sensual style to the decadence of rock 'n' roll and the horrors of juvenile delinquency.

The major problem with Elvis in the eyes of authority figures was the way he used his performing style to whip his largely female audiences into a frenzy during his concert performances. His gyrating pelvis, leg movements, and continual motion were considered far too provocative for mainstream audiences. Sometime during 1956, Elvis was dubbed "Elvis the Pelvis," a nickname he despised.

Elvis often teased the crowds by moving so close to them that he was within their grasp.

The press almost always described an Elvis concert as mass hysteria, paying particular attention to the manner in which the girls screamed and cried uncontrollably. At times, the crowds stormed the stage to get to Elvis, who urged them on by leaning over the stage toward the crowd until he was almost—almost—close enough to touch. Police were assigned to surround the area just below the stage to keep the crowds away

Elvis' unique performing style inspired a number of nicknames. The Colonel dubbed his boy "the Atomic-Powered Singer," while the press called him "Elvis the Pelvis."

from him. Focusing on the hysteria generated by his performing style, newspaper stories painted Elvis as a catalyst for misbehavior among his fans.

Elvis was not the only rock 'n' roll performer receiving negative press. In June 1956, a concert by Bill Haley and the Comets erupted into pandemonium when teenagers began dancing in the aisles. Fights broke out, and chairs flew across the floor. Such incidents were considered proof that rock 'n' roll music was destructive.

Inevitably, part of the perceived problem was blamed on the rock 'n' roll beat, which critics referred to disparagingly as a

"jungle beat." The reference to jungle music implied that teenagers had no sense of social decorum when exposed to "the beat"—just like uninhibited natives of the jungle. There was an implicit racism in these comments, too, which surfaced in a more direct way when some critics referred to rock 'n' roll as "Negro music." "It's that jungle strain that gets 'em all worked up," pronounced the manager of the auditorium where Bill Haley and the Comets performed in June 1956.

Elvis' long ducktail haircut—heavy on the pomade and accented by sideburns—spelled "juvenile delinquent" to mainstream America.

In addition to Elvis' performing style and his music with a "jungle beat," other aspects of his image were decried or derided. Much was made of his Southern background. Articles that year commonly referred to Elvis as a "hillbilly"

or to his music as "hillbilly music," even though he was clearly singing rock 'n' roll. *Life*'s coverage of Elvis began with the blaring headline, "A Howling Hillbilly Success" and focused on an event in Texas in which fans supposedly broke through a plate glass window to request autographs on various body parts. Sometimes Elvis' peculiar tastes in clothing and his ducktail haircut with sideburns—which were called tasteless—were attributed to his Southern background. Articles ridiculed his Southern accent by phonetically spelling out the lyrics of his songs as he pronounced them or phonetically spelling out the words he spoke in an interview. In *Time* magazine, a caption under a photo of Elvis in the recording studio read, "Elvis Presley: 'Hi luh-huh-huh-huv yew-hew.'" Identified as a Southerner by

Teenage girls mobbed Elvis at every opportunity—a reaction many parents found disturbing.

the mainstream press and the entertainment industry, Elvis was described in terms that presented him as alien, and therefore even more threatening.

At the dark corners of this view of his Southern background lies the image of the male from the backwoods who seeks out and takes an adolescent girl as his bride. Part of the controversy and threat that Elvis represented must have been related to that negative stereotype. In other words, conservative, middle-class America saw Elvis as a long-haired, powerfully attractive "hillbilly" who thrust his pelvis and growled provocative lyrics at their all-too willing teenage daughters—and conservative, middle-class America was afraid.

BEST CONTROVERSIES ABOUT ELVIS

Andreas Cornelis van Kuijk

ONE CONTROVERSY surrounding Elvis Presley actually had very little to do with him directly. Colonel Tom Parker, who managed Elvis for 22 years and then continued to "manage" him in death, was accused in 1981 of having mismanaged Elvis during the last few years of his life.

It began in May 1980 when lawyer Blanchard E. Tual was appointed by the probate court to represent Lisa Marie Presley after the executors of Elvis' will needed clarification on their dealings with Colonel Parker. As Tual investigated, he discovered several disreputable acts by Parker that hurt Elvis' financial security. Among the findings was that Parker failed to register Elvis with the performing rights society BMI, so Elvis did not collect royalties from songs in

Elvis on the Colonel: "People say the Colonel has a good thing in me. Sure he has. And I've got a good thing in him."

which he had a writing credit. Also, Elvis' catalog of 700 songs was sold to RCA in 1973 for $5 million, and Parker received half of that money. This represented an unusual deal, according to Tual, because RCA did not own the master tapes from any of its other artists. Besides, Elvis was only 37 at the time, so it would be illogical for someone so young to sell what would have been a lifetime annuity for him. Thus, the deal benefitted the Colonel but was a detriment to Elvis. Parker also had separate deals with RCA for consulting and promotion, which represented a conflict of

Hal Wallis on the Colonel: "I'd rather close a deal with the Devil."

interest for him. According to Tual, if Parker was being paid by RCA for other deals, then it would be difficult for him to objectively negotiate with RCA on Elvis' behalf. Also, Elvis was booked with the International Hotel from 1969 to 1972 at the same rate, when other entertainers with less drawing power were earning much more.

Among Tual's recommendations was that the court direct the Presley estate to file a complaint against RCA over the sale of the master tapes. He also suggested that the estate's lawyers file suit against Parker in order to void his merchandising contracts with Presley. A judge ordered the Presley estate to sue the Colonel and demanded an auditing of Parker's merchandising company, Boxcar Enterprises. The news that Parker may have betrayed his one and only client hit Elvis' fans hard.

Adding to the controversy was a bizarre fact uncovered in court records. It seems the Colonel was not Tom Parker at all but Andreas Cornelis van Kuijk of Breda, Holland. Parker had always told reporters that he hailed from Huntington, West Virginia, which was a difficult fact to verify since the West Virginia state courthouse had burned down sometime in the past, destroying all records.

The Colonel, 1960s: "Anybody who will pay my boy a million dollars can make any kind of [motion] picture they want."

In truth, Parker immigrated to America illegally about 1929, perhaps jumping from a Dutch ship docked in Florida. He served in the U.S. Army from 1929 to 1932. When he swore allegiance to America during induction, he renounced his Dutch citizenship, but he was never naturalized as an American citizen.

After his discharge, he began cruising the Southern carnival circuits, doing everything from selling cotton candy to working as a barker. He founded two carnivals, the Great Parker

The Colonel, 1981: "I [owned] 25 percent of Elvis alive, and I own 25 percent of him dead." He actually owned 50 percent.

Pony Circus and, later, Colonel Tom Parker and his Dancing Chickens. The "Colonel" in Parker's name does not refer to military rank. It comes from the peculiar Southern custom of bestowing that title on a gentleman as an honor from a particular state, which in Parker's case was Louisiana and Tennessee.

By the 1950s, Parker was working in country-western music, eventually managing Eddy Arnold and then working as a promoter for Hank Snow. He met and worked with Elvis in 1955, becoming his manager on March 15, 1956. The Colonel's fee for managing Elvis was 25 percent— a tidy sum for a manager. But in 1967, Parker's share became an unheard-of 50 percent when he

The Colonel on the news that Elvis died: "Oh, dear God."

signed a new contract with Elvis, which was one more bit of business that Blanchard Tual thought excessive.

The Presley estate did sue the Colonel in 1981. During the two years of litigation, the Colonel's lawyers tried a number of delaying tactics, including moving the trial to New York state. Ever the slippery carny, Parker at one point used the defense that he was not a U.S. citizen but a man without a country, and therefore, he could not be sued in an American court. The case was eventually settled out of court, but Parker was forced to surrender all connections to the Elvis Presley name.

By the 1990s, the Presley estate and Parker had mended their differences, and Parker sold his files, photographs, and memorabilia to Graceland. Detractors like to paint the Colonel as the villain in the Elvis Presley story, but it is difficult to dispute Parker's success in guiding "his boy's" career.

BEST CONTROVERSIES ABOUT ELVIS
The Memphis Mafia

AFTER ELVIS' discharge from the army, the entertainment press discovered that he was accompanied by an entourage of friends and associates wherever he traveled. The press dubbed the entourage "the Memphis Mafia" or "the Tennessee Mafia," just as they had called Humphrey Bogart's group of buddies and cohorts "the Holmby Hills Rat Pack" and deemed Frank Sinatra's gang of celebrity friends "the Rat Pack." However, the differences between the Rat Pack and the Memphis Mafia became apparent as Elvis' career in Hollywood continued, and the press never quite grasped the Mafia's relationship to Elvis.

Sonny West (left), *Joe Esposito* (behind Sonny), *and Red West* (behind Elvis' shoulder) *maneuver Elvis through a crowd.*

Most of the members of the Mafia were not fellow entertainers but hometown boys from Memphis, family members, or friends Elvis had met in the army. Many of them actually lived with Elvis, whether he was in Memphis or in Hollywood. They accompanied Elvis to the set, drove him to and from the studio, and worked as bodyguards to keep fans and press away from him. The closeness of this group of friends and employees made Elvis feel at home in Hollywood or on the road, but it also isolated him from industry insiders and fellow entertainers who could have been a positive influence on him.

Gossip columnist Hedda Hopper spoke of the Mafia as guardians of

Red West (with back to camera) *had worked for Elvis for almost 20 years when Vernon fired him in 1976.*

Elvis in a 1965 column called "Hedda Says Elvis Still the King in Hollywood," but she also hinted at the strangeness of the situation. She declared that Elvis couldn't be safer if he were behind the Notre Dame line, but she noted that they "jealously seal him off from all intruders."

Elvis' insistence that his friends tag along often caused controversy on the sets of his movies. The boys tended to engage in water fights, shaving cream attacks, and other more destructive antics on the set, distracting Elvis and interrupting the shooting. MGM executives sent down a memo just before the start of *Stay Away, Joe,* warning the group about their behavior. During the 1970s, when Elvis resumed touring, some of the Memphis Mafia acted as bodyguards. On more than one occasion, they got too rough with spectators or fans, and lawsuits ensued. The bodyguards, specifically Red and Sonny West, were criticized at the time for their heavy-handed tactics, but few realize the number of death threats and strange encounters that Elvis experienced in those years. Nonetheless, the Wests and Dave Hebler were fired by Vernon Presley in 1976, prompting the trio's tell-all book *Elvis: What Happened?,* which did more damage to Elvis than any stranger could ever have done.

BEST CONTROVERSIES ABOUT ELVIS
Doesn't Drink, Seldom Smokes, Doesn't Cuss

TOWARD THE END of Elvis' movie career, his management team, as well as some studio executives in the movie industry, were aware that the singer's image had not kept pace with the fast-changing 1960s. Producer Hal Wallis chose not to renew Elvis' contract when it expired in 1967 because, as Wallis noted, "It's not so much that Elvis is changing, but that the times are changing. There's just not the market for the no-plot musicals that there once was."

Surprisingly enough, some studios did attempt to modernize Elvis' movies, but they met with some resistance by fans and conservative members of the entertainment press. Though no studio wanted to alter the formula for an Elvis Presley musical comedy too much, they did update the dialogue and the stories in them to include harsher language and sexual situations. One of the first movies to present a more mature Elvis Presley was *Stay Away, Joe*. In the film, Elvis' character not only swears but also manages a bedroom romp with the character played by costar Quentin Dean. In an atypical portrayal, Elvis' character was less than chivalrous. The change prompted Associated Press writer Gene Hansaker to inquire in a newspaper article, "Is Elvis Presley asking for more criticism?" It was

Despite the tameness of this bedroom scene in Stay Away, Joe, *some conservative fans were offended.*

Elvis' later movies, such as Live a Little, Love a Little, *were not immune from the sexual revolution of the 1960s.*

common for reporters to note that even in real life Elvis did not drink, rarely smoked, and did not swear, but now it seemed that clean-cut Elvis Presley was submitting to the new Hollywood freedom—at least on the screen.

Live a Little, Love a Little was a hip sex farce along the lines of *The Swinger* and *A Guide for the Married Man*. Again, Elvis' character swore, and the script made it clear that the leading female character, played by Michele Carey, had been sexually active prior to meeting Elvis. The storyline called for Elvis and Carey to move in together and even sleep together, though they do not engage in sex. The franker attitude toward sex was a surprise to some critics and fans, who had always considered Elvis' films to be family entertainment. Elvis made only a couple of movies after *Live a Little, Love a Little*, and this minor controversy over his more mature characters quickly faded away.

BEST CONTROVERSIES ABOUT ELVIS
Cardiac Arrhythmia vs. Polypharmacy

SHORTLY AFTER Elvis Presley died on August 16, 1977, Dr. Jerry Francisco, the chief medical examiner of Shelby County, announced that Elvis had died of coronary arrhythmia, an irregular heartbeat resulting from hypertensive heart disease or myocardial infarction. His findings were the result of a three-hour autopsy that his office had conducted at the request of Vernon Presley. Little did Francisco realize that his announcement and the autopsy would start a 20-year controversy over the role of drugs in Elvis' death—and in his life.

Tennessee medical examiner Jerry Francisco testifies before the state medical board hearing for Dr. George Nichopoulos. Francisco never swayed from his opinion that Elvis died from cardiac arrhythmia.

Because the autopsy had been a private one requested by the family, the exact findings were not made public. All reports, notes, and photos related to the autopsy disappeared forever by August 19, and the contents of Elvis' stomach were destroyed before further analysis was done. Any concrete evidence of a drug-related death could only be found in the sealed autopsy report.

On September 13, 1979, the ABC-TV news magazine *20/20* aired a report called "The Elvis Cover-Up," and the details surrounding Elvis' death began to take on the character of a mystery novel. The investigative report, which was produced by Charles Thompson and reported by Geraldo Rivera, marked the first major national media attention devoted to the rumors of a drug-related death. The show attempted to pinpoint the exact cause of Elvis' death and had filed a lawsuit on August 10 to obtain a copy of the autopsy report from Francisco. When Francisco refused to hand over the report, *20/20* accused him of participating in a cover-up. The medical examiner held a news conference declaring that he was not involved in any cover-up. After the *20/20* report, county officials were pressured to open a criminal investigation of the case but ultimately declined to do so. The lawsuit filed by Thompson and

Despite Francisco's announcement, rumors of a drug-related death surfaced almost immediately, probably because of the August 1 release of a book entitled *Elvis: What Happened?* Written by Steve Dunleavy, the book detailed the tragic story of Elvis' decline by drug misuse through the experiences of three former bodyguards, Red and Sonny West and Dave Hebler. As fate would have it, an interview given by Sonny West to syndicated newspaper columnist Bob Greene just prior to Elvis' death was printed the day he died. In many newspapers, the column appeared alongside stories about Elvis' death, fueling sensationalized rumors of a drug-related demise.

local Memphis reporter James Cole eventually made it all the way to the Tennessee Supreme Court. In 1982, the court ruled that Francisco was not obligated to release the autopsy results because the post-mortem had been requested by the family.

Meanwhile, Elvis' Memphis physician, Dr. George Nichopoulos, was brought before the Tennessee Board of Medical Examiners on several charges related to overprescribing drugs to Elvis Presley and other patients. In January 1980, the board suspended his license for three months for indiscriminately prescribing and dispensing controlled substances for ten people, including Elvis and Jerry Lee Lewis. Though the board's conclusions did not challenge Francisco's official ruling about the cause of Elvis' death, the inquiry did reveal stories about the singer's extensive drug use to the public. The exaggerated rumors that had been floating around for over two years paled in comparison to the damning details that surfaced in Dr. Nick's testimony: Elvis was prescribed over 12,000 pills and vials of potent drugs in the last 20 months of his life; he was hospitalized several times because he was swollen from head to foot from drug misuse; he carried three suitcases of pills and supplies whenever he toured, which his whole entourage used freely. These stories resurfaced in November 1981 when Nichopoulos was officially charged in a criminal court with 11 felony counts of over-prescribing drugs to nine patients, including

Elvis and Jerry Lee Lewis. He was acquitted. Five new charges were brought against him in 1992 by the state of Tennessee for overprescribing drugs to Elvis. This time, the State Department of Health was determined to revoke the doctor's medical license permanently.

Over the years, the cause of Elvis' death has generally been recognized as polypharmacy, or the interaction of several drugs, based on the information revealed by the Nichopoulos trials as well as on statements to that effect by Dr. Eric Muirhead, pathologist at Baptist Memorial, and Dr. Noel Foredo, who was present at the autopsy. Meanwhile, the struggle to have the autopsy results made public continued. In 1991, ABC went to court again to force Francisco to surrender the autopsy report. In May 1993, the Shelby County Commission filed a lawsuit to force the state of Tennessee to reopen an investigation into Elvis' death. As a result, the autopsy notes—but not the report—were given to a forensic pathologist to help settle disputes about the actual cause of death.

The debate over the role of drugs in Elvis' death matters little to fans, who largely ignore the darker side of his life and career. Those still determined to ferret out the exact facts seem to have a personal agenda that does not consider Elvis' contributions to 20th-century music or his impact on our culture.

Top: *The book* Elvis: What Happened? *exposed Elvis' drug abuse to the general public.*
Above: *Dr. Nick* (left of Elvis) *was frequently a part of Elvis' entourage.*

BEST COSTUMES

GOLD LAMÉ SUIT

At the request of Colonel Tom Parker, famed Hollywood clothing designer Nudie Cohen created a gold lamé suit for Elvis for his 1957 tours. It consisted of gold slacks and a jacket woven from spun gold thread. Nudie had established a reputation among county-western stars for his brightly colored western-style costumes with elaborate embroidery. While colorful stage attire was typical of country performers, the mainstream press simply was not ready for Elvis and his glittering raiment, and they used its conspicuous nature to attack Elvis. As the tour progressed, the reported cost of the suit grew higher and higher. The St. Louis *Post-Dispatch* claimed it cost $2,500; the Fort Wayne *News Sentinel* reported that the jacket alone cost $2,000; by the time he crossed the border, Canadian papers valued it at $4,000. Elvis never liked the suit because it was heavy and uncomfortable. When he ripped the pants during a performance, he never wore the entire suit again.

"TEDDY BEAR" COSTUME

Elvis' purported fondness for teddy bears was likely just a publicity stunt manufactured by the Colonel in the 1950s. One offshoot of the story holds that Kal Mann and Bernie Lowe composed the song "Teddy Bear" for Elvis supposedly as a response to the rumors. Elvis performed the song in his second film, *Loving You,* which was shot in glorious Technicolor. The cinematography, with its rich, saturated colors, proved the perfect vehicle to exploit the film's 1950s-style costumes.

For the "Teddy Bear" number, Elvis wore a silky, maroon and white, western-style outfit. The engaging love song combined with the endearing ensemble served to soften Elvis' rebellious persona. Aside from being a fan favorite, the costume gained attention when it was discussed on *You Bet Your Life,* a television game show hosted by Groucho Marx. The president of the San Diego Elvis Presley Fan Club, who had purchased the costume, appeared on the show, and Groucho teased her about her passion for Elvis and her unusual acquisition.

LEATHER ENSEMBLE

For one segment of the television special *Elvis*, Scotty Moore and D.J. Fontana reunited with Elvis onstage for an informal jam session. Elvis reminisced about his early career and belted out several of his famous hits with fresh and exciting new arrangements. The black leather ensemble that he wore in this segment is the most famous costume from "The '68 Comeback Special." Designed by Bill Belew, the costume is so familiar that it is a virtual icon for the special, and it has become synonymous with Elvis' creative comeback in the late 1960s. Like the new arrangements to his famous hits, the black leather outfit recalled the past but did not duplicate it. The comeback special aired at the close of 1968, when flower children held love-ins and wore paisley and posies. In the midst of the Age of Aquarius, a drop-dead handsome Elvis Presley strolled onstage in black leather, with a guitar cocked on his hip, and he reminded us that rock 'n' roll was not about peace and harmony. It was about sex and rebellion.

BURNING LOVE JUMPSUIT

Elvis wore a bright red jumpsuit onstage during his fall tour in 1972. The costume quickly became a fan favorite and one of his most famous stage costumes. Fans began referring to it as the "Burning Love" jumpsuit, perhaps because of its color. Also, the song "Burning Love" had been a recent hit for Elvis, and he included it in his song selection while on tour that year. Confusion exists about the "Burning Love" jumpsuit because the white costume and cape worn onstage at the Madison Square Garden engagement had once been given the same name. Elvis appears in the white suit on the cover of the album *Burning Love and Hits from His Movies, Volume 2*, which is why that costume had originally been christened with "Burning Love." However, the title seemed better suited to the red stage costume, and over time, the red suit usurped the cherished nickname. Elvis donated the red suit to the National Cerebral Palsy Telethon in 1972. In October 1995, the suit sold at a Las Vegas auction for a record $107,000.

BEST COSTUMES

ALOHA FROM HAWAII JUMPSUIT

The landmark television special *Elvis: Aloha from Hawaii* was telecast live to several countries via satellite. Elvis wanted a costume that signified America, so designer Bill Belew produced a white jumpsuit with an American Eagle patterned in red, gold, and blue gems. The costume's spectacular calf-length cape proved to be too cumbersome during rehearsals, so Elvis ordered a hip-length cape to replace it. A belt decorated with gold American eagles accented the ensemble. During the show, Elvis threw the belt into the audience and later threw the cape into the cheering crowd as he finished the closing song. Elvis ordered a second cape and belt for the jumpsuit and wore the outfit in later performances. The original belt has never surfaced, and the original cape is now in the hands of a private collector. By the end of 1974, Elvis stopped wearing capes onstage. Not only were they heavy and uncomfortable, but members of the audience tended to grab the edges of them while he was performing, resulting in some near accidents.

TIGER JUMPSUIT

Elvis wore the Tiger jumpsuit, also known as the Mad Tiger, around 1973 or 1974. The Tiger and Dragon suits were two of the first to be made without capes. This white jumpsuit with a high collar sported an open V-neck, flared sleeves, and belled pant legs. The dominant design was a jumping tiger, which wrapped around the front of the suit from the bottom left to the top right. The suit was accented with tiger stripes down the sides of the legs and on the belt buckle. Though perhaps not as ostentatious as some of the other Presley jumpsuits, the Tiger is significant because it represents something personal about Elvis. One of Elvis' hobbies was karate, which he first became interested in while he was in the army. He dabbled in the sport for almost 20 years. His karate nickname was Tiger.

Most of the suits that Elvis wore during the 1970s were made of 100 percent gabardine wool from Milan, Italy. Bill Belew prefered this material because it moved with the body while retaining its shape, as can be seen in the photo at the left.

PEACOCK JUMPSUIT

The Peacock jumpsuit, used during a 1974 tour, proved to be one of Elvis' personal favorites. A white jumpsuit with a V-neck and high collar, the Peacock features a large blue and gold bird rendered in a stylized design on both the front and back. Blue stylized peacock feathers fall down the sides of the pant legs. The peacock was the most expensive jumpsuit Elvis ever had made, costing over $10,000. The peacock designs were hand-embroidered with gold thread. The belt includes gold medallions that alternate

with designs that look like the eye of a peacock feather. Elvis eventually gave the Peacock suit to Paul Lichter, who still has it in his possession.

Elvis was attracted to peacocks because they represent eternal life. At one time, he kept a few of the birds at Graceland, but he gave them to the Memphis Zoo after one of them ruined the surface of his Rolls-Royce. Inside Graceland, a set of stained-glass windows with a peacock design separate the living room from the music room.

BEAR CLAW JUMPSUIT

Bill Belew designed the Bear Claw jumpsuit for Elvis for his June 1975 tour. Elvis had met Belew in 1968 when the costume designer made the black leather ensemble for the NBC television special *Elvis.* When Elvis returned to regular live performances in Las Vegas and on the road, he asked Belew to design stage costumes for him. The stereotype of Elvis during the 1970s consists of the singer wearing an open-necked white jumpsuit with a high collar. However, Belew actually designed a variety of

jumpsuit styles in an array of colors for Elvis.

The Bear Claw, also known as the Sabre Tooth, is a navy-colored jumpsuit with a scoop neck and baby blue sleeves. The suit is decorated with designs that simulate those found in Native American arts and crafts. The dominate motif is a bear claw. Bear claws encircle the neck like a necklace and adorn the front of the suit as well as the large flared area of the pant legs.

BEST QUOTES ABOUT ELVIS

Forbidden fruit.

"He's just one big hunk of forbidden fruit."

> teenage girl to Mae Boren Axton in mid-1950s, reprinted in *Elvis World*, 1987

"When I first knew Elvis he had a million dollars worth of talent. Now he has a million dollars."

> Colonel Tom Parker in 1956, reprinted in *Elvis! The Last Word*, 1991

"Despite repeated efforts by critics to cool his sex-hot flame, Elvis Presley has remained the most incendiary figure in the world of rock 'n' roll."

> "Inextinguishable," *Newsweek*, August 27, 1956

"I'll not have him at any price—he's not my cup of tea."

> Ed Sullivan before Elvis' ratings-busting appearance on *The Steve Allen Show Time*, July 23, 1956

"I want to say to Elvis Presley and the country that this is a real decent fine boy, and we've never had a pleasanter experience on our show with a big name than we've had with you."

> Ed Sullivan to Elvis in front of the studio audience after Elvis' third appearance on *The Ed Sullivan Show*, January 6, 1957

"[Elvis] can't go out for a walk. He can't drop a dime in a jukebox and drum his fingers on an oilclothed tabletop. He can't press his nose against the windows of haberdasheries. He can't take the top down on any of the Cadillacs and cruise in the moonlight. He can't ask a girl to dance or share a coke with him. He can't do any of the things he'd really like to do. He has to stay in that hotel room, a prisoner until early morning when he can escape again."

> Hal Kanter in his article "Inside Paradise," *Variety*, January 9, 1957

"Last night's contortionist exhibition at the Auditorium was the closest to the jungle I'll ever get. But it isn't the Memphis wiggler who's the 'missing link', it's his audiences..."

> Helen Parmelier reporting for the *Ottawa Journal*, April 4, 1957

"When I originally saw the act, I was horrified.... Elvis was rolling around on the stage floor of the Pan Pacific Auditorium in Hollywood with his arms and legs wrapped around the microphone as though they were bride and groom."

> Hedda Hopper in her autobiography *The Whole Truth and Nothing But*, 1962

"He is no longer the sneering, hip-twitching symbol of the untamed beast that resides in 17-year-old breasts. He has come back from the Army easygoing, unassuming, orderly..."

> "Rock-a-Bye Role for Presley," *Life*, October 10, 1960

"It would be unpatriotic of Elvis to go below that figure

Back from the army.

[90% tax bracket]. I got to keep this boy making three movies a year. There's a war in Vietnam, and it costs money to fight it. Elvis shows his patriotism by helping to finance the Government."

> Colonel Tom Parker quoted in "Elvis: Why They Call Him Mr. Clean," *Weekend*, September 15–21, 1965

Elvis and his mike: bride and groom.

"So Elvis Presley came…sowing seeds of a new rhythm and style in the white souls of the new white youth of America, whose inner hunger and need was no longer satisfied with the antiseptic white shoes and whiter songs of Pat Boone. 'You can do anything,' sang Elvis to Pat Boone's white shoes, 'but don't you step on my Blue Suede Shoes.'"

Eldridge Cleaver in his land-mark book *Soul on Ice,* 1968

"A long-gone folk hero often leaves behind the legend that someday he will return to his people. Barbarossa still sleeps, and the horn of Roland has not sounded

Long-gone folk hero.

again, but Elvis Presley is appearing in the flesh before an audience for the first time in nine years."

on Elvis' shows at the International Hotel "Return of the Big Beat," *Time,* August 15, 1969

"A young writer from *New York* magazine radiates love. 'When I was in sixth grade,' she says, 'we used to ask each other who we would let feel us up. I used to say I would only let Elvis feel me up.'"

"Absolutely Free," *Harper's,* November 1969

"…I've never had a losing Presley picture. They were all successful."

Hal B. Wallis quoted in *Dialogue on Film,* March 1975

"But it's hard to imagine Elvis Presley's success com-ing anywhere but here. He molded it out of so many American elements: country and blues and gospel and rock, a little Memphis, a lit-tle Vegas, a little arrogance, a little piety….How could we ever have felt estranged from Elvis? He was a native son."

Charles Kuralt in a CBS News Special on Elvis Presley, August 18, 1977

"One night I went into the casino after the show, and I saw [Bobby Darin] standing there with Elvis Presley… both of them were beautiful, polite, talented kids. I

thought I'd make them laugh. So…I whispered, 'I see you fellows are alone. If you need any help meeting girls, don't be embarrassed to ask me.' Presley thought I was serious. 'Thank you, Mr. Burns,' he said. Toughest audience I ever worked to."

George Burns reprinted in *Elvis! The Last Word,* 1991

"…[Elvis] came around, apologized for the way he'd changed 'Blue Moon of Kentucky,' and I told him that if it would help him get his start and give him a dif-ferent style, I was for him a hundred percent."

legendary blue-grass artist Bill Monroe reprinted in *Elvis! The Last Word,* 1991

"Maybe it's ironic that after that first appearance [on the 'Grand Old Opry'] the head of the Opry suggested that Elvis try to find a day job, and that Elvis cried all the way to Memphis after the Opry show. Then he went on to become the biggest star since Hank Williams. There's some kind of justice in that, I think."

Hank Williams, Jr., reprinted in *Elvis! The Last Word,* 1991

"When I first heard Elvis' voice, I just knew that I wasn't going to work for any-

Bobby Darin and Elvis in Vegas.

body; and nobody was going to be my boss….Hearing him for the first time was like busting out of jail."

Bob Dylan reprinted in *Elvis! The Last Word,* 1991

"…Elvis was and remained a working class hero, a man who rose from obscurity and transformed American popu-lar art in answer to his own needs—and who may have possibly been destroyed by the isolation that being an American celebrity some-times entails. He was as much a metaphor as a maker of music, and one of telling power and poignancy."

John Rockwell, *The New York Times* reprinted in *Elvis! The Last Word,* 1991

BEST BOOKS

MYSTERY TRAIN AND DEAD ELVIS

Greil Marcus examined the cultural contributions of a handful of legendary performers in *Mystery Train: Images of America in Rock 'n' Roll Music*, a unique work that is part history and part commentary. In the section on Elvis, Marcus describes him as a seminal figure who made a profound impact on American music and culture. The book is remarkable because it was written in 1975—before Elvis died. As such, it countered the image of Elvis as an over-the-hill Vegas entertainer. While

Mystery Train examines Elvis Presley the musical legend, Marcus' 1991 book *Dead Elvis: A Chronicle of Cultural Obsession* looks at images of Elvis that have evolved since his death. Using examples from bestsellers, tabloid headlines, television, advertisements, art, and other media, *Dead Elvis* suggests that these images reveal more about American culture than they do about Elvis. Together, the two books provide a sense of how America's view of Elvis the legend has changed in the 16 years between their publication.

WHEN ELVIS DIED

Published in 1980, *When Elvis Died* by Neal and Janice Gregory offers a riveting overview of the response by the press, public, and celebrities to the news of Elvis' death. The Gregorys exhaustively searched through hundreds of newspapers, magazines, and news scripts and organized the material into a detailed chronological account. The book opens with the moment the news was reported over the Associated Press wire and concludes with the many published tributes that flooded the newsstands in the

wake of Elvis' death. The way the television networks handled the story provides one of the most interesting tales. Conservative CBS, which dominated the ratings in those days, refused to lead off their evening news with the Elvis story. Millions of viewers switched to another network almost immediately, a phenomenon monitored by the Arbitron ratings service. The Gregorys' serious examination of Presley stood out at its release amidst a sea of dubious anecdotal biographies by Elvis' former friends and associates.

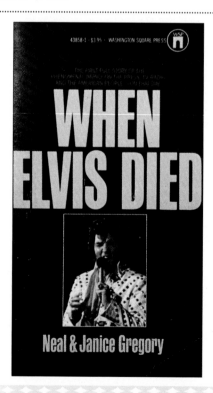

ELVIS

In 1982, the year after Albert Goldman published *Elvis,* a mean-spirited, inaccurate, and highly speculative biography, Dave Marsh released his version of the singer's life and career, which was also titled *Elvis.* Marsh's sympathetic, astute analysis of Elvis' music and career balanced and even challenged Goldman's highly prejudiced account. Marsh, one of the writers for *Rolling Stone* and cofounder of *Creem* magazine, focuses on the development of Elvis' sound and the changes in his music over time. In 1982, few rock crit-ics were exploring Elvis' music with any depth, and Marsh's career biography filled that gap despite an effusive style that sometimes sacrifices facts for flavor. However, Marsh devotes little space to Elvis' movies, and what he does write is seldom positive. The oversized biography features many black-and-white photographs, some of which were rare at the time, though the photos often lack sufficient explanation. The unusual cover design of the book features a striking close-up of Elvis and does not display the title or author's name.

ELVIS FOR BEGINNERS

Elvis for Beginners belongs to a series of books called the Beginners Documentary Comic Books, which are published by Writers and Readers Publishing in association with Unwin Paperbacks. Others in the series included *Marx for Beginners* and *JFK for Beginners.* The series uses everyday language to describe the cultural significance of key historical figures who made an impact on the 20th century. Using an ultrahip writing style, some photographs, and striking black-and-white woodcut illustrations, *Elvis for Beginners* describes the context in which Elvis' music was developed and then follows through with an analysis of the technological and social changes that made a mass phenomenon like Elvis possible. Opinionated, with some offbeat ideas and occasionally inaccurate details, the 1986 book is interesting precisely because it has a point of view. Fans may find that point of view harsh; others will come away with a deeper understanding of Elvis as a cultural phenomenon.

BEST BOOKS

ELVIS: HIS LIFE FROM A TO Z

The best reference source on Elvis Presley, *Elvis: His Life from A to Z* by Fred L. Worth and Steve D. Tamerius, is an exhaustive tome filled with facts and figures on Elvis' life and career. The encyclopedia features more than 2,000 entries and is divided into three sections: "The Man," "The Performer," and "His Music." The first section offers annotated entries on people, places, and things related to Elvis. The second section features details on his movies and television appear-

ances. Also included is a comprehensive listing of his concert performances and information on Elvis-related projects that were never completed. The last section is a thorough listing of his singles, EPs, albums, bootlegs, and other music information. Chart listings, composers, and trivia are included in each entry. This book contains over 200 photos, some of which had never been featured in a book. Published in 1988, *Elvis: His Life from A to Z* focuses on data, not analysis, but even the hard-core Elvis fan will find new facts here.

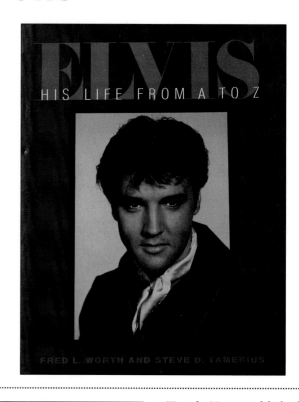

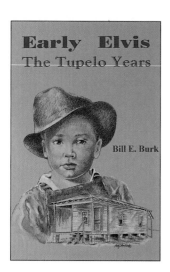

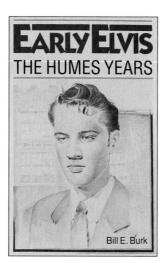

EARLY ELVIS SERIES

Bill E. Burk, a former reporter for the *Memphis Press-Scimitar*, is the founder and publisher of *Elvis World* magazine. In the course of his reporting career and during his years with *Elvis World*, Burk has met and talked with hundreds of people who knew and loved Elvis. Tapping into that rich resource, he has created a series of anecdotal biographies that flush out the details of Elvis' early life. Burk wrote *Early Elvis: The Humes Years*, published in 1990, and *Early Elvis: The*

Tupelo Years, published in 1994. The series will continue with a volume on Elvis' teen years in Memphis. The appeal of the books is the personal accounts by the people "who knew him when," including classmates, teachers, coaches, neighbors, and friends. Also, little-known facts and colorful stories about Elvis emerge from the pages of these unpretentious bios, while well-known myths are shattered. Fans of Elvis who have read countless biographies and career overviews will appreciate the detail and the rare photos.

ELVIS ALBUM

Several compilations of newspaper and magazine articles on Elvis Presley have been published over the years, including *The Elvis Clippings* by Karen Loper and *Long Lonely Highway* by Ger Rijff. The reproductions in these compilations are sometimes of poor quality, making them difficult to read. The full-color *Elvis Album*, published in 1991, offers reprints of clippings about Elvis Presley from 1954 through 1990, along with a variety of familiar, unusual, and even rare photographs of Elvis. The material is laid out to look like a scrapbook—as though a loyal fan has gathered clips and pictures on Elvis from the beginning of his career through his death and into the 1990s. The only text in the book consists of the hand-written captions below the photos. Every controversy, pivotal career move, and major event in Elvis' life and career is covered in the articles, which are actual pieces from well-known, little-known, and even unknown newspapers and magazines. Leafing through the pages is like reliving the era.

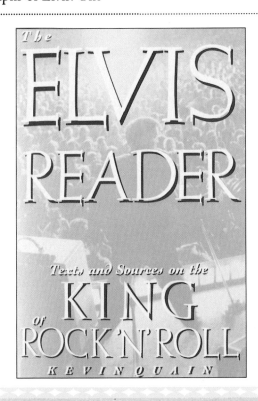

THE ELVIS READER

A collection of essays, interviews, short stories, reviews, and musings, *The Elvis Reader: Texts and Sources on the King of Rock 'n' Roll* serves as commentary on the myth of Elvis Presley, rather than the man. The articles are divided into sections based on subject matter. For example, "The Southern Elvis" features essays that analyze how Elvis' Southern background affected his image and career. Included in this section is Linda Ray Pratt's well-known and acclaimed essay "Elvis and the Ironies of a Southern Identity." "The Mythical Elvis" features articles that attempt to sum up what Elvis means to American culture. This section includes some of the famous newspaper and magazine articles from the time of his death, such as "A Lonely Life Ends on Elvis Presley Boulevard" by Clark Porteous in the *Memphis Press-Scimitar* and "Last Stop on the Mystery Train" by Jay Cocks in *Time* magazine. A handy and insightful reference section is located at the back. Published in 1992, *The Elvis Reader* was compiled by Kevin Quain.

BEST BOOKS

ELVIS: THE SUN YEARS

Popular Culture, Ink., specializes in reference books on seminal rock 'n' roll figures, including Elvis Presley. *Elvis: The Sun Years* by Howard A. DeWitt provides an example of the detailed research and specific focus their books often employ. A few introductory chapters address Elvis' childhood and high-school years, but the bulk of this 1993 book details his recording sessions for Sun, his tours on the Southern country-western circuits, and his stint with the *Louisiana Hayride*. The book also discusses some of the blues and rhythm-and-blues artists that influenced Elvis and provides background information on Sam Phillips and others involved in Elvis' early career. DeWitt depends heavily on interviews, including those with friends and acquaintances of the Presleys, musicians of the era, and others who were witnesses to the period. Some of those interviewed, such as Doug Poindexter, Marion Keisker, and Freddie Bell, are familiar names in Elvis lore and literature, but they have rarely been given a voice.

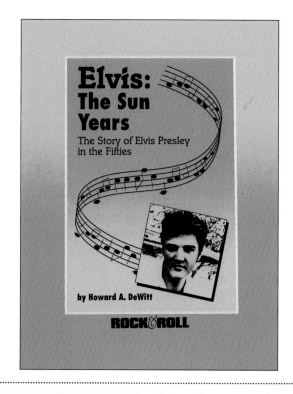

LAST TRAIN TO MEMPHIS

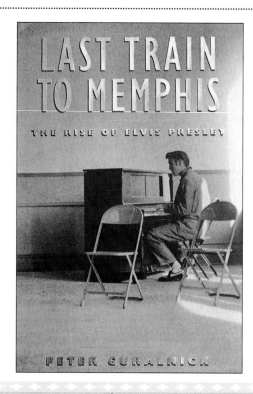

Music journalist and historian Peter Guralnik has authored the best biography of Elvis to date, *Last Train to Memphis: The Rise of Elvis Presley*. Published in 1995, *Last Train to Memphis* is more accurate and professional than the anecdotal tell-all biographies by former friends and associates of Elvis. The book begins with the birth of Elvis and his twin brother in 1935 and ends with the singer's departure for the army in 1958. A second volume by Guralnik that covers the rest of Elvis' life and career is planned for the future. Indigenous Southern music is Guralnik's area of specialty, and he has written extensively about country music, blues, and rhythm and blues in *Lost Highway, Feel Like Going Home,* and *Searching for Robert Johnson.* His analysis of the development of Elvis' sound is one of the book's strengths. Without the standard rock hyperbole of Dave Marsh and other *Rolling Stone* alumni, Guralnik writes a detailed, insightful account of Elvis' early career with conviction and authority.

BEST ELVIS HEADLINES

Early Career

"A Winnah! Presley Hot as $1 Pistol on Victor"
Billboard, March 3, 1956

"A Howling Hillbilly Success"
Life, April 30, 1956

"Disks Jump Presley Groove"
Variety, October 10, 1956

"Is Rock 'n' Roll Making Savage Sex Sinners of Simple Teen-agers? Is Young Elvis Presley the Big Answer?"
Private Lives, December 1956

"Presley Brings Delirium Tremors to 25,000"
Hamilton Spectator, April 3, 1957

"What Is Presley Doing to Our Children"
Canadian Home Journal, June 1957

"Elvis' New Song! You're in the Army Now"
The Chicago American, March 15, 1958

"Farewell to Priscilla, Hello to U.S.A."
Life, March 14, 1960

Mid Career

"Elvis Presley: Idol or Idiot"
National Enquirer, October 21, 1962

"I'm Looking for a Wife... But I Can't Find One"
National Enquirer, April 4, 1965

"If the Queen Doesn't Want to Meet Elvis— Then We Don't Go"
Colonel Tom Parker's reason for not visiting England
London Daily Mirror, September 14, 1965

"Presley: From Backwoods Phenom in 1956 to Polished Superstar in 1972"
Variety, June 14, 1972

"Elvis: Everybody Gets Enough of What They Want To Get What They Need"
Rolling Stone, August 31, 1972

Death

"All Roads Lead to Memphis"
London Evening Standard, August 17, 1977

"The King Is Dead"
Tupelo Daily Journal, August 17, 1977

"A Lonely Life Ends on Elvis Presley Boulevard."
Memphis Press-Scimitar, August 17, 1977

"L'adieu à Elvis"
France-Soir, August 17, 1977

"Last Stop on the Mystery Train"
Time, August 29, 1977

"Elvis Has Left the Building"
Stereo Review, January 1978

After Death

"The King Is Dead, Long Live the King"
Chicago Sun-Times, August 9, 1987

"UFO Alien Sang 'Love Me Tender'"
Sun, February 9, 1988

"Statue of Elvis Found on Mars"
Sun, September 20, 1988

"Ain't Nothin' But a Charge Card"
on the Elvis MasterCard
Esquire, February 1989

BEST TV APPEARANCES
Stage Show (March 17, 1956)

IN DECEMBER 1955, Colonel Tom Parker and RCA gambled that television would make an excellent medium to introduce Elvis Presley to a national audience. When Elvis charged in front of the cameras for the first time on Tommy and Jimmy Dorsey's *Stage Show* on January 28, 1956, he began a love-hate relationship with the television industry that kept his name on the front page for most of that year.

Big-band leaders Tommy and Jimmy Dorsey hosted the weekly variety series, which was produced by comedian Jackie Gleason as the lead-in for Gleason's sit-com *The Honeymooners.* An array of acts paraded into the studio each week and performed for a studio audience as well as in front of the *Stage Show* cameras. Elvis had originally contracted to make four appearances, but based on the audience response to his first show, he was signed for two additional shows.

Whoever snapped this publicity photo did not see the clash of generations represented by the image. Rock 'n' roller Elvis and big-band leaders Tommy and Jimmy Dorsey represented popular music from two different eras.

The Dorsey Brothers Orchestra backed Elvis on "Heartbreak Hotel" for his Stage Show *appearance on February 11, 1956.*

With each appearance, Elvis grew more at ease in front of the cameras, and he became more aware of the reaction of the studio audience to his performance. By his fifth and best appearance on March 17, 1956, more of an interaction between Elvis and the studio audience occurred. Elvis chose to sing "Heartbreak Hotel" and "Blue Suede Shoes" for this show. He had sung "Heartbreak Hotel" on his third appearance, but he had been backed by the Dorsey Brothers Orchestra. On his fifth appearance, the song sounded more like Elvis' recording of "Heartbreak Hotel," which was climbing up the charts. When Elvis strummed the opening chord to the song on his guitar, he paused for a second as screams and applause broke out. He was much more mobile during this performance, shaking his shoulders

*A more confident Elvis appeared on **Stage Show** on March 17. He teased the audience with his body movements and provoked a fervent response.*

Stage Show aired opposite the enormously popular *Perry Como Show*. Elvis' appearances on *Stage Show* helped improve its ratings, though the show never came close to beating Como. The January 28 show had garnered an 18.4 rating; by the March 24 appearance, the ratings had increased to 20.9. More significantly, Elvis' performances on *Stage Show* established precedents in terms of his future TV appearances. Elvis, the Colonel, and RCA would use television to showcase the singer's latest singles, and various shows would use him as a weapon in the ratings battle between variety programs despite the controversy he generated.

In 1956, Elvis became a weapon in the ratings war between variety shows, resulting in some of television's most notorious moments.

and moving his legs throughout the song instead of holding back until the instrumental break as he had done on earlier appearances. During the break, he stepped back and shook his entire body much like before, but he tagged on a rolling leg movement, sending the audience into a brief screaming frenzy. Elvis' smiles at the reaction he elicited suggested he both expected and enjoyed the response. During the chorus of the song, he reached down into the lower registers of the scale to sing, "I'm so lonely, baby. I'm so lonely, baby, I could die," and the audience screamed and cheered.

BEST TV APPEARANCES
The Milton Berle Show (June 5, 1956)

MILTON BERLE, nicknamed Mr. Television because his variety programs had dominated the airwaves since 1948, had moved his program to Los Angeles in September 1955. The 1955–56 season would be the last for his long-running series, which ended with the June 5 telecast starring Elvis Presley. Considering the impact of Elvis' performance on the program, Berle left the air with a bang, not a whimper.

Aside from Elvis, the guests on the show were exactly the kind of entertainers America expected to find on a variety program—actress Debra Paget, comedian Arnold Stang, TV actress Irish McCalla (star of *Sheena, Queen of the Jungle*), and seven-year-old singer Barry Gordon. Much of the comic patter between the guests centered around Elvis and the sensation he was causing. Little Barry Gordon did an imitation of his singing style, while Paget swooned over Elvis much to the comic chagrin of Berle. The comic routines involving Elvis focused on his sex appeal or his effect on women, with Berle getting his clothes torn off by a group of "Elvis fans" because he stood too close to the singing sensation. The highlight of the show—and the biggest controversy of Elvis' early career—was his provocative rendition of "Hound Dog." Performing the song on television for the first time, Elvis sang it without his guitar, which had begun to serve more as a prop anyway. Without his guitar to clutch, swing, or bandy about, Elvis grabbed the microphone throughout the performance, bending it over and straddling it between his legs. At times, he stopped, bowed his head, and then cast his eyes upward to point

Elvis happily poses for publicity shots with Irish McCalla, who starred in TV's Sheena, Queen of the Jungle.

Milton Berle, who had developed his act in vaudeville and on the burlesque circuit, had no qualms about having Elvis on his show.

his finger at the studio audience, which always resulted in full-volume screaming. Elvis teased his audience with his hip-swiveling, provocative performing style, going beyond what he had done on *Stage Show*. By this point in his career, the female fans expected certain moves from Elvis, and when he complied, they responded to him. The relationship between Elvis and his audience was like an elaborate seduction: Elvis teased and tempted the women, and no matter how far he went, he left them wanting more.

This type of interaction, which he had fine-tuned while touring across the country, threatened to break down the barriers between audience and performer. And this threat was at the core of the controversy over his performance on the Berle show. For the climax of "Hound Dog," Elvis slowed down the tempo to repeat the chorus. While belting out this final verse to a blues beat, he turned his body in profile to the audience and thrust his pelvis at some imaginary tar-

get. Accentuating the pelvic movements was the fact that his hand was resting next to the crotch of his pants. If some audience members had not yet made the connection between Elvis' performing style and sex, then these few seconds on national television made them see the light.

The next day, columnists and critics were ruthless in their descriptions of Elvis' performance, most often comparing it to a striptease. In doing so, they gave it a lurid or lewd connotation, suggesting it was out of the realm of mainstream entertainment. Throughout the summer, several publications and spokespersons for prominent institutions criticized or complained about Elvis and his effect on audiences. The Berle performance served as a concrete event around which to base certain accusations brewing against Elvis, particularly involving the sensuality of his performing style and the hysterical reactions of the fans. His burgeoning image as a dangerous rock 'n' roller had just been made solid.

  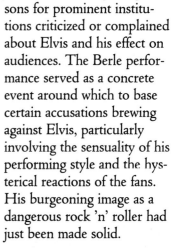

Elvis sang "Hound Dog" for the first time on **The Milton Berle Show** *on June 5, 1956. This single performance solidified his burgeoning image as the country's most notorious rock 'n' roller.*

BEST TV APPEARANCES
The Ed Sullivan Show (October 28, 1956)

DESPITE earlier statements to the contrary, Ed Sullivan signed Elvis for three appearances on his legendary variety series. Elvis' first appearance occurred on September 9, 1956, though Sullivan himself was not there because he had been in a car accident. The veteran showman and entertainment columnist did, however, serve as host for Elvis' second engagement on October 28. Legend has it that Sullivan would allow Elvis to be shown only from the waist up for his program, but this restriction occurred only for Elvis' final appearance on the show on January 8, 1957.

Of the three appearances, the October performance provides an excellent example of the interaction between Elvis and his audience. He sang three times on this show, beginning with "Don't Be Cruel" and "Love Me Tender," returning a short time later to sing the ballad "Love Me," and concluding with "Hound Dog." Throughout the first two sets, in which Elvis chose low-key numbers, he held back from his customary hip and leg movements and body shakes. A series of hand gestures elicited screams from the female fans in the

Elvis checks over his cue cards in rehearsal for his October 28 appearance on **The Ed Sullivan Show.** *Sullivan's show was considered the pinnacle of variety series.*

audience as did his rendition of "Don't Be Cruel," in which he exaggerated the syncopation of the lyrics more than in the recorded version. With each hiccup sound, the audience responded with squeals and applause. At certain intervals, Elvis positioned himself as though he were going to break into his more frenzied performing style, but then he backed down, in effect teasing his audience.

Returning to the stage a final time, Elvis played on the audience's expectations for a frenzied performance and carried out the suspense as long as possible: While introducing his final number, he teased, "I'd like to tell you that we're going to do a sad song for you. This song here is one of the saddest songs we've ever heard. It really tells a story, friends. Beautiful lyrics. It goes something like this." Still keeping everyone on edge, he swung his arm in the air as though he were about to break into song, then looked at the audience and stopped. He repeated the gesture—again, another false start. At last, he launched into a fast-paced, raucous rendition of "Hound Dog," the song that had caused perhaps the most memorable controversy of

The Sullivan appearances generated much hype and publicity.

could not have chosen a song that had more significance, given his TV appearances over the last year, and he could not have given a more explosive performance of that signature song.

THE STEVE ALLEN SHOW

Steve Allen's variety series, which debuted on June 24, 1956, aired opposite the immensely popular *Ed Sullivan Show*. Allen knew that to beat the veteran variety series in the ratings, he needed the hottest performer in the country—Elvis Presley. He signed Elvis for his second show, which aired July 1. Allen was also mindful of the controversy surrounding Elvis. In a clever maneuver designed to give him his ratings and a family program too, Allen neutralized Elvis' sexuality through the use of comedy. For example, dressed in a tux and a pair of blue suede shoes, Elvis gamely sang "Hound Dog" to a basset hound wearing a top hat and a bow tie. Restricted from moving by his attire, the setting, and by Allen, Elvis offered a version of the song that was devitalized. Throughout most of the show, Elvis was the punch line to a joke orchestrated by Allen: His blue suede shoes were out of sync with the tuxedo; he sang to a dog, whose pitiful expression almost upstaged him; he appeared in a sketch that made fun of his Southern background. By not allowing Elvis control over his own act and by using his image as a target at which the show's comedy was aimed, Allen defused the sensuality associated with Elvis and orchestrated Elvis' worst television performance. But Allen did get what he wanted—he beat the Sullivan show in the ratings.

Steve Allen and Elvis rehearse the "Range Roundup" sketch, which poked fun at Southern radio shows.

The Colonel negotiated a cool $50,000 for Elvis' three appearances on the Sullivan show.

the rock 'n' roll era when he performed it a few months earlier on *The Milton Berle Show*. Whereas on that program, he had slowed down the song on the final verse to perform an erotic version, this time his frenzied rendition exploded across the stage and screen. Every hip and leg movement was exaggerated as he belted out the lyrics at an ever-increasing pace. He

BEST TV APPEARANCES
Elvis

IN EARLY 1968, Colonel Tom Parker closed a deal for Elvis to appear in his own television special for NBC, which eventually aired on December 3. The Colonel's vision of the special consisted of Elvis walking in front of a Christmas tree, singing everyone's favorite, familiar carols, and then wishing everyone a happy holiday. Fade out.

Steve Binder, the producer of the special, had a different vision. With this program, he hoped to capture what he felt was Elvis' genius—the adaptation of rhythm and blues to the tastes of mainstream audiences. He wanted to prove that Elvis' original music had been essential to the development of rock 'n' roll and that Elvis was not a relic of the past. Binder had gained a reputation for capturing the high-powered energy of rock music on film with *The T.A.M.I. Show*, a 1964 concert movie featuring a range of acts from the Rolling Stones to James Brown. He had also directed several episodes of NBC's prime-time rock music series *Hullabaloo*. Binder's credentials and conviction helped convince Elvis to defy the Colonel's idea and go along with the young producer's vision.

The opening of Elvis' television special recalled his notorious image from the 1950s without duplicating it.

The Blossoms backed Elvis during the gospel tribute.

Elvis consists of two concert segments performed before a live audience interspersed with four elaborate musical productions. Two of the production numbers represent the influence of gospel and country-western music on Elvis' music. The gospel segment opens with a dancer interpreting the spiritual "Sometimes I Feel Like a Motherless Child." Elvis then appears onstage to sing the gospel numbers "Where Could I Go but to the Lord" and "Up Above My Head," backed by the female vocal trio the Blossoms. Elvis, the Blossoms, and the Claude Thompson Dancers conclude the segment with a rousing rendition of the rhythm-and-blues number "Saved." Without a word of dialogue, this production number suggests the evolution of black spirituals to rhythm and blues to the music of Elvis Presley.

The country-western segment focuses on the secular influences of Elvis' music, specifically honky-tonk. This production number tells a simple story through song and dance in which Elvis—as the "Guitar Man"—roams the honky-tonk strips and carnival midways of the South looking for a chance to sing. At first he has little but the guitar strapped to his back, symbolized by the blues-tinged "Nothingville." His adventures are related through song as he encounters carny toughs in "Big Boss Man" and the temptations of women in "Little Egypt." At the end, the Guitar Man walks off into a promising future—suggested by the set, which is a road paved in lights.

The production number that begins the show refers to Elvis' past. He opens the program—his first TV appearance in over eight years—with "Trouble" from the movie *King*

Elvis as the Guitar Man roams the honky tonks of the South in the country-western segment.

The most acclaimed segment featured a leather-clad Elvis singing informally to a live audience.

Creole. Dressed in black, Elvis looks every bit the dangerous rock 'n' roller of the previous decade as he sings one of his early hits. The final production number points Elvis to the future because it is representative of the large-scale sound that characterized the next phase of his career. Elvis concludes his special with "If I Can Dream," a modern-day hymn with a gospel-soul arrangement.

The two segments performed before a live studio audience comprise the most famous moments of the show. In these segments, Elvis and four musicians, including his long-time band members Scotty Moore and D.J. Fontana, sit on a small stage surrounded by an audience of mostly female fans. Elvis wears the famous black leather suit designed by Bill Belew, and his hair is fashionably long, though reminiscent

of the past. The majority of songs performed during the live segments were his past hits— "Hound Dog," "All Shook Up," "Blue Suede Shoes," etc. However, new arrangements, plus Elvis' lower vocal range, result in a slightly different sound. The effect is powerful, as an energized, charismatic Elvis thrills the audience with his first live performance in eight years. In retrospect, these live segments, which are a clever weaving of the old and the new, signify

Elvis concluded with the moving "If I Can Dream," though the Colonel lobbied hard for "Silent Night."

a specific moment in Elvis' career—a turning point. They symbolize the moment when the notorious Elvis the Pelvis returns from the past to reclaim his crown as the King of Rock 'n' Roll. Small wonder that the special is more popularly known as "The '68 Comeback Special."

Left to right: *Director Bones Howe, producer Steve Binder, Elvis Presley, and executive producer Bob Finkel.*

BEST TV APPEARANCES
Elvis: Aloha from Hawaii

TAKING ADVANTAGE of advances in global communications, *Elvis: Aloha from Hawaii* was beamed by the Intelsat IV satellite to countries all over the world on January 14, 1973. Broadcast at 12:30 A.M. Hawaii time, the special was seen in Australia, New Zealand, the Philippine Islands, Japan, and other countries in the Far East. Even parts of Communist China supposedly tuned in. The next day, the show was rebroadcast to 28 European countries. The special consisted of a concert performance by Elvis in front of a live audience at the Honolulu International Center Arena. After the audience left the arena, Elvis was filmed singing five more songs, which were to be included in the U.S. edition of the concert. NBC's broadcast of the show on April 4 included only four of the additional songs, however. The American broadcast of the special was watched by 51 percent of the television viewing audience, which was more people than watched the first walk on the moon. Eventually, *Elvis: Aloha from Hawaii* was seen in 40 countries by at least a billion people.

Elvis did a full dress rehearsal on January 12, which was not televised. After seeing a tape of his performance, he decided he needed a haircut. The difference in hairstyles provides a way for the Elvis fan to distinguish between photos of the

Some estimates say Elvis: Aloha from Hawaii *was seen by 1.5 billion people, which, in 1973, was about every third person in the world.*

rehearsal and photos from the special. Both shows were a benefit for the Kuiokalani Lee Cancer Fund. Lee was a Hawaiian composer who had died of cancer, and Elvis performed Lee's song "I'll Remember You" in his honor. About $75,000 was raised for the fund.

The special provides a good example of his stage show from the 1970s, a period in which he embodied the term "superstar." His band and orchestra began the performance with the opening strains from Richard Strauss' symphonic poem "Thus Spake Zarathustra," also recognizable as "The Theme from *2001: A Space Odyssey*." The sonorous sound of the kettle drum solo, which signaled the conclusion of that segment of "Zarathustra," segued into the driving rhythms of "See See Rider," Elvis' opening number. At that point, Elvis bounded onstage, strutting back and forth in front of the audience and showing off his costume, complete with cape. Grabbing a guitar, which he rarely played but used as a prop, Elvis began singing the chorus to "See See Rider."

Elvis sang a variety of songs throughout the concert special, including his current hits, such as "Burning Love" and "Suspicious Minds," as well as the past hits "Hound Dog," "Love Me," and "A Big Hunk o' Love." He also sang "My

Elvis' arrival by helicopter at the Hawaiian Village Hotel was filmed for the opening of the show.

Way," "Steamroller Blues," and other pop and rock tunes as well as the moving country classic "I'm So Lonesome I Could Cry." During the course of the evening, he removed his cape, and while singing "An American Trilogy," he tossed his studded belt into the audience.

For the finale, Elvis sang his standard closing number, "Can't Help Falling in Love," which built up to the large-scale sound typical of his style of that era. By the time this number had begun, Elvis had resumed wearing his cape, which typically

The 1973 special captures Elvis at one of his best moments in this phase of his career.

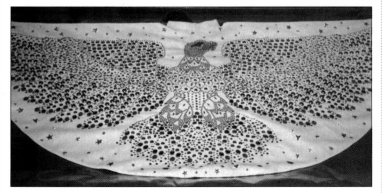

To the surprise of the audience and his entourage, Elvis threw this cape into the crowd.

signaled the end of the show for his band and the audience. Usually, he concluded the number by dropping to one knee in the spotlight, grabbing the ends of his cape in his hands, and spreading the garment out behind him—a grandiose gesture befitting the World's Greatest Entertainer. On this night, he added an extra touch by throwing the gem-laden cape into the crowd, where it was caught by a lucky fan. As the orchestra reprised "See See Rider," Elvis left the stage. As usual, he did not return for an encore. It was simply too hard to top the effect of such sublime imagery.

FANS

ELVIS ALLOWED HIS FANS a remarkable degree of access. He was never too tired for a photo or autograph; he flirted with all, regardless of age or beauty; he could remember by name those who followed him from concert to concert; and he never openly complained about his lack of privacy. The fans have repayed Elvis with their undying loyalty and devotion . . . even 20 years after his death.

BEST FAN STORIES
I Gave a Letter to the Postman

THE LYRICS to Pat Geiger's favorite Elvis Presley song, "Only Believe," include the line "All things are possible, if you only believe." The song reflects the long, hard struggle behind Geiger's campaign for an Elvis Presley stamp. The effort took eight years and 11 months, though it is not the longest campaign in stamp history. That honor belongs to Shirley Thomas, a professor at the University of Southern California, who lobbied the post office for 26 years for a stamp for Theodore von Karman, a Hungarian-born mathematician and a pioneer aeronautical researcher.

Geiger began her campaign in 1983, with a letter to the U.S. Postal Service suggesting that Elvis Presley be the subject of a stamp. Before she was finished, at least 50,000 people signed petitions in support of the stamp, more than 60,000 letters were written by Elvis stamp supporters, and five different postmaster generals had taken office.

"It was a wonderful experience," declared Pat Geiger, regarding her successful campaign for an Elvis stamp. (Photo by Toby Talbot.)

from Mississippi, Tennessee, and other states. Geiger wrote to 50 celebrities seeking their help, but only Ann-Margret and her husband, Roger Smith, responded. When 1987 rolled around, a frustrated Geiger learned that Elvis wasn't in serious consideration for a stamp. The stamp campaigners were not even close to achieving their goal.

The situation improved when Anthony M. Frank became postmaster general. When he commented, "I think an Elvis stamp would be fun," the media became interested in the campaign. The attention proved to be a double-edged sword. While focusing interest on the campaign, it also increased the efforts of the opposition. Those opposed to the stamp, including members of the

Geiger learned some very basic information with that first letter—with the exception of former presidents, a person had to be dead ten years before being eligible for a stamp. Elvis would not be eligible until August 16, 1987, so Geiger used the intervening four and a half years to organize her efforts. She notified fan clubs about her campaign and enlisted their help in writing letters to the postmaster general, the Citizens' Stamp Advisory Committee, and senators and representatives

Citizens' Stamp Advisory Committee and various politicians, felt Elvis' abuse of prescription drugs and the rumors about his bizarre lifestyle did not send the proper message to children. Geiger and the campaign began to focus on countering the accusations of the opposition. Their efforts were boosted by positive events related to Elvis, such as the release of well-received videos or CDs.

As the media attention increased, Geiger became adept at fielding questions by the press. From 1989 to 1993, she was the focus of 65 radio interviews, ten television appearances, and dozens of articles. During that period, she also endured personal insults by those who opposed the stamp and by insensitive reporters looking for angles for their stories. A reporter for *The Columbus Dispatch* openly ridiculed her in a 1990 article, suggesting that she "get a life." Like many reporters who write about aspects of the Elvis phenomenon, this journalist had a condescending and uninformed view of fans who devote time and energy to Elvis-related causes.

Finally, on January 9, 1992, Frank announced that an Elvis stamp would be issued in 1993, despite the reluctance of the Citizens' Stamp Advisory Committee to recommend such an action. Though Geiger was relieved at the announcement, the specifics of the stamp's issue were less than desirable. Elvis' stamp was going to be part of a book that included stamps of other performers. The stamp campaigners believed he was entitled to an individual issue. The U.S. Postal Service eventually changed its decision, opting to issue Elvis' stamp as a genuine commemorative on a sheet of 40. Later, it was included in a book honoring rock 'n' roll and rhythm-and-blues artists.

The post office decided to let the general public get in on the fun. Two stamp designs were chosen as finalists, and the public was encouraged to vote on which design they preferred. In the choice between a young, rock 'n' roll Elvis and a mature, Vegas-style Elvis, Geiger chose the latter. However, she was not too disappointed when her choice was not selected for the actual stamp. Later, the original poster for the unused design, by artist John Berkey, was given to Geiger for spearheading the stamp campaign. She loaned the poster to the Elvis Presley Memorial Trauma Center in Memphis for permanent display so that other fans could enjoy it.

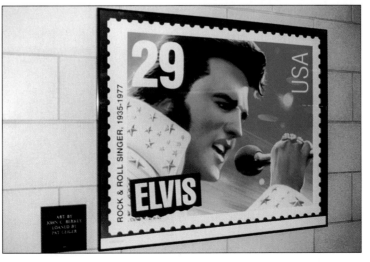

Above: Geiger displays part of her collection of Elvis images. (Photo by Toby Talbot.) **Far left:** *Geiger poses with Mark Stutzman, who painted the winning design for the Elvis stamp.* **Left:** *John Berkey painted the other design that was in final contention for the stamp. The original poster for the unused design is now a part of Geiger's Elvis collection. It hangs at the Elvis Presley Memorial Trauma Center.*

BEST FAN STORIES
King of the Whole Wide World

AMANIA EXISTS in America for all things Elvis. Fans organize conventions to share insights, information, and collectibles, and academics study Elvis in the classroom as part of our contemporary culture. This kind of interest is not restricted to America, however. Fans throughout the world share this passion for Elvis Presley and participate in Elvis-related events, ranging from fan conventions to scholarly investigations.

In Thailand, Dr. Nitaya Kanchanawan, who has a Ph.D. in linguistic studies, combines her lifelong interest in Elvis with her academic pursuits. A professor of Thai language studies, Kanchanawan was asked by the U.S. Information Service to present lectures on Elvis at Thailand's American University Alumni Association Language Centre in 1985. The talks drew hundreds of fans, many of whom expressed a desire to participate in other Elvis-focused activities. In response, Kanchanawan organized huge parties for the Elvis fans of Thailand at the Narai Hotel in Bangkok. More than festive gatherings, the "parties" were small conventions, where fans had the opportunity to discover new Elvis videos, tapes, and CDs. Prizes were awarded for Elvis-related activities, and Kanchanawan displayed items from her personal Elvis collection. Ideas and analyses of Elvis' music and cultural impact were freely exchanged at these parties, which prompted the press to refer to them as "semi-academic gatherings."

In 1988, Ramkhamhaeng University asked her to produce an educational series on Elvis, which became one of the most popular educational programs in Thailand. She has also lectured about Elvis in Asia and in the United States. In Thailand, she has spoken about Elvis in American history and black literature courses. In 1994, she served as a guest lecturer at the University of Iowa for a course called Elvis as Anthology. Recently, she translated *When Elvis Died* by Neal and Janice Gregory into Thai. In her capacity as an academic, Kanchanawan not only introduces young people to the music of Elvis, but she also provides a context for understanding his importance.

Left: *Dr. Nitaya Kanchanawan combines her interest in Elvis Presley with her academic endeavors.* Above: *Kanchanawan (behind podium) became well known in her native Thailand for organizing Elvis conventions where participants could exchange ideas and information. In addition to lectures and discussions, the gatherings also featured displays of memorabilia and exhibitions of Elvis-related documentaries and programs.*

BEST FAN STORIES
Crying in the Chapel

JANELLE MCCOMB knew Elvis Presley from the time he was born until he died. Over the years, Elvis and McComb exchanged gifts, views, and ideas. She wrote a poem for Elvis for Lisa Marie's fourth birthday entitled "The Priceless Gift," and he presented her with irreplaceable tokens of his esteem and friendship, including a diamond ring and a TLC necklace.

McComb and her husband once asked Elvis how he would like to be honored in his hometown. He thoughtfully replied that he would like to have a chapel built in his name so that fans could have a place to meditate. Shortly after Elvis died, she committed herself to raising the money to construct a chapel behind the Presley birthplace in Tupelo. Though in declining health, McComb undertook the task with dedication and perseverence because ". . . I had made a commitment to a young boy who had very few friends in life."

Top: *The Elvis A. Presley Memorial Chapel in Tupelo.* Bottom: *The chapel's 12 pews were donated by Elvis' friends and associates.*

equal enthusiasm and appreciation. One couple from California recycled aluminum cans to find the extra money to donate to the chapel. During construction, McComb even slept on the site to prevent souvenir hunters from stealing materials.

The groundbreaking ceremony occurred on Elvis' birthday in 1979, and the Elvis A. Presley Memorial Chapel was dedicated on August 17, the day after the anniversary of his death. More than 4,000 people attended the dedication, including Mississippi governor Cliff Finch and Kathy Westmoreland, one of Elvis' backup singers. Westmoreland moved the audience to tears with her rendition of "My Humble Father Watches Over Me." Also in attendance were Mrs. R. L. Laukoff, who dedicated the large stained-glass window, and Colonel Tom Parker, who had arranged for the purchase of the organ. Vernon Presley had donated the family Bible to the chapel before his death in June 1979.

She traveled around the country, drumming up money to start construction. The first donations came from people in Tupelo who had known the Presleys before they moved to Memphis. As word of her mission spread, donations arrived from Colonel Tom Parker, the Official Elvis Presley Fan Club of Great Britain, and the Elvis Now Fan Club of San Jose, California. Large and small contributions were accepted with

The Elvis Presley Commission was formed in 1977 to govern the administration of the Elvis A. Presley Memorial Chapel and the Elvis Presley Youth Center. Over the years, there have been dozens of weddings in the chapel while fans from all over the world have dropped in to remember Elvis. Having fulfilled her goal, McComb reflected, "He lived and died, and during that time I always knew I had a friend."

BEST FAN STORIES
Mansion over the Hilltop

AT 3764 ELVIS PRESLEY Boulevard in Memphis, Tennessee, the white-columned portico of Elvis Presley's Graceland is visible behind a clump of trees atop a small hill. At 605 Riverland Road in Roanoke, Virginia, the white-columned portico of Kim Epperly's Miniature Graceland is visible behind a clump of shrubbery atop a smaller hill.

Miniature Graceland is a downsized version of Elvis' legendary home located in the Epperly yard

Kim Epperly poses beside Miniature Graceland, which she and her husband began building in 1984.

in an unassuming residential section of Roanoke. Landscaped with small shrubs to simulate the real Graceland's shady surroundings, Epperly's version even includes the music gates and gate house. Behind the mansion is a small swimming pool with a stone patio, which connects to a tiny Meditation Garden, complete with fountain and classical arcade.

Over the years, Epperly and her husband, Don, added other Elvis-related sites to the arrangement, including Elvis' birthplace home. A scaled-down version of the shotgun shack sits close to a small country church, similar to one Elvis might have attended in his hometown of Tupelo. The Memphis home of Vernon Presley is located behind Miniature Graceland, and the Heartbreak Hotel restaurant and the Auto Museum are nearby. Roanoke's Civic Arena, where Elvis performed in concert many times, is also included, which adds a touch of Epperly's own hometown to Miniature Graceland. When the roof is lifted, an audience of dolls represent fans who sit enraptured as an Elvis doll performs onstage. The latest addition includes an ambitious effort to simulate the Memphis Airport, where replicas of three airplanes once owned by Elvis are housed. One plane flies via a cord suspended between the house and a tree. Cement walkways and tiny streets connect the various buildings. Most of the time, Elvis music is piped out of the Epperly home so visitors are

treated to an aural as well as visual treat.

Miniature Graceland was completely handmade by the Epperlys, and it is constructed with care and precision. Don Epperly did most of the construction based on photographs supplemented with sketches and descriptions provided by Kim. Construction began in 1984 after Kim visited the real Graceland. A die-hard Elvis fan since childhood, Kim attends Tribute Week every August in Memphis, and that year she thought it would be helpful if local fans who didn't get to travel to Graceland every summer had a miniature version to visit. Since then, as many as 10,000 visitors show up each year to admire the detailed reproductions. Each August, local fans hold a candlelight vigil at Miniature Graceland to commemorate the anniversary of Elvis' death, reminiscent of the ceremony held in Memphis.

Not surprisingly, Miniature Graceland has attracted the famous, the peculiar, and the extraordinary. People from as far away as Poland, Russia, and Australia have visited Roanoke looking for the site. A young couple became engaged there, with the future bridegroom actually bending down on one knee near the mansion. Former president Jimmy Carter and wife Rosalyn dropped by one evening unrecognized. Kim Epperly did not realize they were there until she saw them on the evening news, when Carter commented that her Graceland was beautiful.

In 1994, vandals, floods, and theft severely damaged Miniature Graceland. After the local newspaper reported the many problems the Epperlys were experiencing, several volunteers and local businesses contributed their time and supplies to restore the display. "Miniature Graceland does take a lot of work," Kim told *The Washington Post*, "but it's worth it. It brings a lot of pleasure into my life."

Top left: *Miniature Graceland takes over most of Epperly's yard in Roanoke, Virginia.* Top right: *The Epperlys have added to their display over the years, including their version of Elvis' Tupelo birthplace.* Middle right: *A replica of an old country chapel sits behind the birthplace.* Above: *An audience of dolls sits in the miniature version of Roanoke's Civic Arena.* Left: *Behind Miniature Graceland is a tiny version of Meditation Garden.*

BEST FAN STORIES
Treat Me Nice

IF ELVIS FANS are intensely devoted, one reason must be because Elvis sincerely appreciated their affection and adoration. Throughout his entire career, he allowed them surprisingly close access considering the magnitude of his stardom.

Fans have gathered at the music gates at Graceland since Elvis purchased the property in 1957. Not only did he tolerate their presence, but he often went out of his way to talk to them, sign autographs, and openly flirt. Beth Pease of Memphis remembers a time in 1957 when she and her girlfriend were at the gates, waiting for Elvis to drive by. He roared up in a black Cadillac, stopped the car by the gates, and then got out to greet the small group. He walked over to Beth's girlfriend, gathered her flaming red hair in his hands, and called her beautiful. Beth grabbed the bottom of his coattail, and she boldly ran her hand up his back. When she told a surprised Elvis that she just couldn't resist, he winked and said, "That's all right, baby."

On occasion, he allowed fans to join his all-night movie excursions at the Memphian Theater. Sharon Fox of Chicago was in the right place at the right time when she, her mother, and a friend were told by the guard at the music gates that Elvis was going to the movies that night. The trio showed up at the Memphian, and one of Elvis' bodyguards allowed them inside. When the movies ended at about 7:00 A.M., Elvis obliged Sharon by posing for a couple of photos with her. Marty Lacker, one of the Memphis Mafia, even took them.

During the 1970s, Elvis was known to throw his expensive jewelry to the fans in the audience and occasionally even to buy a car for a lucky fan. When Mennie Person complimented Elvis on his Cadillac limousine, he bought her a gold and white Eldorado to call her own. When he discovered it was her birthday, he threw in some money so she could buy some clothes. Generous, grateful, and appreciative, Elvis never became too famous to attend to his fans.

Generous to a fault, Elvis made headlines in the 1970s by giving away luxury cars to fans. He gave an Eldorado to Mennie Person of Memphis (top) *and another Cadillac to TV newsman Don Kinney of Denver* (above).

BEST FAN STORIES
Steadfast, Loyal, and True

ELVIS PRESLEY fans share a reputation for donating their time and money for worthy causes, keeping Elvis' popularity quotient high, and pulling together for other fans. Many fan clubs use their memberships to raise money in Elvis' name for charities, because Elvis donated so much to so many charities during his lifetime. Fans with large memorabilia collections lend them for fund-raising events or museum exhibits, usually in Elvis' name.

Robin Rosaaen of San Jose, California, owns one of the largest Elvis memorabilia collections in the country, consisting of 40,000 items. From rare 1950s pieces to recent souvenirs, her collection includes a wide range of artifacts, keepsakes, and memorabilia. Rosaaen has loaned parts of her collection to universities, hotels, and other institutions for special exhibits as well as to fund-raising events to promote worthy causes. She is also a storehouse of information about Elvis Presley and serves as a consultant for various Elvis-related projects.

Fans return Elvis' generosity and honor his memory by participating in worthy causes in his name. Avid collector Robin Rosaaen frequently uses her Elvis memorabilia for fund-raising events.

Elvis fans are also known to consistently chip in when an unassuming soul experiences mishap or misfortune, just as Elvis had always done. When the Celebrity Room restaurant of Mechanicsville, Virginia, went into bankruptcy, owner Alan Serafim had to liquidate most of the memorabilia that decorated the restaurant's 50-seat Elvis room. He was able to reopen 13 months later at a new location. After the reopening, many people who purchased the memorabilia loaned it back so the new restaurant could feature an Elvis wall.

Elvis fans contributed their own brand of good will toward Russia after the political changes in that country allowed its citizens to more openly express their admiration for western entertainers. When Raisa Gorbachev, wife of Soviet leader Mikhail Gorbachev, visited America and admitted she was a big Elvis fan, a fan club called the Elvis Special Photo Association sent her a collection of memorabilia. Around the same time, Russian artist Kolya Vasin told the press he had always wanted to visit Graceland. A fan club in England called Elvisly Yours raised the money for him to go.

BEST FAN CLUBS

ELVIS' ANGELS

Begun by young Linda Rae in Los Angeles around 1960, Elvis' Angels epitomized the typical Elvis fan club from the era. Angels was established simply because the members were devoted fans of Elvis Presley. Their newsletter, titled *The Voice of the Angels*, was typed on plain white paper and then mimeographed for national distribution. The pages were filled with news items and details about Elvis as well as scoops about his upcoming movies. In addition, members contributed original poems expressing their love and devotion to Elvis and telling of exciting first-hand encounters with their idol. Tips on where to get Elvis photos and collectibles served as filler. The group is now defunct, but the members of Elvis' Angels, and others like them, represent the core of Elvis' fans. Devoted and sincere in their affection, most of these girls remained fans as adults, and many of them passed down their affection for Elvis to younger generations.

ELVIS MEMORIAL CLUB OF TEXAS

Eddie Fadal founded the Elvis Memorial Club of Texas, and it was Fadal who made this fan club special. Fadal was a disc jockey when Elvis met him after performing at the Heart O' Texas Coliseum in 1956 in Waco, Texas. While stationed at Fort Hood, Elvis liked to visit Fadal and his family. As a matter of fact, Elvis was there so often that Fadal built an extra room onto his house, which he painted pink and black. He also obtained a piano for Elvis to play. Fadal taped some of the songs that his famous friend played at that piano, and they later found their way onto a bootleg album called *Forever Young, Forever Beautiful.* The day Elvis died, Fadal moved. He formed the Elvis Memorial Club of Texas and opened his Elvis room to the public. A minimuseum with Elvis photos and memorabilia, the room was distinguished by a brightly colored stained glass window. Sadly, the attraction was closed down and the fan club folded when Fadal passed away in 1994.
(*Left*: Anita Wood, Elvis, and Fadal.)

THE ELVIS PRESLEY BURNING LOVE FAN CLUB

In the spirit of Elvis' generosity, the Burning Love Fan Club exists to raise money for two charities that Elvis himself had something to do with. In the process, they intend to keep Elvis' name remembered. The fan club's motto "Just Carrying on Where Elvis Left Off" attests to their purpose. As of 1996, this Chicago-based group had raised a total of $138,000, for LeBonheur Children's Medical Center and the Elvis Presley Memorial Trauma Center. In addition to raising money for these two medical facilities on a regular basis, the club donates 200 teddy bears to children's hospitals every Christmas. The Burning Love Fan Club was started in 1983 by Bill DeNight, who has been an Elvis fan since he was ten years old. The 1,600 members of the club have published cookbooks, held auctions, and sold candy bars to raise funds. Often, DeNight donates items from his personal collection of Elvis memorabilia *(pictured)* to auction off for charity.

ELVIS PRESLEY TANKERS FAN CLUB

Gary Pepper *(pictured, with Elvis)* organized the Elvis Presley Tankers Fan Club while Elvis was in the army. "Tankers" referred to Elvis' stint in a tank unit, though Elvis was a jeep scout driver. Pepper, a victim of cerebral palsy, was one of the first people to greet Elvis at Union Station in Memphis after he was discharged. Elvis admired Pepper's courage in the face of his debilitating condition, and he treated him more as a friend than a fan. Elvis invited Pepper to parties at Graceland and in Hollywood, so the fan club president always had the inside scoop for his newsletter, *The Tankcaster*. When Gary's father, Sterling, lost his job, Elvis hired him as a guard at Graceland. Elvis also hired Gary as Fan Club Coordinator and Foreign Correspondent, a job that involved writing letters and magazine articles for fans. In 1966, Pepper tried to get the Memphis Coliseum renamed the Elvis Presley Coliseum, but the city refused. He stayed on the Presley payroll until Elvis died in 1977. Pepper died in 1980.

BEST FAN CLUBS

ELVIS WORLD

Though not a fan club, *Elvis World* is a Memphis-based fan organization that includes about 6,000 members from all 50 states and all over the world. *Elvis World* publishes a glossy, four-color magazine featuring contributions from an international writing staff. Its stories about fans and fan clubs from around the world remind readers of the global impact of Elvis Presley. *EW* includes news of the latest Elvis-related events, and the regular columns "Shopper's Corner" and "Elvis Book Shelf" offer tips on gift items, collectibles, and books. The inclusion of rare photos of Elvis, some never before published, makes *EW* a collectors' item as well as a magazine. *Elvis World* was founded by Bill E. Burk *(pictured, with Elvis)* in August 1986. Burk, a photo-journalist and friend of Elvis', serves as publisher, while his wife, Connie Lauridsen Burk, is the editor. Burk organizes fan activities each August during Tribute Week in Memphis, including breakfast meetings that showcase leading Elvis biographers. A percentage of the *EW* profits is contributed to charity.

E.P. CONTINENTALS

The E.P. Continentals became famous because Elvis named them himself. Inspired by his favorite automobile at the time, he dubbed the group the E.P. Continentals sometime in the mid-1950s, and eventually the organization grew into a large fan club with several chapters. Earl Greenwood served as copresident of the E.P. Continentals and later wrote a biography about Elvis called *The Boy Who Would Be King*. After Greenwood resigned as president, he asked two sisters from Chicago, Jean and Pam Drew *(left)*, to take over. Though the girls experienced some administrative problems, they finally became national copresidents in 1961. The Continentals represent one of the oldest Elvis Presley fan clubs in existence: A version of the club is still active in Kissimmee, Florida.

E.P. CONTINENTALS-Chicag
Jean and Pam Drew-Co-Pre
Taken July, 1960

OFFICIAL ELVIS PRESLEY FAN CLUB OF GREAT BRITAIN, WORLDWIDE

Founded by Jeannie Seward in 1956, the Official Elvis Presley Fan Club is supposedly the world's oldest established Elvis fan club. Albert Hand, publisher of *Elvis Monthly*, became president of the group in the 1960s. Hand established ties with Colonel Tom Parker and members of the Presley family as well as with the movie studios and RCA. Hand died in 1972, and Todd Slaughter took over as president of the club and publisher of *Elvis Monthly*. Slaughter is also the author of a 1977 book titled *Elvis Presley* and has written liner notes for British-released Elvis albums. The enterprising Slaughter has gained a reputation as an Elvis authority, and he often contributes to Elvis-related books and video projects. Slaughter and Ernst Jorgensen worked as researchers for the album *Essential Elvis—The First Movies*, and the album was dedicated to the Official Elvis Presley Fan Club. Julie Mundy took over the operations of the fan club in 1996.

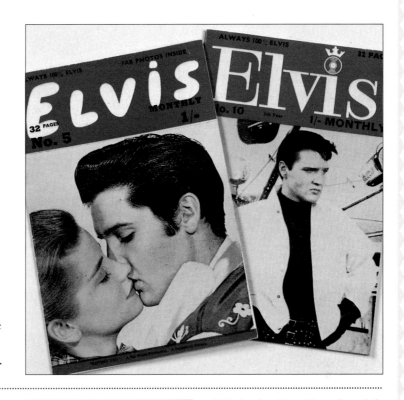

Our King Fan Club

OUR KING

Begun in the 1960s, the Our King fan club of Alva, Oklahoma, was taken over by Jim Hannaford in 1964. At the time, Hannaford was a struggling college student who devoted every free moment to putting out the fan club newsletter. Despite being a simple, hand-typed newsletter like those from other fan clubs, the publication's content was not just the usual fawning and fussing over Elvis Presley. Well written and thoughtful, the newsletters often featured editorials on proper behavior and the virtues of discipline. While the Our King fan club no longer exists, Hannaford is known among Elvis fans because of his later work as a writer. He has written articles for several music magazines, including *Goldmine, Discoveries,* and *Live Music Review,* and he authored *Inside Jailhouse Rock,* a close-up look at the making of Elvis' most famous movie. Hannaford is also a noted collector of Elvis memorabilia and photographs, which have been published worldwide.

BEST FAN CLUBS

THAT'S THE WAY IT IS

A recent fan club compared to most, That's the Way It Is was formed in 1986 and includes about 300 members. Despite its small numbers, the club consists of dedicated individuals who want to present a positive image of Elvis by raising money for charity in his name. Based in Chicago, the group had raised about $10,000 by 1996 for various charities, including the Elvis Presley Memorial Trauma Center, the Make-a-Wish Foundation, and the St. Jude Children's Research Hospital. Unlike most fan clubs, who tend to compete against each other when trying to raise money, That's the Way It Is generously contributes to the charitable drives of other clubs. For their dedication as well as their spirit of cooperation, the club was named Fan Club of the Year by *Elvis World* magazine in 1995. Carol Hopp, president of the club, states, "...we try to carry on the way we think Elvis would have wanted. We enjoy each other and the greatest entertainer of the century."

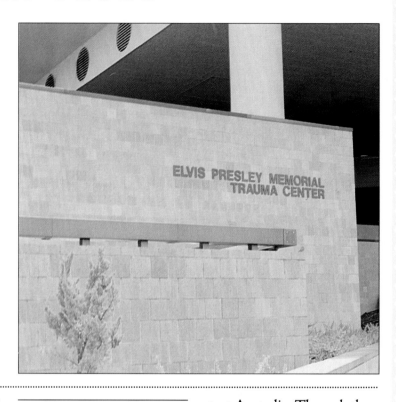

FOREIGN FAN CLUBS

After Elvis returned to live performances in 1969, fans from other countries sometimes journeyed to the States to see him in person and to lobby Elvis and the Colonel to tour overseas. Although Elvis never did perform outside North America, he still became a tremendous international star with a loyal following. During his lifetime, dozens of fan clubs were established all over the world, from the King "O" Mania Fan Club in nearby Canada to the Elvis Presley Fan Club of Tasmania in distant Australia. Through the efforts of magazines such as *Elvis World*, current European fan clubs have a higher profile and enjoy increased interaction with American clubs. One of the oldest European fan clubs still in existence is Germany's EPG Club, which was established in 1973. Other major clubs include Sweden's Tidskriften Elvis, the United Elvis Presley Society of Belgium, and a club from Holland called For Elvis Fans Only. (*Left:* Ngvar Home of Norway's fan club presents Elvis with a plaque.)

BEST GRAFFITI AT GRACELAND

IN THE YEARS since Graceland has been open to the public, fans who visit Memphis frequently express their devotion through an unusual medium—graffiti on the fieldstone wall that borders the property. Sometimes touching, sometimes insightful, sometimes funny, these notes pay tribute to Elvis as well as comment on the many ways that he touched the lives of his fans.

"Loving you makes a lonely street a lot easier."

"Every mountain I have to climb, Elvis carried me over on his back."

"In memory of our Mom and Dad ... Our home was filled with your music."

"We can't stand still anymore either, Elvis. Thank you. Go cat Go."

"Coming back from Lubbock
I thought I saw Jesus on the plane,
But it might have been Elvis, They look kinda the same."

"God needed rock 'n' roll, so he called him home."

"I heard the call, I made the pilgrimage, I came to Graceland."

"I came here a non-believer, but I am leaving here a fan."

"I've been to Mt. Vernon. I've been to Monticello. I have to say, though, our Founding Fathers don't have anything on Graceland."

"Wherever you are, Elvis is ..."

"[*Elvis* author Albert] Goldman is a son of a bitch."

"It's like Gail-Brewer [sic] Giorgio said, Elvis *Aron* Presley is not dead!"

"Elvis we love you so much that we named our little boy Chadwik after you in *Blue Hawaii.*"

"Elvis, Let's go to Denver for sandwiches sometime."

"Elvis, I fondle your hair in my dreams."

"Elvis, I wish I was your belt buckle for a day!"

I, Kid Nitro, tagged your jet. That's what you get, Mr. Rock [Star], but I still [love] you."

"You wouldn't have liked the way Caddies look today, anyway."

"Elvis, How 'bout that son-in-law?"

"Elvis, I know you're alive! Call me, we'll do lunch."

"Dear God: Bolton and Cyrus for Presley?!? Let's trade!!!"

A fan expresses herself on the wall that borders the property of Graceland.

Language barriers don't prevent international visitors from participating in the tradition.

Billy Idol got carried away when writing on the wall. Graceland caretakers left it up for a while because Lisa Marie was a fan of Idol.

BEST ELVIS LANDMARKS

GRACELAND

Elvis Presley's home for 20 years, Graceland served as his retreat from the personal and professional pressures of an increasingly demanding career. The small Southern-style mansion with a white-columned portico was built in 1939 by Dr. Thomas Moore and named after his wife Ruth's aunt, Grace Toof. Elvis bought the 13.8 acres of land with its house, barn, smokehouse, and wellhouse in 1957 for slightly over $100,000. He renovated the house and gradually made additions to the property until Graceland consisted of 23 rooms and the grounds included the Trophy Room and Meditation Garden, as well as a carport, bath house, and racquetball court. Opened to the public in 1982 and placed on the National Register of Historic Places in 1991, Graceland draws approximately 700,000 visitors per year. On almost any given day, flowers and fan mementoes are left on Elvis' grave in Meditation Garden, which attests to the passion and loyalty of his fans. A visit to Graceland offers a glimpse of both Elvis the man and Elvis the phenomenon.

LAUDERDALE COURTS

In contrast to the space and opulence of Graceland is the stark poverty of Lauderdale Courts, a federally funded housing project that was home to Elvis from September 1949 to January 1953. The Presleys, including grandmother Minnie Mae Presley, lived at 185 Winchester Street, Apartment 328, a two-bedroom, ground-floor apartment costing $35 per month. At Christmastime in 1952, the housing authority told the Presleys that they were making too much money to stay at Lauderdale Courts. It had been an endless cycle for the Presleys since they had moved in: Elvis, Gladys, and Vernon all tried to work to support the family, but when they got a little bit ahead, they were threatened with eviction. The Presleys left Lauderdale Courts on January 7, 1953—the day before Elvis' 18th birthday. They moved in with relatives on Cypress Street. While not an entertaining landmark to visit, Lauderdale Courts is a reminder of the poverty that the Presleys had endured and from which they escaped.

HUMES JUNIOR HIGH SCHOOL

Two days after Elvis recorded his first song for Sun Studio, "That's All Right," disc jockey Dewey Phillips played the tune on his rhythm-and-blues radio program *Red Hot and Blue* and then called the young singer down to the station for an interview. Phillips asked Elvis what high school he attended, and he replied that he had gone to Humes. In 1954, Humes was an all-white school, and by asking this question, Phillips was subtly letting the audience know that Elvis was a white

singer, despite having recorded an R&B tune. The Dewey Phillips story has been repeated many times, and Humes has become a part of Elvis lore and literature. Now a junior high school, Humes is proud of its most famous graduate. The auditorium has been renamed the Elvis Presley Auditorium, and the school has an Elvis room, which includes copies of the 1953 yearbook along with copies of his junior and senior high school diplomas.

BEALE STREET

Memphis has always been a musical crossroads, where the South's indigenous styles of music rub up against each other on hot sultry nights. The beating heart of the Memphis music scene was the clubs on Beale Street, where blues and rhythm-and-blues artists honed their craft. Though Elvis was known to visit the performers on Beale, his connection to that legendary strip of seedy joints and tiny clubs has probably been exaggerated. Clearly he was influenced by the sounds that were played there, because they

permeated the Memphis music scene, but his exposure to the music most likely came through the radio. Sadly, by the 1970s, Beale Street had become a shadow of its former self. The clubs were gone, and empty storefronts dominated the area. Two decades later, the city mounted an effort to bring back Beale, albeit in a sanitized form. Look for the Music Walk of Fame, which consists of brass musical notes mounted on the sidewalk. The notes feature the names of prominent Memphis performers, including Elvis.

BEST ELVIS LANDMARKS

SUN STUDIO

Called the "Cradle Where It Rocked," Sun Studio may be the world's most famous recording studio. From it came a sound that changed the course of popular music, and the music of Elvis, Jerry Lee Lewis, Carl Perkins, Johnny Cash, and Roy Oribson still seems to echo inside its walls. Sam Phillips moved Sun Records from 706 Union to 639 Madison in the late 1950s. In 1969, he sold Sun to Shelby Singleton, who moved the operation to Nashville. The historic Sun building was sold and became the site of a plumbing company and later an auto parts store. After Elvis died, Grayline Tours purchased the building and partially restored it. Though currently a working studio, Sun takes advantage of its fabled past by offering tours. The studio is furnished with musical and recording equipment from the 1950s, as well as photos of the legends who made history there. Taylor's, the restaurant next to the studio where Elvis filled up on cheeseburgers, is now the Sun Studio Cafe.

CENTER FOR SOUTHERN CULTURE

The Center for Southern Culture is located on the former site of the famous Lansky clothing store. Owned and operated by Bernard and Guy Lansky, Lansky's Clothing Emporium at 126 Beale Street specialized in loud, hip attire. The clientele included local Memphis musicians, rhythm-and-blues singers, and Sun recording artists. Elvis began shopping at Lansky's in 1952, while still in high school. When Elvis died 25 years later, the Lanskys provided suits for the pallbearers at his funeral. The store closed in the 1980s, and the building stood empty. During the 1990s, the Center for Southern Culture opened in the old Lansky store. Though small, the museum offers a thoughtful collection of exhibits highlighting Southern heritage and history, including the music of the South. The huge, colorful mural celebrating the glory of Memphis that adorned the outside of the building when it was Lansky's is faded but still visible. (*Left:* Elvis shops at Lansky's.)

LIBERTYLAND

Located at the Mid-South Fairgrounds, Libertyland was called Fairgrounds Amusement Park in the 1960s. At that time, Elvis' fame had become so enormous that he could not venture into public without causing a near riot. His solution was to privately rent entertainment facilities for the evening. Sometimes it was a movie theater, sometimes a roller rink, and sometimes it was the Fairgrounds Amusement Park—which cost him $2,500 per night. The Zippin Pippin, a wooden roller coaster, was Elvis'

favorite ride. In 1975, the old Fairgrounds Amusement Park was remade into a historical, educational, and recreational amusement park called Libertyland. After the huge facility was completed in 1976, Elvis would rent Libertyland just as he had the old park, except he rented it for his daughter, Lisa Marie. Elvis' last visit to Libertyland was eight days before he died; he reportedly rode the Zippin Pippin for two hours. Libertyland plays host to several Elvis-related events each August during Tribute Week. (*Right:* Elvis at Libertyland.)

THE PLAYHOUSE (MEMPHIAN THEATER)

When not in the mood for a midnight ride on the Zippin Pippin, Elvis would go to the Memphian Theater for private showings of movies. As with the Fairgrounds Amusement Park, he rented the theater for the entire night to avoid the general public. His group, which included Priscilla, members of his family, some of the Memphis Mafia, and their wives or girlfriends, would arrive around midnight or after. They usually stayed till dawn. Occasionally, fans

were allowed inside the theater to watch the movies as long as they did not disturb Elvis. During one of his midnight excursions to the Memphian in 1972, Elvis was introduced to Linda Thompson by George Klein, and she became his companion for several years. The Memphian was proud of its association with Elvis, and a small brass plate marks the chair where Elvis most often sat. In 1981, the docudrama *This Is Elvis* premiered at the Memphian. The theater has since changed its name to the Playhouse.

BEST ELVIS LANDMARKS

POPLAR TUNES

Poplar Tunes, founded by hardworking Joe Coughi, epitomizes the 1950s record shop. Located near Lauderdale Courts, the one-story brick building was a hangout for Elvis and his friends during their high school years. As a youth, Elvis purchased singles at Poplar Tunes to add to his ever-growing record collection. When he went from being a record collector to a recording artist, Poplar Tunes began selling his Sun singles. Most claim it was the first store to sell an Elvis Presley record. Because Elvis was from the neighborhood, his singles sold like wildfire, and he enjoyed signing autographs at the store for the local customers who supported him. Poplar Tunes still sells Elvis' records, and it looks much the same as it did in 1954. The walls of the store are lined with dozens of rare and interesting photos, including a telling shot of Elvis, Dewey Phillips, and Coughi that captures that fleeting moment when Elvis—standing between obscurity and legend—was just a boy from the neighborhood who made good. (*Right: Elvis at Poplar Tunes.*)

BIRTHPLACE IN TUPELO

The site of Elvis' birthplace includes the original two-room house, the Elvis A. Presley Memorial Chapel, the Elvis Presley Youth Center, and Elvis Presley Park. When Vernon built the house during the Depression, it was an unpainted shotgun shack sitting on a dirt plot on Old Saltillo Road. After the city of Tupelo opened the house as a tourist attraction in 1971, they turned it into a quaint bungalow located on the newly renamed Elvis Presley Drive. City officials furnished the house with amenities that the Presleys never could have afforded, and they hung inappropriate or ill-suited adornments on the wall. Structural changes were made, including the addition of a picturesque porch, and the grounds were landscaped to include small dells with such charming names as Gladys Glen and Lisa Lane. Despite the white-wash, Elvis' birthplace remains a fascinating site because the shotgun shack is steeped in Elvis folklore. It is also a nostalgic glimpse back in time to a simple childhood in the rural South.

TUPELO HARDWARE COMPANY, INC.

Legend has it that the first guitar Elvis Presley ever owned was purchased for him by his mother at the Tupelo Hardware Company. The story had become so embellished over time that Forrest L. Bobo, the man who sold the guitar to Gladys, wrote it down in a letter in 1979, which is now displayed in a glass case inside the store. The letter isn't the only attraction the store at 114 West Main Street has to offer, however. The Tupelo Hardware Company has not changed much over time, and walking through its door is not much different than when Elvis walked through it so many years ago. As a matter of fact, it's still the same front door. The counter Elvis leaned on is still the same, as are the display cases throughout the store. For a small price, visitors can buy a guitar-shaped key holder that reads, "Tupelo Hardware: Where Elvis Bought His First Guitar."

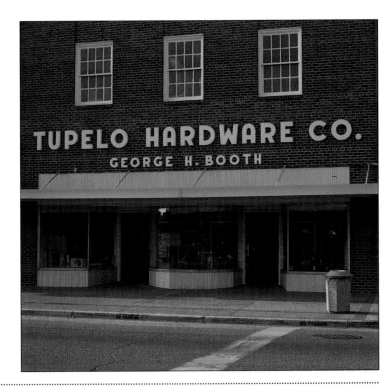

TUPELO McDONALD'S

One of the two McDonald's restaurants in downtown Tupelo offers a surprisingly tasteful tribute to Elvis Presley. The restaurant's decor includes an elegant-looking glass divider that separates the counter from the tables, with three depictions of Elvis etched into the glass. Each depiction represents a different phase of Elvis' career. Offbeat information about Tupelo's famous native son is arranged on the walls thematically. The complete TCB oath is framed and hung prominently, along with quotes by and about Elvis. Written insights into various aspects of his career are framed alongside photos. A very unusual piece includes a copy of Colonel Tom Parker's arrangement with the Hilton Hotel that contractually bound Elvis to play the hotel for years without a raise in pay. In addition, a display case contains books, trading cards, records, commemorative plates, and other collectibles. The McDonald's tribute features enough information to keep even the most knowledgeable fan interested.

BEST ELVIS LANDMARKS

ELVIS' STAR ON THE WALK OF FAME

A familiar attraction in the heart of America's movie capital, Hollywood's Walk of Fame immortalizes the entertainers of the past and present. Located along Hollywood Boulevard and Vine Street, the monument consists of bronze name plaques in pink terrazzo stars embedded in the sidewalk. The stars pay tribute to the famous, the notorious, and the forgotten who made contributions to the entertainment industry. Businessman Harry Sugarman proposed the idea for the Walk of Fame in 1958, and the first eight celebrities to receive stars were announced at that time. Construction was completed in 1960, and the Walk of Fame was dedicated on February 9. At that time, 1,500 other performers received stars, including Elvis Presley. Currently, more than 2,000 stars make up the Walk of Fame. Each star is identified by one of five icons—a movie camera, a radio microphone, a TV set, a record player, or theatrical masks. Elvis earned his star for his contributions to the recording industry.

HOLLYWOOD HOME

While making movies in Hollywood, Elvis rented homes in the Los Angeles area, most notably a house in Bel Air that had once been occupied by the Shah of Iran. In 1967, he purchased his first Hollywood home, which was located at 1174 Hillcrest Road in Trousdale Estates. Elvis paid $400,000 for the six-year-old faux chateau, which included an Olympic-sized swimming pool and a guest cottage. A multilevel, three-bedroom home in the French Regency style, the property still looks much the same as when Elvis owned it. An iron gate keeps intruders from getting too close, and over the years, fans have developed the habit of writing on the gates much like they do on the wall surrounding Graceland. The fan phenomenon of expressing opinions and feelings about Elvis via graffiti is as interesting as the house itself. Elvis purchased the home with Priscilla in May 1967, but the family lived there less than a year, opting to move after Lisa Marie was born.

174

HONEYMOON HIDEAWAY

After Elvis and Priscilla were married amid much flurry and fanfare in Las Vegas on May 1, 1967, they borrowed Frank Sinatra's jet and escaped to the tranquility of 1350 Ladera Circle, a Palm Springs estate that Elvis had leased. Home movie footage exists of Elvis carrying Priscilla over the threshold of the house and picking a rose for her from the garden. Considered avant-garde during the 1960s, the estate has an unusual elliptical design, and there is not a single square room in the house.

The house is now owned by an investment group called the Boston Investors, which has restored it to its original 1960s decor and added posters, photos, and artifacts related to Elvis and Priscilla. Renamed the Honeymoon Hideaway, the estate is not open to the general public, though bus tours drive by it twice a day. The Boston group leases it to corporations for major events, and they hope to sell it to a foundation or collector who will preserve it as Elvis' home.

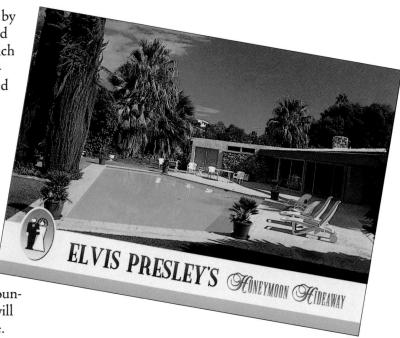

BLUEBERRY HILL

Visitors to the Blueberry Hill Restaurant will find more thrills there than just burgers and beer. To walk through the doors of this St. Louis landmark at 6504 Delmar is to take a crash course in American pop culture. The restaurant is filled with memorabilia and collectibles from popular music and television, including a downstairs room devoted to Elvis. The Elvis Room displays photos, backstage passes, Las Vegas menus, guitars, jewelry, the original issues of Sun records, and other collectibles. Each year, the restaurant holds a party on Elvis' birthday and another on the anniversary of his death. At the birthday parties, trivia and impersonator contests keep the customers entertained before they share the giant guitar-shaped cake. For the August parties, professional performers impersonate Elvis, Priscilla, the Colonel, and other members of Elvis' family. Owner Joe Edwards also uses his high profile as the proprietor of the Blueberry Hill to promote the achievements of various local musicians and celebrities.

Best Fan Photos

HYSTERIA

After Elvis appeared on national television in 1956, his life became a rocket ride of fame, fortune, and fan hysteria. As an old friend said at the time, "Elvis belongs to his fans." And there was no turning back.

AUTOGRAPHS

From the time he cut his first record in the summer of 1954 until the day he died, Elvis rarely refused an autograph, and fans were always eager to take advantage of the opportunity to get one.

BEST FAN PHOTOS

PERSONAL TOUCH

Sincerely touched by the devotion of his fans, Elvis interacted with them in an intimate, physical way few stars ever dared.

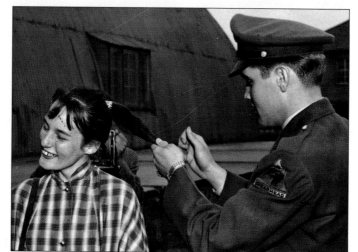

DEVOTION

Even Elvis fans themselves can find it difficult to account for the extent of their devotion. As one put it, "I can't describe what it's like to fall in love, but I know when it's happening to me. That's how it was with Elvis."

LEGEND

SINCE HIS DEATH IN 1977, Elvis has been absorbed into the popular culture that he helped to define. The resulting image of him is so powerful that it can be exploited as a cash cow, venerated as an icon, or studied as a phenomenon. That image reverberates with a significance that Elvis himself could scarcely have imagined . . . whether it appears in pop art, in an academic lecture, or on a bubble-gum card.

CAREER HIGHLIGHTS

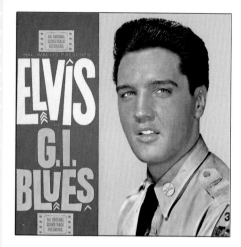

During his 22-year recording career, Elvis had 67 Top-20 hits and 14 number-one records on *Billboard*'s Top 100/Hot 100 charts.

"Hound Dog" became only the second single in history to reach number one on the pop, rhythm and blues, and country-western charts. The first record to accomplish this feat was Carl Perkins' "Blue Suede Shoes" in 1956.

"Jailhouse Rock" was the first record that ever entered the NME British singles chart at number one.

"Don't Be Cruel"/"Hound Dog" was the number-one single in America for 11 weeks, longer than any other singles release in the rock era.

During his 22-year recording career, Elvis had 38 Top-20 albums and 25 Top-Ten albums.

Elvis Presley, Elvis' first album, was the first LP ever to go gold.

Four of Elvis' albums remained on the charts for a year or more: *G.I. Blues* (111 weeks), *Blue Hawaii* (79 weeks), *Elvis Is Back* (56 weeks), and *Aloha from Hawaii Via Satellite* (52 weeks).

Around 1995, Elvis passed the half-billion mark in total career record sales, according to Paul Williams, the Vice President of Strategic Marketing for RCA and a member of that company's Elvis Presley Worldwide Committee.

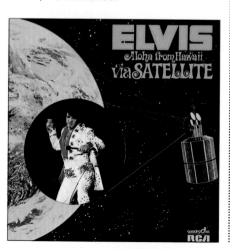

Elvis admires one of the seven gold records he received for his 1956 singles releases.

As of 1992, Elvis' recordings have garnered 111 gold and platinum certifications from the Recording Industry Association of America (RIAA). The Beatles have the second-most certifications, with 44. The Rolling Stones place third with 39 certifications, Barbra Streisand ranks fourth with 37, and Elton John places fifth with 36.

Elvis won three Grammy Awards during his career, and he was nominated 11 other times. After his death, Elvis received two nominations: "Softly As I Leave You" was nominated for best country vocal performance by a male, and *Elvis Aron Presley* was nominated for best album notes.

The total box-office gross for Elvis' feature films is reportedly $150 to $200 million dollars. (This does not include video revenue.)

In 1965, Elvis ranked as the highest-paid actor in Hollywood, earning more

Elvis in Hollywood: The highest-paid actor of 1965.

THE FLOPS

Elvis' accomplishments and amazing career statistics speak for themselves. However, the legendary entertainer experienced his share of flops. Two that made a profound impact on him personally were his performance on the *Grand Ole Opry* in 1954 and his engagement in Las Vegas in 1956.

Based on the regional success of "That's All Right," Elvis and the Blue Moon Boys were booked on the legendary radio show for September 4, 1954. Elvis appeared on Hank Snow's segment and sang both sides of his first Sun single. The audience reaction was polite but not enthusiastic. When Jim Denny, head of Opry talent, suggested he go back to driving a truck, 19-year-old Elvis grew visibly upset. He was so upset that he left his clothes in a gas station restroom on the way home.

Two years later, Elvis experienced a similar audience reaction when he played the New Frontier Hotel in Vegas. As a result, his two-week engagement was cut to one week. Elvis swore that he would never play Vegas again, which, fortunately, was a vow he did not keep. In both cases, Elvis was the wrong performer for the audience. *Grand Ole Opry* audiences expected traditional country, not rockabilly; Vegas crowds expected pop music, not rock 'n' roll.

than $2,700,000 that year. For his films, he generally received a salary plus a percentage of the profits.

Attendance for Elvis' 1969 engagement at the International Hotel in Las Vegas topped 101,509, which broke existing Vegas attendance records. The gross receipts amounted to $1,522,635, which also set a record.

Elvis: Aloha from Hawaii was billed as "the first international satellite telecast." While TV satellite transmission had been used in the entertainment industry previously, it had never been done on such a scale, where a program taking place in one country was beamed to various countries across the world.

At the International, Elvis broke existing Vegas attendance and receipt records.

Liberace and his brother clown with Elvis backstage at the New Frontier Hotel, where Elvis flopped in '56.

BEST RUMORS AND MYTHS
The Mississippi-Alabama Fair and Dairy Show

THE MISSISSIPPI-Alabama Fair and Dairy Show looms large in the Elvis Presley story. In 1945, when he was ten years old, Elvis entered the fair's talent show, supposedly winning a prize for singing "Old Shep." In 1956, Elvis returned to the fair for two sold-out performances and donated the proceeds to the city of Tupelo. Tupelo used the money to purchase the Elvis Presley birthplace and to fund a youth center for the underprivileged children of the area. Taken together, the two incidents make a near perfect sentimental tale. The fair earns the distinction of inaugurating Elvis' career by bestowing an award on him long before anyone else discovered his talent, and the hometown boy validates the fair's judgment of him through his enormous success in 1956 and then returns to the scene of his initial triumph as a sign of gratitude.

Throughout most of Elvis' career and long after his death, the 1945 appearance at the fair was used as a benchmark to prove that he had talent and ambition from the beginning. In early tellings of the story, such as in his 1959 studio biography, he was declared to be the first-place winner of the talent show. As late as 1967, this version of the story was still trotted out for the press, specifically in publicity for the film *Double Trouble*. After Elvis died, biographies "corrected" the mistake by declaring that he had not won first

Vernon and Gladys Presley beam after Elvis' triumphant return to the Fair and Dairy Show in 1956.

Did ten-year-old Elvis really win a prize for singing "Old Shep" at the fair?

place. Instead, he took home second-place honors, which included $5 and free rides at the fair for the rest of the day.

To the surprise of most Elvis fans, who know his biography inside and out, a 1994 book by Bill Burk entitled *Early Elvis: The Tupelo Years* reveals that Elvis probably left the fair's talent show empty-handed. While conducting interviews for his book, Burk discovered that Shirley Gillentine Jones won first prize in 1945, Nubin Payne placed second, and an unidentified boy won third. In an old faded photo of the proceedings, the three winners show their prizes to the camera while a ten-year-old, sober-looking Elvis stands beside them. Elvis may have placed fourth or fifth, but he won no trophy, no money, and no free pass for the fair's rides. There was no mention of the talent show or its winners in the Tupelo newspaper. Apparently, they didn't think it was interesting enough. Digging through old newspaper articles, Burk uncovered an interview in which Gladys Presley offhandedly mentioned to Memphis reporter Robert Johnson that Elvis had come in fifth that day.

Ultimately, it matters little whether Elvis won a prize that day at the fair. The embellishment of this story reveals the way that a major piece of the Elvis Presley myth was woven from the mundane fabric of his everyday life.

BEST RUMORS AND MYTHS
A Record for His Mother's Birthday

A SHY, 18-YEAR-OLD Elvis Presley entered the Memphis Recording Service on a Saturday afternoon in the late summer of 1953. He was on a lunch break from Crown Electric, so he was driving the company pickup truck, which he parked in front of the recording studio. The motto of the studio was "We Record Anything—Anywhere—Anytime," and they meant it. For four dollars, anyone could walk in off the street and record a two-sided acetate, and that was precisely what Elvis had come to do.

Rock 'n' roll folklore holds that a naive young Elvis went to the studio that day to make a record for his mother's birthday. As late as 1968, an article by respected music critic Robert Hilburn about "The '68 Comeback Special" repeated this apocryphal story. Since Gladys Presley's birthday was April 25, however, the timing in this version of the story does not add up. While no one knows for sure what prompted Elvis to go to that studio, one likely explanation paints him as being more ambitious than he was shy and more shrewd than he was naive.

"We Record Anything—Anywhere—Anytime."

The Memphis Recording Service was one of several small businesses in Memphis that would have accommodated Elvis' request to make a record for a small fee. This particular business, however, was owned and operated by Sam Phillips, who also ran Sun Records, an independent record label that had been recording rhythm-and-blues artists for several years. In the early 1950s, rhythm and blues was called "race music," because R&B musicians were predominantly African-American. Phillips firmly believed that the rhythm-and-blues sound could win a mass audience, and he had been known to proclaim, "If I could find a white man who could sing with the sound and feel of a black man, I could make a billion dollars." Phillips' reputation was built on the recordings of R&B and blues artists, but he had just begun to work with country singers when Elvis walked into his recording service.

Elvis chose the Ink Spots' "My Happiness" for his first recording and backed it with another Ink Spots tune, "That's When Your Heartaches Begin." His choice of material—two songs by the Ink Spots, an established R&B group—suggests that Elvis knew of Phillips' statement, and he selected the producer's recording service in the hopes that Phillips would take notice. More than likely, Gladys' birthday was the last thing on his mind, because Elvis was looking to get discovered.

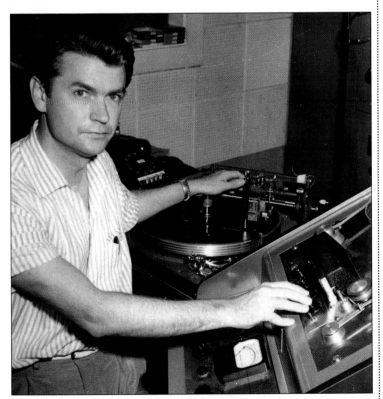

Unfortunately for Elvis, Sam Phillips was not behind the controls the first time he walked into the Memphis Recording Service.

BEST RUMORS AND MYTHS
Elvis the J.D.

IN 1956, ELVIS burst onto the national scene with the force of an explosion, knocking the country right off its feet. Looking back, it all seems so harmless, but Elvis appeared at a time when rock 'n' roll music was attacked in the popular press on a daily basis. During the spring and summer of 1956, many national magazines published articles that claimed a direct link between rock 'n' roll and juvenile delinquency. Elvis' music, his performing style, and his physical appearance were equated with the decadence of rock 'n' roll, which was blamed for the increase in juvenile sex and crime.

Rumors about Elvis were generated by those who wanted proof that he was a negative influence, and these rumors were spread in the press. Some of the stories are only slight embellishments of actual incidents, while others are so exaggerated that they border on hysteria. Teenage girls liked to have their arms and hands autographed by Elvis, but this harmless fad was depicted as an attempt by Elvis to seduce gullible girls. *Confidential* magazine warned girls to "beware of Elvis Presley's doll point pen," and claimed that he was coaxing young girls to take their shirts off so he could autograph their breasts with "Elvis on the Righty, Presley on the Lefty."

More than one rumor claimed that Elvis' sensual performing style had to be the result of some drug. Teenagers in Texas spread the rumor that he actually "peddled dope," while other stories insisted that he indulged in marijuana in order to work himself into the necessary frenzy that constituted his onstage performing style. Because of his personal appearance, which many reporters associated with the working-class South, there was an assumption that he had been in jail, and even "in and out of jail" several times.

Looking every bit the notorious rock 'n' roller, Elvis snarls for the cameras.

Real-life j.d.? Elvis is all smiles after being acquitted of assault and battery and disorderly conduct for a 1956 fight with two gas station attendants in Memphis.

The rumors were so rampant that reporters felt compelled to pursue them no matter how extreme they seemed. In doing so, they only brought more attention to the negative publicity plaguing Elvis. When New York television talk-show host Hy Gardner interviewed a weary Elvis via telephone, he brought up one of the more troublesome stories. "What about the rumor that you once shot your mother?" asked Hy, in all seriousness.

BEST RUMORS AND MYTHS
A Really Big Show

ELVIS APPEARED on *The Ed Sullivan Show* three times during the 1956–57 television season. On September 9, 1956, Charles Laughton substituted for Sullivan as host, because the legendary columnist and TV personality had been injured in a car accident. Sullivan himself hosted Elvis' October 28 appearance, and during his segment, the hot new singer was presented with a gold record for "Love Me Tender." However, it is Elvis' final appearance on *The Ed Sullivan Show* on January 6, 1957—in which the television cameras shot Elvis only from the waist up—that represents a cornerstone in the Elvis Presley mythology.

Speculation runs rampant as to why Sullivan and the censors chose to shoot Elvis from the waist up for his *third* appearance. He had been appearing on national television for a year, and though his TV performances usually created controversy, it seems that censoring him during his third appearance on the Sullivan show was akin to shutting the barn door after the horse had already escaped.

The most common explanation suggests that Sullivan had received more negative feedback from Elvis' earlier appear-

ances than he had expected. He wanted to prove that he was sensitive to those who found Elvis offensive, but he still needed the ratings that Elvis' appearance would generate. The waist-up-only edict seemed a viable solution to his dilemma. An alternative explanation is offered by David Marsh in his biography *Elvis*.

Behind the scenes of The Ed Sullivan Show, *Sullivan offers some advice for appearing on his program. The Colonel, wearing a genuine Elvis T-shirt, listens intently.*

He hints that Sullivan's actions were related to the antics of Colonel Tom Parker, who had supposedly forced Sullivan to apologize on the air for negative remarks made about Elvis during the previous summer. The waist-up-only order was Sullivan's retaliation. Jane and Michael Stern offer a humorous but dubious explanation in their book *Elvis World*. According to a director for *The Ed Sullivan Show*, Elvis had put a cardboard tube down the front of his pants during the October appearance and manipulated it in an overtly sexual way to make the studio audience scream. To avoid a repeated occurrence, a furious Sullivan ordered strictly above-the-waist coverage for Elvis' final engagement.

None of these explanations offers any insight into Sullivan's motivations, but all of them add to the folklore surrounding the event, thereby enhancing Elvis' notorious rock 'n' roll image from this stage of his career.

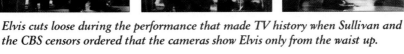

Elvis cuts loose during the performance that made TV history when Sullivan and the CBS censors ordered that the cameras show Elvis only from the waist up.

BEST RUMORS AND MYTHS
I Want to Be Your Teddy Bear

IN 1956 OR EARLY 1957, a rumor ran rampant that insisted Elvis collected teddy bears. Fanzines were thrilled at the contradiction that this bit of news seemed to indicate. What would a notorious, swivel-hipped rock 'n' roller be doing with a collection of teddy bears? It was fodder for fanzines and reporters for months. Fans sent Elvis teddy bears by the hundreds, which he in turn donated to children's hospitals or organizations such as the National Foundation for Infantile Paralysis. Publicity was then generated about his generosity, which prompted more teddy bears from his fans. A more perfect publicity gimmick could not have been invented.

Hedda Hopper claimed that the rumor was started when a reporter saw Elvis winning teddy bears for kids at a fair. Actually, Elvis' stunt of winning bears for kids at the Memphis Tri-State Fair was a result of the rumor—not the start of it. A much more likely explanation connects the teddy bear story to the shrewd promotional tactics of Colonel Tom Parker.

Not so coincidentally, the Colonel mentioned Elvis' alleged hobby in an interview on January 24, 1957—the very day that Elvis recorded the song "Teddy Bear." The song was one of the musical numbers in

Back in 1957, Elvis—the notorious rock 'n' roller—decorated his room in pink and accented it with stuffed animals.

Elvis just wants to be their teddy bear.

Loving You, which had just begun filming in Los Angeles. The tune "Teddy Bear" was supposedly written for Elvis by Kal Mann and Bernie Lowe because they had heard of his fondness for the stuffed creatures, though this tidbit of information may well have been invented. The publicity about Elvis' extensive teddy bear collection certainly didn't hurt the song's chances of hitting the top of the charts, which it did in July 1957.

The teddy bear rumor may have been more than just an attempt to bolster sales of the single or promote Elvis' recent movie. In 1957, the Colonel made an effort to counter the negative reports about juvenile delinquency that were swirling around "his boy" by presenting another side to Elvis Presley. That year Elvis attended charity events, donated large sums to charities, and gave away personal belongings to be auctioned for benefits. His solid relationship with his parents was given a high profile, and few articles failed to mention that he did not smoke, drink, or swear. The teddy bear rumor seems an extension of this effort to soften Elvis' notorious persona with positive publicity. After all, how could anyone attack a man who collects cuddly teddy bears and then gives them to sick kids?

BEST RUMORS AND MYTHS
Is Elvis Alive?

OFTEN, AFTER THE DEATH of a notable figure, rumors begin to spread that the person is not actually dead. Stories of this nature surfaced after the deaths of Adolf Hitler, James Dean, Jim Morrison, John Kennedy, and countless others whose lives had changed history or made a cultural impact. And so it was with Elvis Presley.

A masked Orion (Jimmy Ellis) fueled the Elvis rumors by performing incognito.

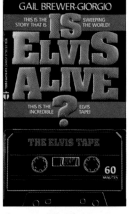

A tape with Elvis' voice (supposedly) was included with each book.

Rumors began to stir in 1979 when Gail Brewer-Giorgio wrote a novel titled *Orion,* in which the main Presley-like character arranged his own death in order to find peace and privacy. The novel generated very little attention, except that unknown singer Jimmy Ellis took the name Orion after the character in the book and then recorded several albums. For several years, he performed in public in a mask to hide his true identity, though whether he was trying to get audiences to believe he was Elvis is not known. In 1981, a book by Steven C. Chanzes claimed that a terminally ill Elvis impersonator had been interred at Graceland—not Elvis. Brewer-Giorgio's novel and Chanzes' book both flopped, and any rumors that had begun to surface about Elvis quickly faded.

In 1987, Brewer-Giorgio revived the rumors once again with her self-published book *The Most Incredible Elvis Presley Story Ever Told.* In this book, she claimed her novel *Orion* failed because it had been squelched by important Presley people. It seems the novel had gotten too close to the truth. Her claims that Elvis was still alive were based on a few unexplained mysteries in Elvis' life that she supposedly researched and then explained. Her book was republished the next year as *Is Elvis Alive?,* and her position was supported by Texas-based record producer Major Bill Smith. The resulting publicity started a full-scale media blitz, culminating in Elvis sightings in fast-food restaurants, at cheap motels, and even at Chernobyl shortly after the nuclear disaster. Explanations as to why Elvis would fake his own death ranged from his desire for peace and privacy to his need to escape the death threats stemming from his work as a government agent. Many Elvis fans were appalled at the way the rumors exploited Elvis, while the media claimed the craze was caused by fans who refused to let him die. Brewer-Giorgio managed another book out of the hype surrounding her, while two syndicated TV specials were produced before the furor died down.

Why did the media go to such lengths to fuel the rumors with publicity, specials, and "news" reports? Why did the rumors spark the collective imagination of the general public? The real mystery of this story seems to stem not from Elvis but from the public's intense fascination with the ridiculous rumors.

BEST COLLECTIBLES: 1950s

ELVIS PRESLEY LIPSTICKS

Elvis Presley Enterprises was established in the summer of 1956 by Colonel Tom Parker in a deal with Hank Saperstein. Saperstein had successfully merchandised Wyatt Earp, the Lone Ranger, Lassie, and other icons of American pop culture. The Colonel and Saperstein approved 18 licensees, who produced about 30 products. Among them were Elvis Presley Lipsticks, which Saperstein claimed would be so popular "they would walk off the counter."

Shades included Hound Dog Orange, Heartbreak Pink, Cruel Red, Tender Pink, Tutti Frutti Red, and Love-ya Fuschia. Each lipstick came attached to a card with a picture of Elvis and the tag line, "Keep me always on your lips." The lipsticks are a popular collectible today, partly because the colors were named after Elvis songs. A tube attached to the original card is quite valuable, while the lipstick chart that lists all the colors is extremely rare.

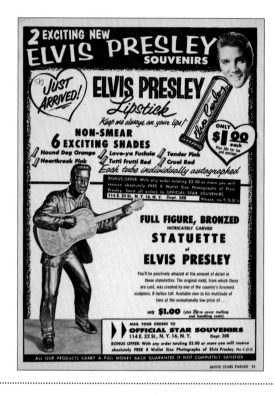

ELVIS PRESLEY SNEAKERS

After the Saperstein deal, fans could literally dress themselves from head to toe—hats to shoes—in Elvis Presley merchandise. Elvis Presley Enterprises licensed the Randolph Manufacturing Company to make Elvis canvas sneakers in 1956.

Two different colors were available, a green and black pair and a black and white pair. The former are the most valuable, though sneakers in both colors are rare and highly sought collectibles. The tan-colored box that the sneakers came in featured a photo of Elvis on the front and the back. The photo on the front was a shot of Elvis performing, which was the famous pose used on his first album cover. The photo on the back was a dreamy portrait, with "Love Me Tender" printed at the top and Elvis' signature at the bottom. The box is now considered extremely rare. A pair of sneakers in the box is currently worth between $1,350 and $1,500. (*Left:* Elvis and merchandiser Hank Saperstein show off an Elvis sneaker.)

ELVIS PRESLEY RECORD PLAYER

Two models of the "Elvis Presley Autograph" record player were produced in the fall of 1956 by RCA Victor. Both were covered with blue vinyl contrasted with a light blue-gray tweed material, and both were distinguished by Elvis' signature, which was stamped in gold on the top.

The more sophisticated model, which sold for $47.95, could play up to fourteen 45-rpm records automatically. Those on a budget could put down one dollar and pay one dollar per week at participating RCA dealers. A bonus was included with this model in the form of an Elvis three-record EP set that featured 12 songs.

The other record player was a four-speed model that cost $32.95, or 75 cents down and 75 cents per week. The less expensive model came with a two-record EP set with eight songs. Both record players came with an instruction booklet titled "How to Use and Enjoy Your RCA Victor Elvis Presley Automatic 45 Victrola Portable Phonograph."

LOVE ME TENDER NECKLACE

Several pieces of jewelry were manufactured by Elvis Presley Enterprises in 1956, including a charm bracelet, a pair of earrings, a pin, and the Love Me Tender necklace. The necklace was issued to coincide with the release of Elvis' first movie, though nothing about the design of the trinket relates to the film.

Available in a gold or silver finish, the heart-shaped pendant bore an engraving of Elvis playing the guitar. The card to which the necklace was attached is dark blue and white and contains a printed list that names four of Elvis' songs from 1956.

The necklace and card together make a nice keepsake commemorating that all-important year for Elvis. The gold finish version is slightly more valuable than the silver finish to collectors today, and a necklace still attached to its card increases the value of the item by almost twice as much.

BEST COLLECTIBLES: 1950s

THE PINK ITEMS

In 1956, Elvis Presley Enterprises issued an autograph book, diary, scrapbook, photo album, and record case as a set of must-have accessories for every teenage girl. All of the items were dusty pink and featured the same black line drawing of Elvis with white highlights. The collectibles are commonly referred to as the pink items. The material used to make the items was a simulated leather called "leatherette."

The drawing was based on the photo that adorned the cover of his first album, *Elvis Presley*. A small hound dog also graced the covers, which was a reference to Elvis' biggest hit single of 1956.

The scrapbook and photo album are the largest items in the set, but the diary is extremely difficult to find, making it the most valuable collectible.

THE ELVIS PRESLEY HAT AND HEAD SCARF

The 1950s was an era of crew cuts and curly pony tails, and Elvis Presley Enterprises licensed several hats and scarves to take advantage of the fashions of the day. The head scarves, which were made of a blend of rayon and silk, featured a four-color print of Elvis. The largest scarves measured 32 inches square and cost under $2. Women's kerchiefs and hankies were also available, as was a more exotic-looking form of head gear—the Elvis turban! Comfortable and casual, crew hats became popular among teenage boys. Even Elvis was known to don one on occasion. Elvis Presley Enterprises sold two different styles of gabardine crew hats. Both featured titles of popular Elvis songs in the wide band around the crown. The more common style included a portrait of Elvis inside a yellow burst; the other showed a picture of Elvis clasping his hands by his face. The latter is currently higher in value, and both hats inflate in value if the original price tag is still attached.

ELVIS PRESLEY BUBBLE GUM CARDS

In 1956, Elvis Presley Enterprises authorized the Topps Gum Company to produce a set of Elvis cards to add to its line of collectors cards. The color cards sold in packages of five for a nickel, bubble gum included. Single cards sold for a penny.

The complete set contains 66 cards, which are divided into two parts. The first set includes cards 1–46 and is referred to as the Ask Elvis Series. Each card in this part features a question for Elvis and his answer and signature on the back. Cards 47–66 depict scenes from Elvis' first film, *Love Me Tender*, and feature details about the movie on the backs.

All of the cards are colorized black-and-white photographs. Counterfeit reproductions of this set of cards were produced in black and white, which makes them incredibly easy for collectors to identify.

TEDDY BEAR PERFUME

Teen-Age, Inc., came up with Elvis Presley's "Teddy Bear" Eau de Parfum in 1957, licensed by Elvis Presley Enterprises. The name was undoubtedly inspired by the success of Elvis' hit single, "Teddy Bear," as well as by the rumors that he collected teddy bears.

The tall, slender bottle with a white cap featured a photo of a smiling Elvis from the mid-1950s. The perfume came in a plain yellow box with a look that was sup-posed to simulate cork. There was no writing on the box.

Later, Elvis Presley's "Teddy Bear" Eau de Parfum was reissued with the bottles bearing a 1957 copyright. However, the photo of Elvis on the label was clearly from the 1960s. Also, the bottle shape is square, and the cap is a metallic color. The date of reissue is not known, but the reissued perfume is worth considerably less than the original.

BEST COLLECTIBLES: 1950s

ELVIS PRESLEY GUITAR

Elvis was credited with starting a boom in guitar sales that reached mammoth proportions by 1957. Elvis himself generally used his guitar more as a prop than a musical instrument, but popular imagery of the era usually associated him with a guitar. That year, Elvis Presley Enterprises licensed the Emenee Music Company to manufacture several different toy guitars bearing Elvis' name and likeness.

The "Teddy Bear" and "Hound Dog" models origi-nally sold for $12 and came in both four-string and six-string versions. The "Love Me Tender" guitar was more elaborate. The two-tone plastic body measured about three feet long and came in a carrying case. The "Love Me Tender" model, which was sold only through Sears stores and catalogs, also included a small songbook and an automatic chord player. The four-string versions of all three guitars are more rare and therefore more valuable.

DOG TAG JEWELRY

To commemorate Elvis' induction into the army, or more likely to exploit it, Elvis Presley Enterprises issued jewelry reproductions of his dog tags, complete with his proper serial number—55310761. The dog tag jewelry included two styles of bracelets, sweater holders, anklets, necklaces, and key chains. The jewelry featured a chrome finish over a brass base.

Currently, the sweater holder is the most valuable piece. Several years ago, many boxes of dog tag jewelry were uncovered, and consequently, the jewelry is not as valuable as other Elvis collectibles. The dog tags remain popular items, however, because they represent Elvis' stint in the service.

In 1977, reproductions were produced, which were not made of chrome over a brass base but instead were tinted gold. The originals have a copyright date of 1956, though they were not issued until 1958.

TEENZINES

Among the most delightful of all magazines about Elvis Presley are the teenzines (teen magazines) from the mid to late 1950s. They are also among the most valuable because they cover the burgeoning days of rock 'n' roll, an exciting period in American popular culture. This period is of interest to a variety of collectors in addition to the Elvis fan.

Teenzines fall into two groups: single publications that focus entirely on Elvis Presley and regularly issued magazines that feature cover articles about Elvis. One of the most sought-after single-issue magazines is *Elvis Presley: Hero or Heel?*, which addresses the question all parents wanted to know in 1956. Another is *Elvis Answers Back*, which included a 78 rpm flexi-disc recording with the voice of Elvis attached to the magazine. The most colorful regularly issued teenzines of the era include *Dig* and *Hep Cats*.

MOVIE MEMORABILIA

Elvis' first four films represent the oldest and most popular phase of his film career, making the 1950s movie memorabilia the most valuable. The most sought-after movie collectible is probably the one-sheet—a poster that measures 27×41 inches. At almost $800, the one-sheet for *Jailhouse Rock* is the most valuable. Lobby cards, which measure 22×28 inches and come in sets of eight, follow one-sheets in popularity. Complete lobby-card sets for the 1950s movies are scarce, making them worth a great deal. The set from *Love Me Tender* is valued at about $850. However, the set was reissued after Elvis died, and the reissues, which are marked with an R preceding the date in the lower right corner, are not nearly as valuable. Generally speaking, the memorabilia for *Jailhouse Rock* is the most valuable of Elvis' films. The movie *King Creole* was rereleased in 1959, with a whole new set of posters and lobby cards. The 1959 memorabilia is not as valuable but features a better selection of images.

BEST COLLECTIBLES: 1960s AND 1970s

RCA POCKET CALENDARS

From 1963 through 1980, RCA Records printed pocket calendars with Elvis' picture on one side and a 12-month calendar on the other. To promote good will, as well as Elvis' singles and albums, RCA issued the calendars to fan clubs and to record stores as give-aways for their customers. Versions of the calendars were printed for foreign markets as well, including Germany and Japan. The promotion proved to be a popular one, particularly after Elvis died. The rarest and most valuable

calendar is the 1963 issue, while those from the years 1976 to 1980 are worth less than any others. In 1980, RCA celebrated 25 years of releasing Elvis Presley records. They issued authentic reproductions of all 18 calendars for individuals who ordered the 25th Anniversary limited-edition Elvis Presley box set. The reproductions feature small imperfections and differences, making it possible to spot the reissues. The pocket calendars remain a popular RCA collectible because they are inexpensive and part of a series.

RCA CATALOGS AND BONUS PHOTOS

Promoter extraordinaire Colonel Tom Parker convinced RCA that they should more actively tout their top artist by offering slick-looking annual catalogs to list available Elvis records. Issued throughout Elvis' career, the catalogs were compact booklets that not only promoted Elvis' music but were also collectibles. Some were printed vertically and stapled in the spine, and others were printed horizontally and spiral-bound. RCA also offered bonus photos

with many of Elvis' albums though only for a limited time. Sometimes, bonus photos served the same function as the catalogs because lists or photos of available Elvis albums were printed on the backs to promote the singer's records. Because they were offered for a limited time, bonus photos have a higher value than the catalogs. Currently, the photos offered in the *Gold Records Volume 4* and *It Happened at the World's Fair* albums are worth over $100, making them the most valuable.

HOLIDAY POSTCARDS

Every year at Christmas, Colonel Tom Parker printed greeting cards as gestures to fan clubs, lesser business associates, the media, and miscellaneous contacts. Occasionally, one of these postcards ended up as a bonus in an Elvis album. Sometimes Elvis was pictured alone on the cards, but often the Colonel was pictured alongside him, usually in a Santa Claus suit. As the years went by, stranger versions of the annual Christmas postcard began to appear. One card from the early 1970s showed Elvis performing in his white jumpsuit on a snowy rooftop while the Colonel, dressed in a Santa suit, popped out of the chimney. The most valuable are the two Christmas cards issued while Elvis was in Germany. The Colonel had Easter postcards printed between 1966 and 1969, though they lack the humor and imagination of most of the Christmas cards. The holiday postcards are an interesting collectible because they typify the Colonel's carny-style promotional tactics.

MOVIE MEMORABILIA

All but four of Elvis' narrative films were released in the 1960s, so movie collectibles best represent his career during this decade. One-sheet movie posters and lobby card sets remain the most popular collectibles, because they are relatively easy to obtain. Perhaps the most entertaining movie collectibles are the miscellaneous items given away as promotion. Each movie slated for promotional gimmicks inspired a different trinket, with the wackier items bearing the mark of the Colonel. Some of the most interesting items include a lei with a color photo of Elvis to promote *Blue Hawaii*, pens with feather tips to advertise *Tickle Me*, and a brown paper army hat to tout *G.I. Blues*. When the promo items for *It Happened at the World's Fair* ran out, the Colonel struck a quick deal with a novelty manufacturer to make Psycho-Sticks—two flimsy sticks that were rubbed together to spin a propeller on the end of one of the sticks. While certainly a memorable promo item, they bore absolutely no connection to the movie.

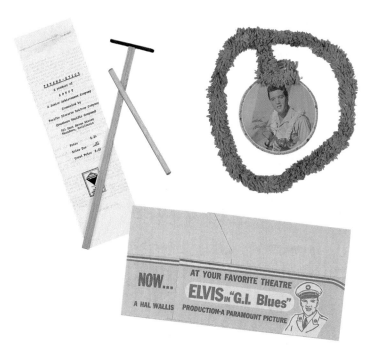

BEST COLLECTIBLES: 1960s AND 1970s

BOOKS INTO MOVIES

Elvis' movies are frequently criticized as quickly produced, formulaic musical comedies written by Hollywood hacks. While some of his films had original stories, many were based on popular novels. In general, books that were made into movies are desirable collectibles, and those that inspired Elvis' movies are no exception. Several of the books are difficult to find today, though most are not very valuable. The paperback version of *Wild in the Country*, written by J.R.

Salamanca, is perhaps the most sought after because the cover shows a photo of Elvis and costar Hope Lange. Other books include *A Stone for Danny Fisher* by Harold Robbins *(King Creole); Charro!* by Harry Whittington; *Pioneer, Go Home* by Richard Powell *(Follow That Dream); Flaming Lance* by Clair Huffaker *(Flaming Star); Kid Galahad* by Francis Wallace; *Mister, Will You Marry Me?* by Frederick Kohner *(Girls! Girls! Girls!);* and *Chautauqua* by Day Keene and Dwight Babcock *(The Trouble with Girls).*

'68 COMEBACK SPECIAL PROMOTIONS

Elvis, the 1968 television special sponsored entirely by the Singer Company, marked a turning point in Elvis' career. The success of the special inspired him to return to live performances and helped revive his recording career. In retrospect, the program was his finest hour, and it is known in Presley lore and literature as "The '68 Comeback Special."

Promotions for *Elvis* were not particularly clever or attractive, but they are wor-

thy because of the special's significance. The best collectible is a 32-page, 4×9-inch booklet that listed every television station carrying Elvis' special on December 3, 1968, and every radio station airing his half-hour Christmas radio special, also sponsored by Singer, two days later. Other "Comeback Special" collectibles include electric store displays of the album cover, posters, ads for the special, and insert cards given away at Singer stores.

ALBERT HAND PUBLICATIONS

One of the most collected publications about Elvis Presley is a fan club magazine from England titled *Elvis Monthly*. Albert Hand, who was the president of the Official Elvis Presley Fan Club of Great Britain, launched the magazine in February 1960. The first 18 issues were 5½×8½ inches and contained 24 pages, but the size was changed permanently to 5×7 inches with 32 pages in August 1961. The content consisted of fluffy, fan-targeted stories about Elvis and his family, but the professional-looking production values made this fan publication highly respected. Todd Slaughter took over the presidency of the fan club and the publication of *Elvis Monthly* after Hand died in 1972.

From 1963 to 1982, *Elvis Monthly* issued an annual covering Elvis' activities for that year. The hard-cover annual, titled *Elvis Special*, featured rare photos, cartoons, poetry, and complete lists of every Elvis song, single, and album released in England.

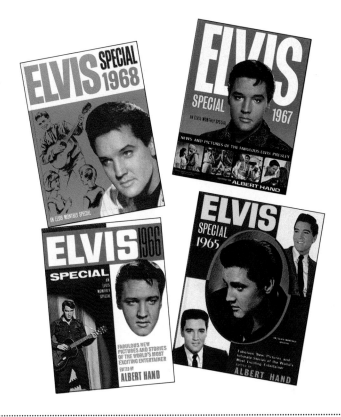

CONCERT SOUVENIRS

After Elvis returned to live performances in 1969, a whole new field of collectibles appeared. Whenever Elvis performed, souvenir stands were erected in the lobbies of venues where he appeared in concert. The souvenir stands sold tour books, pennants, posters, pins, scarves, and other trinkets.

Among the better concert souvenirs were the tour books, also called concert photo folios. Because a new tour book was featured every year, they serve as a chronicle of this phase of his career. Usually 16 or 24 pages in length, the tour books contained color photos of Elvis in performance. Shows at the Las Vegas Hilton always generated additional souvenirs in the form of menus, vinyl or cardboard promo disks that hung from the ceiling, mobiles, and postcards. The menus have since become popular and very valuable collectibles, while the promo disks (which were stolen by adventurous fans from the ceiling areas of the Hilton) have become much sought-after collectibles.

BEST COLLECTIBLES: 1960S AND 1970S

SCARVES

Elvis established the tradition of tossing scarves and towels to the fans in the audience as soon as he began appearing in concert in Las Vegas in the summer of 1969. In the beginning, he threw one or two of his sweat-soaked scarves into the audience per performance. As the habit turned into a ritual, dozens were hurled during each show. Sometimes, fans walked down to the edge of the stage, and Elvis would hand them a scarf. Occasionally, he might pick some lucky soul out of the audience and place the scarf around her neck before kissing her.

Anyone who ended up with the scarves now owns an irreplaceable collectible that is priceless. More than memorabilia, a scarf from Elvis' hands is a virtual relic of a performer whose concerts represented extraordinary personal experiences for the members of the audience. Scarves with Elvis' name printed on them were sold at the souvenir stands in the lobby for those not lucky enough to receive one from Elvis himself.

MATHEY-TISSOT WATCH

The Mathey-Tissot wristwatch represents one of the first jewelry items that Elvis had custom designed. A tastefully designed man's watch that displayed the date, the timepiece featured the name "Elvis Presley" on the beveled edge that encircled the face. Elvis gave the watches as gestures of respect and fellowship to friends and acquaintances.

After being honored as one of the Jaycees' Outstanding Young Men of the Year, Elvis hosted a cocktail party at Graceland for the other nine honorees, and he presented each of them with a Mathey-Tissot watch as they came through the door. A mix-up ensued, and Elvis accidentally gave one to an assistant transportation chairman for the Jaycees. Elvis was embarrassed but would not ask the Jaycee to give the watch back, lest he would embarrass the man as well. Instead, he ordered an additional watch for the ninth honoree. Today, any of the Mathey-Tissot Elvis Presley watches are worth at least $5,000.

BEST COLLECTIBLES: POST 1977

UNUSED CONCERT TICKETS

Elvis was scheduled to leave on another grinding road trip of one-nighters on August 17, 1977. In poor physical shape, he was not looking forward to yet another tour, at least according to some of those around him. He had just completed a tour in June of that year, with his last performance at Market Square Arena in Indianapolis, Indiana, on June 26.

Around 2:00 P.M. on August 16, Elvis Presley was found dead at Graceland. Many of the shows on the tour that never happened were completely sold out or close to it. After the announcement of Elvis' death, promoters offered a refund for ticket buyers. Many fans chose not to return their tickets, keeping them as souvenirs. The fans' reluctance to receive a refund caused a great deal of confusion for promoters who had to account for their losses, pay cancellation fees, etc. Later, many fans decided to sell their tickets for many times the face value.

MEMORIAL ISSUES OF NEWSPAPERS AND MAGAZINES

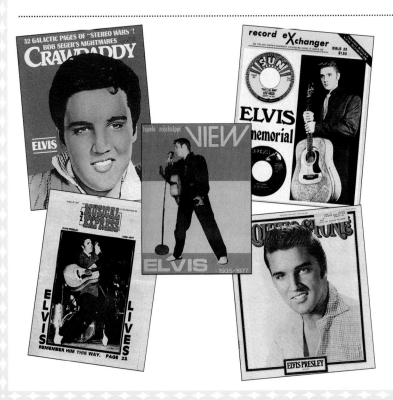

News of Elvis' death dominated the front pages of major newspapers around the country, pushing other prominent stories off the page. These editions of many newspapers have become highly desired collectibles, particularly Elvis' two hometown newspapers. *The Commercial Appeal*'s headline offered a conventional news headline: "Death Captures Crown of Rock and Roll— Elvis Dies Apparently After Heart Attack." By contrast, the *Memphis Press-Scimitar*'s headline read more like a eulogy: "A Lonely Life Ends on Elvis Presley Boulevard." Both of these editions are reprinted regularly, which devalues the originals. The newspapers are not valuable, but they are popular souvenirs among fans. Memorial editions of music magazines such as *Rolling Stone, New Musical Express,* and *Crawdaddy* also make worthy collectibles. Elvis was largely ignored by these magazines in life, but after his death, they assessed and analyzed his contributions to popular music and culture.

BEST COLLECTIBLES: POST 1977

ALWAYS ELVIS SOUVENIRS

"Always Elvis" was a ten-day convention staged by the Colonel and Vernon Presley near the first anniversary of Elvis' death in 1978. Held at the Hilton in Las Vegas on September 1–10, it marked the first organized convention of any type to commemorate Elvis. That year, fans had journeyed to Memphis to pay their respects, but there were no official ceremonies or activities. Typical of the Colonel's approach to marketing, "Always Elvis" featured banners, buttons, photos, programs, copies of a poem that the Colonel had written about Elvis, and other souvenirs—all for a nominal fee. A highlight of the convention was the unveiling of a statue honoring Elvis at the Las Vegas Hilton. After that year, activities were organized in Memphis each August as a tribute to Elvis. The ceremonies and activities grew more elaborate with each passing year. However, the Colonel rarely became actively involved again as per the outcome of the lawsuit brought against him by the Presley estate.

LIQUOR DECANTERS

After Elvis died, McCormick Distilling Company of Weston, Missouri, began issuing liquor decanters in the form of Elvis Presley figurines. The decanters were expensive collectibles even at the time of manufacture and were sold to liquor stores or directly through McCormick Distilling. The suggested retail price at the time was $199.95 per decanter, but many are worth much more. The decanters were often issued in series, with each figurine representing an important phase or key event in Elvis' life or career. One popular series, entitled Elvis' Musical Pets, consisted of figurines of Elvis singing to animals that might remind fans of one of his songs. The series included "Elvis & Hound Dog," which depicted Elvis singing to a basset hound, just as he did on *The Steve Allen Show* in 1956. The base of the decanter was a music box that played "Hound Dog." Another in the series was "Elvis' Teddy Bear," which was in reference to the popular song from *Loving You.*

DOLLS

Dolls of Elvis Presley have been issued as far back as 1956, when Elvis Presley Enterprises licensed a rubber doll in a plaid shirt and jeans—clothing that Elvis himself never wore. The 1956 Elvis Presley doll is now a valuable collectible, perhaps because the "magic skin" that covered the upper torso was made of a lightweight rubber that deteriorated with age. Thus, few exist in good condition.

After Elvis' death, other dolls were manufactured that look more like him. Most of these dolls were made of

durable material, such as vinyl or porcelain, and were intended to be collectibles. The Elvis Presley Limited Doll Series by World Dolls is arguably the most highly regarded series because of the close resemblance to Elvis. The models for the series were sculpted by a noted doll portraitist named Joyce Christopher. Each issue in the series constituted a limited edition and featured Elvis in a different jumpsuit. Some of the pieces included "Flame," "Phoenix," and "All American Elvis."

COMMEMORATIVE PLATES

Several companies have manufactured collector plates since Elvis' death. In 1977, Factors Etc. and the Colonel's company, Boxcar Enterprises, licensed a French company called Limoges to make a commemorative plate with a lithograph of Elvis in brown ink. The expensive Royal Orleans series of collector plates and figurines depicted Elvis in his best-known concerts or jumpsuits. Each plates or figurine was limited to a run of 20,000. The Bradford Exchange, a specialist in collector plates, has done a number of Presley plates over the years, and they are probably the most well known. Among their limited-edition Presley collectibles was the Elvis Presley: Looking at a Legend Series, which included "Heartbreak Hotel" by Nate Giorgio and "Elvis at the Gate of Graceland" by Bruce Emmett. Among Elvis fans, the plates of artist Susie Morton were very well liked. Her richly colored and detailed plate portraits were sold by Ernst.

BEST COLLECTIBLES: POST 1977

BRONZE SCULPTURE

Noted artist Bill Rains interpreted Elvis' career through his bronze sculpture "Journey to Graceland." Three distinct images of Elvis performing are captured in one piece. On one side, a young Elvis sings to the beat of rock 'n' roll as he strums his guitar. Another side features Elvis in a jumpsuit and a cape, which represents his early years in Las Vegas. The final image depicts Elvis in a dramatic pose from his later Vegas period. Three castings of "Journey to Graceland" were done. Bronze I stood 41 inches high and was limited to 42 castings, making those pieces the most rare. Bronze II measured 18 inches high and was released in an edition of 142 castings, while Bronze III topped off at 12 inches in an edition of 1,042 castings. The more castings in an edition, the less valuable the individual pieces. Originally, the Bronze I pieces sold for $25,000 each. "Journey to Graceland" represents an effort to market a tasteful, high-end collectible.

COLLECTORS CARDS

During the 1970s, a relatively new manufacturer of collectors cards, the Donruss Company, was struggling against their main competitor, the Topps Gum Company. In 1978, the license to make Elvis Presley collectors cards was given to the Donruss Company, primarily because they were based in Memphis—Elvis' hometown. The Donruss set includes 66 cards that use both color and black-and-white photos. On October 15, 1992, the River Group released the first of three 220-card series of Elvis Celebrity Cards. The 660 cards were sold individually or in 12-card packs. The cards sold for $1.50 a packet, though prices were inflated almost immediately because they were touted as collectibles. The front of the cards featured photos, with biographical information about Elvis printed on the back. The Donruss cards do not have the same popularity with collectors as the 1956 Topps cards. However, the Topps, Donruss, and River Group sets represent three decades of Elvis cards and offer an interesting comparison and contrast for collectors.

ELVIS WINE

Elvis wine provides an example of the attitude toward the merchandising of Elvis in the months after he died. Most fans know that Elvis rarely, if ever, drank alcohol, so his image and name on a bottle of wine seems out of character. This point was not lost on Colonel Tom Parker, who claimed, "Elvis never drank wine, but if he did, this is the wine he would have ordered."

The Colonel, who had a large measure of control in the licensing, was not very discerning about what type of products were approved. In addition, bootleggers manufactured Elvis products illegally to make a quick dollar off the fans. As a result, many items were produced that were ill-suited to Elvis' image or were just plain tasteless—Elvis Presley Sweat, for instance.

Despite the incompatibility of Elvis and alcohol, the Elvis wine and bottles remain a popular collectible among fans. No longer manufactured, the spritzy white wine was available in 1979 through Boxcar Enterprises, which imported it from Italy via Frontenac Vineyards.

ELVIS COLOGNE

During the 1980s and 1990s, a fashion trend for celebrity perfumes accounted for fragrances named after and endorsed by everyone from Cher to Elizabeth Taylor. At the height of that trend, the Presley estate authorized Elvis cologne, which was issued by Elvis Fragrances, Inc., of Atlanta. Though Elvis cologne was part of a trend, it also harkened back to 1957, when Teen-Age Inc. manufactured Elvis Presley's "Teddy Bear" Eau de Parfum. The Elvis cologne and the Teddy Bear perfume make a pair of significant collectibles, because they are similar items manufactured at different phases of Elvis' career. The former was part of a merchandizing blitz designed to help make Elvis a household name among mainstream audiences, while the latter is in response to his status as a pop culture legend. Teddy Bear perfume was marketed to teenagers, which is apparent from the name and the photo of Elvis on the label. Elvis cologne was marketed to mature men, as indicated by the tasteful packaging and abstract design.

BEST COLLECTIBLES: POST 1977

ELVIS STAMP

Issued by the U.S. Postal Service on January 8, 1993, the Elvis stamp quickly became a popular and inexpensive bit of memorabilia. The stamp ballot, which featured illustrations of the two final stamp designs, has also become a desired collectible. The post office also offered a sheet of 40 stamps in a sleeve that looked like an album cover. Fans soon developed their own schemes for unique stamp collectibles, including writing erroneous addresses on Presley-stamped envelopes so they would be marked "Returned to Sender."

The ultimate collectible is a pad. All stamps are shipped from the printers to the U.S. Postal Service in units called pads, which contain 4,000 stamps. No pad has ever been offered for sale to the public. Before the Elvis stamps went on sale, however, some pads were evidently slipped to collectors, complete with interoffice instructions and warnings from the U.S. Postal Service not to sell any stamps before the designated day. These intact pads are currently worth $2,000.

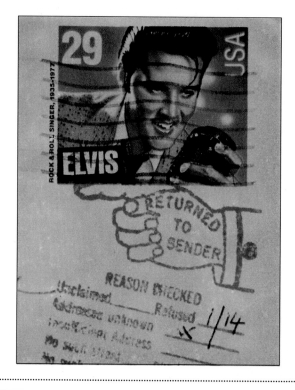

VELVET PAINTINGS

Much Elvis Presley memorabilia over the years has been less than sophisticated or less than tasteful. Some of these gauche items are getting a second look from collectors, including velvet paintings. Of particular interest is the work of fine artists such as Julian Schnabel and Eleanor Dickinson, who began to work in black velvet to blur the line between high art and popular art. A 1994 book entitled *Black Velvet: The Art We Love to Hate* by Jennifer Heath focused attention on painting on velvet, which began in Persia centuries ago. The paintings became kitsch in the 1930s when Mexican-based companies began mass-producing them. One well-known black velvet painting is a giant Elvis *(pictured)* by David Swierz and Dennis Scott. Commissioned by Chicago radio personality Buzz Kilman for his band to use in their stage show, it has been displayed in several Elvis art exhibitions. Why does black velvet attract artists to paint subjects like Elvis, John Wayne, and Clint Eastwood? According to Heath, it is because velvet is the medium of heroes.

Best Bumper Stickers

BEST ELVIS PHENOMENA
Tribute Week

MEMPHIS IN THE MONTH of August finds most natives seeking relief from the sweltering heat and humidity, but the city is generally teeming with tourists who brave the temperatures to attend Tribute Week. Each year on the anniversary of Elvis' death, thousands of fans make the pilgrimage to Memphis to commemorate the life and career of Elvis Presley. Tribute Week began unofficially the first year after Elvis' death when fans showed up in mid-August and mingled outside the music gates at Graceland. That same year, Colonel Tom Parker, with Vernon Presley in tow, held a tribute called "Always Elvis" in Las Vegas. The Colonel's event drew little interest from the fans,

Fans converge on Graceland to participate in the candlelight ceremony.

however, and he never organized another.

Currently, Tribute Week consists of seven days of activities, memorials, and gatherings. Fans visit Graceland, Humes Junior High School, Sun Studio, Beale Street, and lesser-known Presley haunts such as Lauderdale Courts and Poplar Tunes. The city welcomes the Elvis fans, who have helped turn Memphis into a thriving tourist

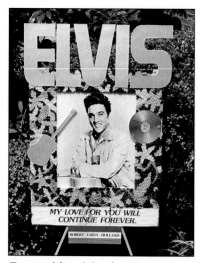

Fans and fan clubs often leave unusual commemorative pieces at Graceland during Tribute Week.

mecca. Other activities include Elvis trivia contests, impersonator contests, collectibles conventions, and book signings by Elvis biographers.

The festivities culminate in a candlelight ceremony, which is the emotional high point of Tribute Week. This ritual has been enacted in some form or another every year since Elvis' death. On the evening of August 15, fans gather in front of the music gates. Elvis' music is piped over a loudspeaker as people mingle and swap Elvis stories before lining up along the graffiti-covered wall. At 11:00 P.M., two or more Graceland employees walk down to the gates with a torch that has been lit from the eternal flame that marks Elvis' grave. As the gates open, the fans, each with their own lighted candle, climb silently and reverently up the hill behind the house, where they walk single file past the grave site. The procession often takes as long as six hours to pass through Meditation Garden. It is not only a gesture of respect for Elvis, but it is proof that Elvis' fans are as faithful after his death as they were during his lifetime.

Meditation Garden during Tribute Week is a sea of flowers.

BEST ELVIS PHENOMENA
Impersonators

THE ELVIS PRESLEY impersonators are probably the most curious off-shoot of the collective desire to keep his name and music alive. Many people are surprised to learn that Elvis impersonators existed long before his death. As far back as 1957, a fanzine article listing 25 important facts about Elvis Presley mentioned that he was the most impersonated entertainer in the world. In 1958, a *Life* magazine article remarked on the increasing number of Elvis imitators in other countries, such as Germany and Japan. Elvis was said to have enjoyed the idea that there were professional Presley impersonators.

After Elvis died in 1977, the impersonation phenomenon blossomed into a mini-industry, and in recent years, the impersonators have become so removed from the real Elvis that they exist as an entity unto themselves. Although various media have taken to ridiculing the phenomenon and, by extension, the fans who enjoy it, no fans expect the impersonators to be as talented or as charismatic as Elvis, or even to look exactly like him. Although fans don't expect impersonators to take Elvis' place, they do enjoy them as a way to remember and relive the excitement of one of Elvis' live performances.

An impersonator's act consists entirely of imitating Elvis' singing and performing style, his appearance, and his mannerisms and speech patterns. Some of the impersonators have had plastic surgery to make their faces and bodies resemble the real Elvis as much as possible. Many have combined their

Singer Rick Saucedo became one of the first Elvis impersonators to garner attention.

names with a part of Elvis' name, including Elvis Bobby Bradshaw, Eric "Elvis" Domino, El Vez, Rob Elvis Dye, El-Ray-Vis, Joe Elvis, Rick Presley, and Jerry El. Most imitators choose to emulate the Las Vegas Elvis, exaggerating the look of that era with coal-black hair, massive sideburns, and the ever-present white jumpsuit. Few imitators try to look like the Elvis of the 1950s or 1960s, an exception being Trent Carlini, who does a mean interpretation of a young Elvis.

Just after Elvis' death, most of the impersonators were professional entertainers with singing and stage experience. Nightclubs and stage reviews hired performers such as Chicago's Rick Saucedo because of their serious interpretation of Elvis' talents. As the years progressed, more and more amateurs joined the ranks of the impersonators, turning this legitimate part of show business into a cultural phenomenon. No longer do the impersonators have to look or sound like Elvis. There are female Elvis impersonators, including Janice K.; black Elvis impersonators, such as Clearance Giddens; and child Elvis impersonators, including little Miguel Quintana.

At one point, the Elvis Presley estate attempted to bring legal action against the impersonators for violating the copyright on Elvis' name and image, but there were so many of them that the lawsuit was dropped. The estate, like most Elvis fans, now accepts the impersonators as an indelible part of Presleyana.

El Vez, the Mexican Elvis, combines Elvis' sound and image with Mexican soul. His band is called the Memphis Mariachis.

BEST ELVIS PHENOMENA
Academic Elvis

I N THE SUMMER of 1995, the University of Mississippi's Center for the Study of Southern Culture held the First Annual International Conference on Elvis Presley in Oxford, Mississippi. The purpose of the six-day event was to establish a forum for discussion between different experts who specialize in popular culture and how it relates to our society, including music critics, Elvis authorities, and scholars.

The primary topics of the conference involved the widespread social and cultural impact of Elvis Presley. Scholars lectured on a range of subjects, including "Elvis and Black Rhythm," "Country Elvis," and "Elvis People." Civil rights author and activist Will Campbell discussed the term *redneck* as a slur against rural, white Southerners; writer David Wojahn talked about his Elvis-inspired poetry; while Peter Nazareth, a professor of English and African-American World Studies, related the story of Elvis Presley to familiar traditions in literature.

In addition to the scholarly lectures, forums, and discussions, the conference also featured live entertainment by top blues and gospel performers, appearances by people who knew Elvis personally, an art exhibit, impersonators, field trips to Tupelo and Graceland, and the sale of souvenirs and collectibles. Fans of Elvis as well as college professors and academic writers

Peter Nazareth, who has taught a course titled Elvis as Anthology at the University of Iowa, and Bill Ferris, director of the Center for the Study of Southern Culture, appeared on a conference panel.

descended on Oxford to learn more about Elvis' cultural significance.

Critics attacked the conference on several levels. Many journalists came to do tongue-in-cheek stories about the intellectuals trying to make something profound out of "Hound Dog" and "All Shook Up." Some academics were horrified at the suggestion that the lowbrow art of Elvis was granted the same honor as the work of famed Southern writer William Faulkner, who also inspires a yearly conference at Ole Miss. Others criticized the inclusion of impersonators and souvenir hawkers at an academic conference, claiming their presence undermined the seriousness of the occasion.

Despite the criticisms and the gentle ribbing by the press, the conference was a success, suggesting the growing interest in Elvis as a subject of scholarly pursuit.

Vernon Chadwick, founder and director of the conference, published a book in 1996 entitled *In Search of Elvis: Music, Race, Art, Religion*, which was related to the conference's central theme. Aside from the conference, several college courses about Elvis, including Icons of Popular Culture I: Elvis and Marilyn at Georgetown University and Elvis as Anthology at the University of Iowa, cropped up in the 1990s, as did academic treatises on his career and music.

BEST ELVIS PHENOMENA
Hollywood Icon

SHORTLY AFTER Elvis Presley died, Hollywood turned its attention to the singer once again, realizing his enormous popularity had not been diminished by death. In 1979, ABC aired the first of several biofilms on the life of Elvis Presley. As directed by John Carpenter, *Elvis* was a solid attempt to encapsulate the singer's contributions to popular music as well as to sympathetically portray Elvis the man. Kurt Russell starred as Elvis in a powerful portrayal that garnered him a well-deserved Emmy nomination.

No actor captured Elvis so convincingly until Michael St. Gerard landed the key role for the short-lived television series *Elvis*. It didn't hurt that St. Gerard looked remarkably like Elvis. The series was based on Elvis' real-life experiences, but each episode contained a deeper meaning. Some episodes were allegories that alluded to Elvis' deeper impact on popular music, while others commented on the long-lasting effects of poverty on his life. Great care went into the production of the series, which was indicated by the beautiful cinematography and the poignant writing.

Expanding on the TV series' evocative use of Elvis as a symbol, a different depiction of Elvis emerged in cinema during the 1980s. Several movies made use of the figure of Elvis Presley because

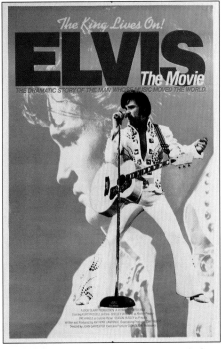

Kurt Russell portrayed Elvis in a made-for-TV biofilm.

Heartbreak Hotel *uses Elvis (David Keith) as a mythic character who solves everyone's problems.*

of the symbolic power his image has come to have. *Great Balls of Fire*, the 1989 biography of Jerry Lee Lewis, used Elvis (played by St. Gerard) to represent the pinnacle of fame and fortune that Lewis aspired to but was never destined to reach. In 1993, *True Romance* featured a spectral figure of Elvis Presley (played by Val Kilmer) who appears at crucial moments to offer sure advice to the main character about what course of action to take. The ultimate use of Elvis as symbol occurred in *Mystery Train*, which tells three separate stories of outsiders who are staying at a run-down Memphis hotel. Elvis never appears in any of the scenes and none of the stories have anything directly to do with him, but his presence haunts the film through the tacky portraits that hang on the wall and the eerie sound of his version of "Blue Moon" that repeatedly plays in the background.

From the wacky Elvis impersonators that run amuck in the comedy *Honeymoon in Vegas* to the darkly heroic, Elvis-inspired main character in David Lynch's surreal *Wild at Heart*, the complex image of Elvis that has become ingrained in American culture offers clever filmmakers a range of interpretations and imagery to explore.

Michael St. Gerard strikes a pose that captures Elvis in looks and attitude.

BEST ELVIS PHENOMENA
Elvis as Art

ELEVATED TO THE LEVEL of myth in our culture, Elvis Presley has been labeled a true folk hero, analyzed as a tragic symbol, and explained as an icon of the American Dream. Writers and artists have used Elvis as a potent symbol for some time, but recent collections and exhibitions of art with Elvis as the subject matter have focused attention on his increased cultural significance.

Several small art centers and galleries, such as the World Tattoo Gallery of Chicago and the Southeastern Center for Contemporary Art, have organized exhibits in which Elvis is the subject of all the art. Most often, the pieces are by artists who, although talented, are relatively unknown, and the audience for the exhibits remains local and limited. In November 1994, a major exhibit entitled "Elvis + Marilyn: 2 × Immortal" was launched at the Institute of Contemporary Art in Boston. Work by prominent artists made up the exhibition, which traveled to major museums around the country from 1994 through 1997. The exhibition and the accompanying catalog brought media attention to the way that artists use popular figures such as Elvis Presley and Marilyn Monroe to express serious ideas.

Key works in the exhibit in which Elvis was the subject matter included *Elvis I and II* by

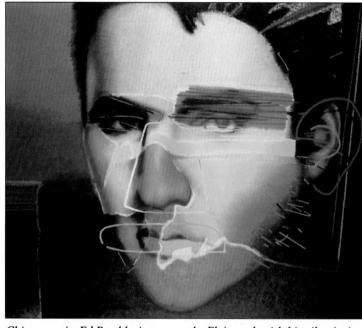

Chicago artist Ed Paschke interprets the Elvis myth with his oil painting entitled **Matinee.**

The exhibit catalogue featured Andy Warhol's Elvis on the cover.

Andy Warhol, a pairing of two sets of silk-screened images of Elvis in an identical pose. These images of Elvis as a cowboy from *Flaming Star* suggest the superficial nature of Hollywood character types, and the fact that Warhol produced the same image repeatedly comments on the lack of individual expression inherent in mass-produced art forms, such as the Hollywood cinema or the silk-screen process. Interestingly, other artists took Warhol's famous silk screen and expanded on it to create new pieces, including Richard Pettibone in *Andy Warhol, Elvis. 1964.* and Jerry Kearns with *Earth Angel.* Other major pieces included Ed Paschke's *Matinee* and William Wegman's *Elvis (Don't Be Cruel).* The catalog that accompanied the exhibition, also titled *Elvis + Marilyn: 2 × Immortal,* includes beautiful reproductions of all the art works plus criticism, commentary, and essays by prominent writers and scholars.

The varied work of those who have creatively incorporated Elvis imagery into their art testifies that Elvis' impact on culture extends well beyond the range of his own art. In life, Elvis blurred the line between black and white cultures with his music; in death, he blurs the line between high and low culture with his image.

BEST ELVIS PHENOMENA
The Elvis Stamp

THE U.S. POSTAL SERVICE announced the approval of an Elvis Presley stamp on January 9, 1992, ending a hard-fought campaign that lasted over eight years. After approval for the stamp was secured, the real fun began. The U.S. Postal Service organized a design competition to select the best stamp rendering of Elvis. More than 50 designs were considered before the field was narrowed to two. Mark Stutzman's effort featured a young, rockabilly Elvis grabbing an old-fashioned Shure Brothers 556S "birdcage" microphone. The other design was created by John Berkey and depicted a mature, 1970s Elvis in a white jumpsuit. To generate good will, interest, and revenue, the U.S. Postal Service announced that they wanted the

The winning design for the stamp featured a young Elvis from the 1950s.

public to select the final design. Ballots showing both designs were distributed by post offices around the country on April 6, 1992, and in the April 13 issue of *People* magazine. Members of the public voted for their choice and mailed the postcard ballots to the U.S. Postal Service.

On June 4, 1992, Priscilla Presley announced that the younger version of Elvis won the competition with 851,200 votes, while the 1970s Elvis received 277,723 votes. Sadly, the design featuring the mature Elvis was too often

described as "the old, fat Elvis" by the media, which unfairly saddled Berkey's interpretation with a negative connotation and may have affected the final tally of votes. Berkey based his rendering of Elvis on a photo taken

Fans lined up hours in advance for the Elvis stamp on its first day of issue.

when the singer was 37 years old and weighed 160 to 170 pounds, and the design clearly does not depict Elvis as being old or unattractive.

The general public voted on one of two designs for the Elvis stamp.

On January 8, 1993, patrons all over the country lined up at post offices before dawn to buy their Presley stamps. Local post offices employed every gimmick to celebrate the day of issue—from offering free coffee to hiring eight-year-old Elvis impersonators. The U.S. Postal Service printed 500 million of the 29-cent Elvis stamps, compared to the 100 million for a typical commemorative stamp. Eventually, Elvis would generate a profit of $36 million for the post office, more than any stamp before or since.

Ultimately, the stamp meant more than just the fulfillment of the stamp campaign's goal. Its success marked a turning point in the posthumous career of Elvis Presley. The many commentaries by fans and experts on the significance of Elvis to the media generated a new appreciation for his music and a renewed interest in the phenomenon.

INDEX